Opening Spaces
Writing Technologies and Critical Research Practices

New Directions in Computers and Composition Studies

Opening Spaces
Writing Technologies and Critical Research Practices

Patricia Sullivan
James E. Porter
Purdue University

Ablex Publishing Corporation
Greenwich, Connecticut
London, England

Printed in the United States of America

Library of Congress Cataloging-in-Publication Data

Sullivan, Patricia, 1951-
      Opening spaces : writing technologies and critical research
   practices / Patricia A. Sullivan, James E. Porter.
         p.   cm. -- (New directions in computers and composition studies)
   Includes bibliographical references and indexes.
   ISBN 1-56750-307-1. -- ISBN 1-56750-308-X (pbk.)
   1. English language--Rhetoric--Study and teaching--Data
   processing.   2. Research--Methodology--Study and teaching--Data
   processing.   3. English language--Rhetoric--Computer-assisted
   instruction.   4. Critical thinking--Study and teaching--Data
   processing.   5. Academic writing--Study and teaching--Data
   processing.   6. Research--Methodology--Computer--assisted
   instruction.   7. Critical thinking--Computer-assisted instruction.
   8. Academic writing--Computer-assisted instruction.   I. Porter,
   James E., 1954-   .   II. Title.   III. Series.
   808'.042'0285--dc21   97-22413
                                                                    CIP

Ablex Publishing Corporation   Published in the U.K. and Europe by:
55 Old Post Road #2   JAI Press Ltd.
P.O. Box 5297   38 Tavistock Street
Greenwich, CT 06830   Covent Garden
                                              London WC2E 7PB
                                              England

Contents

Acknowledgments

An earlier version of Chapter 4 appears as James E. Porter and Patricia Sullivan's, "Working Across Methodological Interfaces: The Study of Computers and Writing in the Workplace" (pp. 294–322) in Patricia Sullivan and Jennie Dautermann's (Eds.), *Electronic Literacies in the Workplace: Technologies of Writing* (Urbana: NCTE & Computers and Composition, 1996).

We thank the readers and reviewers who read all (or part of) this manuscript and offered helpful criticism and encouragement: Ellen Cushman, Gail Hawisher, Gesa Kirsch, Charles Moran, Paul Prior, and Cynthia Selfe. We would like to thank Ann Clark Espuelas and Anne Trowbridge at Ablex for their thorough editorial help with the project, and also Anne Wysocki for her excellent design work. We thank, too, our students from the Spring 1996 seminars in Postmodernism and in Qualitative Research for their reactions to the manuscript, and more generally, we thank the students in the Purdue Rhetoric and Composition Ph.D. Program for challenging our thinking in productive ways.

We thank our colleagues at Purdue (present and past) for their encouragement to pursue this project. It is comforting to work in such a community. We are particularly grateful for Jeanne Halpern and Janice Lauer's early efforts to make methodology an important topic in the Purdue Ph.D. program. We would also like to thank David Caputo and Margaret Moan Rowe for institutional support of the project.

Most of all, we thank our families for their patience and sacrifices; we dedicate this book to them—Peter, Jae, and Elizabeth Fadde; and Gail, Jaime, Kathleen, and Thomas Porter.

Preface

The title of our book—*Opening Spaces: Writing Technologies and Critical Research Practices*—indicates our point of view: we are advocating a postmodern view of research as a critical practice—and in this book we try to show how this thing we call "critical research practices" might apply to the study of writing technologies.

As Chapter 2 will show, if we were to pack our view into a thesis statement it would look something like this: **For the study of writing technologies, we advocate a view of research as a set of critical and reflective practices (praxis) that are sensitive to the rhetorical situatedness of participants and technologies and that recognize themselves as a form of political and ethical action.** We use Chapter 2 to situate the ways in which we mean the terms of this thesis.

This view of research has several characteristics (which are elaborated on throughout the book):

1. It assumes that research ethically begins (or should begin) with the involvement and personal commitment by the researcher to research participants.
2. It acknowledges the rhetorical nature of research activity, which means that it focuses on the role discursive practices play in:

   —framing (and naming) the study;
   —mediating research activities;
   —defining and displacing research relations (a.k.a. ethics);
   —constituting and resisting research power (a.k.a. politics);
   —respect to particular situated moments (i.e., particular subjects, technological medium, historical context, institutional and bureaucratic context, features of scene/environment, etc.).

3. It proceeds through a process of self-reflection and critical inquiry (a constant challenging of assumptions); it acknowledges the possibility of multiple interpretations.
4. It is characterized by a flexible and adaptive approach to design of research; it acknowledges methodological anomalies and divergences.
5. It has as its ultimate aim the betterment of research participants.

This set of characteristics bears considerable resemblance to the research agenda articulated by feminist methodologists like Patti Lather, Liz Stanley, and Sue Wise, and explained by Mary Margaret Fonow and Judith Cook (a connection we explore in Chapter 3). In fact, our theoretical frame owes much to feminist methodology. However, we see our notion of critical research practices as differing from feminist methodology in several important ways. First, we do not think that such approaches to research must necessarily be conducted only by women or focused only on the study of women. (Our approach to methodology is not feminist in the essentialist sense, though we hasten to point out that not all feminist methodology is.) Second, our notion is much more rhetorical in its recognition of the role of language, especially in instituting and challenging ethical and political relations. Third, we pay considerable attention to communication media, especially to the particular features of writing technologies. Fourth, we want to be more self-critical and ironic about method than is most feminist methodology (Fine, 1992).

Our discussion of critical research practices has implications for numerous social science fields that make use of empirical research in developing findings—and especially for those fields which conduct empirical studies of writing activities: computers and composition, rhetoric/composition, professional writing, education, human-computer interaction, usability, and communication. Our intended audience is researchers and methodologists working in and across a number of fields.

The specific site of analysis for this project, however, is the field of computers and composition, whose research identity focuses on the uses of computers to teach and do writing. This group, which is comprised of teachers, researchers, and administrators (mainly in English departments) who work on issues involving writing and writing instruction using computers, includes:

- Teachers and researchers who regularly attend the Computers and Writing Conference
- Regular contributors to and readers of the journal *Computers and Composition* and of NCTE/Computers and Composition collections (such as *Evolving Perspectives on Computers and Composition Studies*) and other similar collections devoted to computers and writing
- Participants on the MegaByte University (MBU-L), ACW-L (Association for Computers and Writing), and WWW-Writing electronic discussion lists and other lists that focus on computers and the teaching of composition.

Our discussion of research practice engages a debate—usually a silent one, though it occasionally surfaces in the form of arguments about theory versus practice or in critiques of methods underpinning controversial studies—that we see as operative within this research community, but also within two other overlapping fields to which we belong: professional writing and rhetoric/composition. A key assumption operating in these discussions might be expressed in terms somewhat like these: Either one can do postmodern theory or one can do empirical research, but it is not possible to do both these things at the same time, because postmodern theory is incompatible, ultimately, with the modernist assumptions of empirical research.

One of us felt this tension keenly while serving as a judge one year for the Best Article award in *Computers and Composition*. The two top entrants for the award used completely different methodological approaches. Article A was a detailed, traditional empirical study focused on the use of the computer for revision. Article B was a postmodern critique of racial and ethnic difference as students articulated and explored these differences in a computer class discussion. Within their particular research paradigms, each article was excellent, and because each article stayed strictly within a particular research paradigm, each article was also limited. Though it was highly systematic in its organization and presentation of research findings, Article A did not sufficiently contextualize itself nor did it sufficiently critique the categories it assumed and the questions it asked. Article B was highly critical and exemplary in its self-reflectiveness, but was not able to articulate clear conclusions or suggest positive, constructive action; it reported its observations in a nonsystematic way.

Let's further complicate these categories. What we have here, of course, is a picture of two different inquiry paradigms: one we might call empirical research, and the other "critical theory." Research, especially the traditional modernist kind, has as its aim the generation of knowledge (usually within specific disciplinary parameters). Theory, especially the postmodern variety, has as its aim critique. Our view in some ways affirms and in other ways subverts both paradigms as it advocates critical interrogation of method.

What we refer to in this book as "traditional empirical research" constitutes a continuum with two extremes, one we call *traditional positivistic* and the other *traditional naturalistic* (see Chapter 3 for a full discussion). Traditional positivistic research is characterized by its reliance on the strict methods of experimental (and usually quantitative) science, as articulated by Donald Campbell and Julian Stanley (1966) and others. This approach to methodology insists that the researcher adopt the role of neutral observer of natural phenomenon, the so-called objective researcher of the scientific method, who describes the world as it is through careful observation of carefully controlled conditions. This is the pure *cogito* imagined by Descartes as the starting point for scientific inquiry—and the paradigmatic ethos of the modern scientific paradigm.

Though a few would still insist that this type of research is the standard to which all empirical research on writing should subscribe (Gross, 1994, for instance), most methodologists now readily acknowledge the limitations of such an approach to research, especially in its application to the study of complex human social behaviors (like writing). We can complain, first, of its ultimate naïveté in assuming that there is any such thing as a position of "neutral observation" (a claim that postmodern theory has aggressively challenged); or that any research activity can operate unaffected by political and economic and institutional constraints (or can safely proceed without acknowledging their intrusion on observation); or that researchers can attain "neutrality" (along with the corollary assumption that it is desirable to do so); or that an experimental or quasi-experimental strategy guarantees the highest degree of knowledge about the phenomena being studied; or that science can somehow escape the taint of rhetoric. From a number of angles, in numerous different fields (including people in philosophy of science, such as Thomas Kuhn and Bruno Latour), the assumptions of this Enlightenment modern, scientific paradigm have been dismissed as untenable.

And yet even as those assumptions are questioned by empirical researchers, they nonetheless persist as the hidden standards by which empirical research typically proceeds. Even those who acknowledge the researcher as participant and who advocate naturalistic approaches to empirical research still buy into an essential premise of the traditional-positivistic position: that our primary job as researchers is to observe phenomena and that knowledge somehow accumulates from detached observation (Strauss, 1987, describes it as the data providing indicators that ground the concepts that emerge through research).

A second view of empirical research—what we call the traditional naturalistic—is characterized by its recognition of the situatedness of the researcher, of her/his involvement in the phenomena being studied. It also posits the view that certain forms of human behavior, especially social forms, are best studied through case studies and ethnographies that openly acknowledge the researcher's intrusion on the social phenomena being studied. Rather than being inferior methods to experiments and quasi-experiments, the argument goes, case studies and ethnographies allow for better in situ study.

This view of research, as articulated by Yvonna Lincoln and Egon Guba (1985) and others, challenges the assumption that experimental method should be the standard for empirical research—but it does not sufficiently challenge (it seems to us) the norm of "neutral observation." Such a view may at least recognize the problematics of neutral observation, may in fact recognize that this ideal is never practically realized, but nonetheless holds this as the standard to which research should adhere. It still tries to train the researcher to be the measurement instrument. It still tries to keep the researcher from contaminating the "naturalness" of the site.

What we want to do is push empirical research beyond its reliance on either of these two traditional forms, to a postmodern empiricism that recognizes more fully the role of power in the research enterprise and that acknowledges as valid the political and ethical relations between researcher and researched; the rhetorical situatedness of all research activity; and the institutional constraints under which research proceeds. In a sense, then, what we are trying to describe is the possibility of a third place beyond the binary between postmodern theory and empirical research. We are trying to articulate a position that acknowledges the strengths of both modes of inquiry and that validates the intersection of both.

We are by no means the first to attempt such a task. Feminist methodologists like Lather and Stanley have been articulating such a position for a while now, and some researchers have made the connections to rhetoric/composition (e.g., Kirsch & Ritchie, 1995). Where our approach is perhaps different is that we locate our discussion in a particular research field (computers and composition), in particular kinds of technologies (the uses of the computer as a writing tool), and in particular institutional and curricular contexts (writing classrooms).

Yet our location of this discussion inside computers and composition is not totally conventional. Our treatment tries to avoid the usual debates in the field of computers and composition. Our chapters are not titled according to the usual categories, which in computers and composition typically means foregrounding the technology involved (e.g., synchronous conferencing, email, hypertext); or the question of the good versus bad uses of computers in the composition classroom; or gender and cultural identity issues; or questions of access, literacy, and democracy. Our book treats all these matters, but none of these topics is our primary frame. Rather we foreground methodology, attempting to promote a reflective and critical approach to the study of computers which, while sensitive to the particular forms of technology in use, is not organized primarily according to those forms.

While our primary focus is computers and composition, we also forge links with professional writing and rhetoric theory/history, because we feel that the three camps have not sufficiently appreciated one another. For example, we feel that many people in computers and composition have not paid sufficient attention to workplace studies in professional writing, and to some extent have even exhibited hostility to the workplace, or at least reluctance to see the workplace as a potential site for change. However, by dismissing workplace practice, computers and composition fails to engage the key site students will inhabit. The field ends up separating the workplace agenda from the social change agenda in the composition classroom, thereby reinforcing an old binary (classroom vs. workplace) that, we contend, is ultimately harmful to students. Perhaps most importantly for computers and composition, we encourage computers and composition people to see themselves as computers and writing people. We hope to encourage researchers to examine not only the first-year composition class but also computer writing classes across the curriculum and computer use in the workplace, and to recognize the potential of electronic writing to radically change the modes of production in both the university and the corporation.

el that researchers in professional writing (who publish in journals such
1al of *Business and Technical Communication, Journal of Business Com-*
munition, Technical Communication Quarterly, and *Technical Communica-*
tion) have neglected the immense influence of computers on workplace writing
practices. Our study argues to this group that computer writing technologies are
not incidental to such practices, but in fact constitute them in fundamental ways
which research must take into account.

We feel that theorists and researchers in rhetoric and composition have not
paid sufficient attention to the distinctive influence of writing technologies. Some
dismiss the technology as incidental to writing practice, seeing the computer as
nothing more than an advanced typewriter. (Some don't see it at all.) Others view
the technology in more dire terms, seeing it as the ally of a capitalist bureaucracy
that must be opposed (e.g., Ohmann, 1985). What we see is that writing via the
various computer technologies—for example, hypertext, electronic networking,
email, computer-aided publishing—actually demands that we develop new theories of rhetoric and composing.

Most important for rhetoric/composition in general, we merge what have typically been considered two distinct approaches to research: theoretical and empirical. Our past work has attempted to heal this unnecessary and counterproductive binary, which, unfortunately, we see reproducing itself in some current research on computers and composition. Our views are not without grounding. We align ourselves with certain postmodern feminist and pragmatic
methodologists like Lather, Stanley, and Lucy Suchman. From this perspective
we try to open a space where theoretical scholarship and empirical research can
intersect. Computers and composition is an especially promising site for such an
engagement and a compatible environment for this kind of inquiry, for several
reasons:

1. Computers and composition foregrounds the relationship of technology to
   writing, unlike work done in either rhetoric/composition or professional writing (which, in privileging the print paradigm, tends to embed or ignore the
   role of technology).
2. Computers and composition focuses on writing in a relatively new and rapidly changing environment; since writing and teaching habits are not as yet
   well formed, it is easier to see practices developing and also to shape those
   practices.
3. Computers and composition is an interdisciplinary field that also bridges the
   technologies/humanities barrier; that is, people in computers and composition
   tend to be technologically oriented humanists, a rare combination.
4. People in computers and composition already think along the lines of "situated uses," especially in the classroom, and they already think of writing as
   production rather than only (or mainly) as critique.

A number of books within the computers and composition community have focused on the rhetoric and ideology of the use of computers as a writing tool (e.g., Bolter's *Writing Space*, 1991; Tuman's *Word Perfect*, 1992; Heim's *Electric Language*, 1987; to some extent Faigley's *Fragments of Rationality,* 1992). Many collections have considered theoretical issues or teaching practices related to the computerized writing classroom (e.g., Hawisher & Selfe's *Critical Perspectives on Computers and Composition Studies*, 1989; Hawisher & Selfe's *Evolving Perspectives on Computers and Composition Studies*, 1991; Hawisher & LeBlanc's *Re-imagining Computers and Composition,* 1992; Handa's *Computers and Community*, 1990; Selfe & Hilligoss's *Literacy and Computers*, 1994). Several works have evaluated the uses of various technologies in the teaching of writing, but none of these treatments has centrally focused on issues of methodology in the study of computer writing.

Computers and composition has yet to explore the methodological implications of studying the computer as a writing tool. Some other ancillary fields have explored the methodological implications of their research. Research in the Computer-Supported Cooperative Work movement (CSCW) has been methodologically reflective in examining how computers assist collaboration in the workplace, but this work has not been much recognized in computers and composition or in professional writing, and this movement itself has not foregrounded cooperative writing activity. Several collections in professional writing have focused on methodological issues. Lee Odell and Dixie Goswami's groundbreaking work, *Writing in Nonacademic Settings* (1985), develops a methodological philosophy for the study of workplace writing practice in professional writing. Almost ten years later, Rachel Spilka's collection *Writing in the Workplace: New Research Perspectives* (1993) followed up on the Odell and Goswami collection and explored new research directions for professional writing. But no book has yet offered a distinct philosophy and rhetoric for the design of studies of computer writing. We feel that such a book is vitally necessary if the computers and composition community is to develop its identity as a research field.

What are our aims in this study? Our efforts in this book are very much influenced by our work in the rhetoric/composition Ph.D. program at Purdue University. Our primary mission as teachers and researchers is, in effect, to train others to become rhetoric/composition teachers and researchers. Thus, to a great extent, our efforts are aimed at changing the way that newcomers in our field—and we define that field broadly to include the overlapping areas of computers and composition, rhetoric/composition, and professional writing—think about research. For starters, we want our graduate students to respect teaching and writing practice. Too often we see them aligning themselves with what they see as one of the two available prestige camps in the field—Theory or Empirical Research—each of which, we believe, tends to (a) underappreciate the contribution of the other area and (b) neglect practice. We do sympathize with the need for alignment. To develop an identity in a research field, one has to develop clear alliances, has to establish a definite identity, and has to work to understand and acquire the inquiry strategies and the values (often implicit) of a given paradigm. But in establishing that identity we do not want our students to adopt a stereotyped persona, become an exaggerated version of the Postmodern Theorist or the Empirical Researcher. We want them to be aware of the limitations of the self, the possibility of the other, the strength of diversity.

Obviously the ultimate aim, the *causa remota*, of producing better writing teachers and researchers is to promote better writers and writing. We are especially interested in advancing the cause of electronic writing, to make it more rhetorically grounded—by which we mean to make it more sensitive to the act of writing as the act of exercising power (politics) and the act of constituting relations (ethics). We want, finally, to articulate a notion of research as practical action (as opposed to the modernistic view of research as generating knowledge). Good research, we are going to argue, has a practical aim. It does something good for somebody. It helps people in a disadvantaged position (and that can be variously defined) achieve some improvement in their circumstances. Research enables that improvement to happen, we argue, to the degree that it attends to the particular situatedness of its participants, to the degree that it is sensitive to human practices and does not subordinate them to Theory, to Method, or to Disciplinary Rules. Good research has to clearly and directly connect itself to the function of teaching (to put this in the terms of another debate), and not simply in a remote way (e.g., "our research results may *eventually* help affect X") but in its day-to-day operation.

As Mark Poster (1990), Andrew Feenberg (1991), and others have pointed out, computer writing technology indeed can potentially be a tool of resistance and transformation—*if* we can figure out what situated uses of it make that possible. Our book argues that the study of writing-with-the-computer requires a situationally sensitive approach to research, and that how this research defines itself and operates is critical to enabling the end we all desire: better research practices serving the aim of better writing practices.

1

Introducing
Critical Research Practices

In this chapter, we introduce the focal topic of this book—namely, critical research practices in computers and composition—through a consideration of why we should bother about/with methodology, and then describe our own methodological standpoint for this project.

In later chapters, we examine in detail the impact of methodology on the study of computers and writing, but we want to start with an example from outside the field: how we might watch, and then research, a college basketball game. Why a basketball game, of all things? Well, to some extent for personal reasons: because both of us are basketball fans, because Pat systematically studies the game, and because Jim used to play it with enthusiasm and modest skill. We think about and talk to each other about basketball, and find the talk interspersed with our workday discussions of methodology.

We have an important professional reason, too: because basketball is not a phenomenon usually studied by researchers in computers and composition (at least they haven't admitted this in print). Its distance from typical computers and composition concerns—and yet, we hope, its overall familiarity to readers—is an advantage to our argument at this point. (Though it may strike you as ironic that we advocate a feminist methodology in this book and start with an example taken from basketball, this game, we assure you, is a *women's* basketball game.)

THE COMPLEXITY OF POSITIONALITY IN
METHODOLOGY

Watching a Basketball Game

Nine members of our two families—Jim, Gail, Jaime, Kathleen, and Thomas; and Pat, Peter, Jae, and Elizabeth—could attend a Purdue women's basketball game and each come away with differing experiences of the game. That's fairly obvious. Peter (who works as video coordinator for the Purdue Athletic Department) would be taping the game for analysis from the crow's nest at the top of Mackey Arena and would have little idea about what happened in whole sections of the game, because attention to videotaping the action limits his ability to follow the game (but he would have stats to report). Jae might be in the halftime foul-shooting contest and thus miss all of the first half as he thought about his strategy; otherwise he would sit for awhile to watch post play and then wander the halls looking for friends. Gail might spend considerable time chasing Thomas (an active three-year-old) in the stands. Elizabeth and Kathleen would sit in the Little Boiler Club on the floor and soak in the ambiance—but they would also ask who won at the end as they contemplated whether they should stay after and try for autographs. Jim and Jaime might watch the forwards intensely because Jaime (who plays JV basketball for the local high school) recently grew and now has to learn how to play forward after a lifetime of being a point guard. Pat would keep a shot chart and report to Peter at halftime about in what specific ways the offense was going awry.

Although everyone attended the same game and "watched" it, the game would turn out to be many events. Part of the fun of watching basketball is talking about it during and afterward, and comparing our various versions of the game. If we asked these nine people to inform us about the culture of Purdue women's basketball, the adults would focus their stories differently than would the children, and the older children who are playing basketball seriously (Jae, Jaime) would tell different stories from the younger ones (Kathleen, Elizabeth), who might focus on the band or the cheerleaders or Purdue Pete or the minibasketballs thrown out after the game.

There are many different ways to focus on a basketball game. As we suggest, these differences can be due to your differing perspective (i.e., age, professional needs, personal interests)—what we call your viewer perspective. There are also different focuses in the game itself. You could follow:

- The intensity (i.e., the noise, the pace, the aggression, the assertion of the point guards' wills, the determination of the post players)
- The ball (where does it go and when)
- "The story of the game" (from a color analyst's view, a journalist's view, a fan's view, a parent's view, or a coach's view)
- Particular players

- Post play
- Offensive movement
- Defensive schemes (i.e., box and one, match-up zone, two-three-two, woman on woman)
- The pageantry (i.e., cheerleaders, band, mascot, banners, how fans dress)
- Friends who are also attending
- The refereeing
- Boilermaker Pete
- Themes that have been reported by others (e.g., Is a particular player being lazy or fighting with the coach?)
- Where the vendors are, if you are hungry

Experienced fans have probably learned to sustain more than one focus, perhaps several—but it would be difficult (and not enjoyable) for anyone to take it all in.

So far, we have identified only beneficent views of the game. We can imagine other, more political views that might not be so sympathetic to the game or to the spectacle of the game. (We can imagine these views because to some degree both of us have adopted them.) A feminist might regard the woman's game positively, and see the 4,000 fans in Mackey Arena as evidence of the improved status of women's sports in intercollegiate athletics, but a more radical feminist vision might also see the game as evidence of a fraud: an appearance of equality that attempts to disguise the inequities that still exist between financial and fan support for the men's and women's teams. Marxists, of course, would never attend a university basketball game, at least not as Marxists, but if one happened to be there, he might see the game as an economic event involving the exploitation of black student athletes for the entertainment and economic advantage of mainly white, upper-middle-class, Republican boosters. (Corporate America—that is, members of the John Purdue Club—occupy the box seats, of course, or they would if any existed at Mackey Arena.) Purdue University gains wealth and prestige—free advertising, more or less—thanks to the hard work of black athletes, the laborers in an exploitive system of production. The Capitalist Republican John Purdue Club Member would see such an arrangement as quid pro quo, free-market enterprise: the black athlete and University working together for mutual economic advantage (no exploitation involved, since participants are "free" to choose).

Here of course we are moving from the conventional realm of watching the game as a spectator into the realm of critiquing the game as cultural event. We are beginning the enterprise of critical and reflective research practice and beginning to question our own motives for being there.

Researching a Basketball Game

However, suppose we were intending to research the basketball game, or analyze it as a coach or sportswriter might. How would we go about it? Obviously the concept of *research* suggests a more systematic and analytic way of processing the event—and it suggests a *reason* for doing so: there are several different strategies we could use. Would we give our two families surveys pre- and postgame, videotape the game, take notes? Would we pay any attention to the game itself, and if so, how would we frame our interest in that game (as observers of what happened, of how fans responded, of how the coaches and players acted on the bench, of what happened in the game, of what prompted noise levels to rise and fall, of how everyone responded to the opposing team, and so on)? Would we study one game or attend the whole season? Would we talk to players, coaches, fans (onetime, new season ticketholders, longtime season ticketholders), band, cheerleaders, photographers, media people, and so on? Would we find out about their lives away from this culture and the ways that these events fit into their lives? What would be our data, and how would we record it?

At this point some of you are thinking, "It's the research question, stupid! Your research questions determine the strategies you use to answer these questions." Yet, we want to ask where do these questions come from? How are they mediated (sometimes unreflectively) by the kinds of questions that everyone else asks (or has asked) while studying this phenomenon? How does your position (as sociologist of family life, or one team's coach, or as feminist who is contrasting male and female college sports experiences, or as parent of an aspiring athlete, or as methodologist interested in deciding how to study this type of event) affect the questions you think to pose? How do your goals (to improve team play, to study family experiences, to examine fan-dom, to critique the male dominance of major college sports for women, or to examine the professionalization of women's sports in Division 1 Programs) interact with the ways that you frame the study and, indeed, what you perceive to be the results?

Saying that a research question directs the choice of method is a form of begging the question. It does not answer the question "Why that question?" and not the 24 others we could have asked but didn't. As we hope we are making clear by now, our interest is in the *why* of research. Our interest is in how research practices, institutional ties, researcher identities, technologies, politics, and ethics percolate together in the events that lead to how we frame our questions and, ultimately, to what we label knowledge. This is not determined solely by the research question(s), nor simply by one's disciplinary affiliation. It's not that easy.

Let's start with the commonplace that our research practices should be understood as complex actions that are taken in situ, that arise out of who we are and what we believe. Indeed, we have no hope of understanding how who we are, what we believe, and what we aim to see affect our sight unless and until we admit to our positioning (and at times take strides to diffuse the impact of our positioning). Let's also admit that our research practices have an ethic: that is, they are motivated by a sense of one's responsibility to a professional community (or communities); that they are tied to one's efforts to establish an identity (a contributing identity) to some community; that they are movitated by a goal, in the form of some imagined beneficial outcome for others (e.g., better teaching practices, better collaborative writing through electronic sharing of texts, better offensive ball movement, better uses of computers as writing tools) and for ourselves (e.g., tenure, promotion, professional fame, pay raises, personal happiness). We see research questions then as an intermediate stage, though in much published research they pretend to be the starting point.

So what's wrong with treating research questions as a starting point? Nothing, when the political and ethical positioning of the questions is made manifest. A lot, when the framing of the research questions appears to make them neutral or innocent. At times, the focus on the question as the motivating factor can block new research avenues, by restricting researchers to asking the same questions, or the same types of questions, again and again (what we have seen happen in much of the research in computers and composition). Disciplinary breakthrough comes when the form of the question itself is challenged, and that can only occur, we argue, by installing methodological reflexivity—what Bourdieu (1988, p. 15) calls "epistemological vigilance"—into the very act of framing the questions.

Let's return to our basketball example and focus on the data gathered about it in order to illustrate the importance of methodological reflexivity in the determination of data-collection strategies. A basketball game is held at a quick enough pace that if you are going to research it (or report on it), you also have to take notes of some kind to formally represent your experience of the game. Those might be video highlights (television news stories are usually crafted to make sense out of the available footage), shot charts (to give you a sense of the offensive strategies and their success), or statistical reports (newspaper stories often try to make sense out of these). Each of these types of notes has differing meanings according to your knowledge level about basketball (and the particular team) and according to your interest in the game. Both a shot chart and a stat report break the chronology of the game for analytic purposes, while video highlights may break the chronology for dramatic purposes; the entire video of the game maintains chronology (though the game will appear to be a different event taped from the crow's nest of Purdue's Mackey Arena than it will taped from courtside: from the top of the arena, players' height and numbers will be obscured; from the court level camera, any patterns of movement and what happens on the other end of the floor will be obscured).

This breaking of chronology (or flow) is significant because basketball is a fluid game with few predictable stops (note that substitutes sometimes wait at the scoring table for as long as four minutes because there is no stoppage of play). Thus, an analytic treatment of a game has to determine when, where, and how to break the game into units for that analysis. It isn't a trivial matter. These framings of the game both block and enable. A key point we want to make related to this form of analysis: All forms of data collection are static snapshots of what is fundamentally a fluid set of events. In general, researchers need to be much more

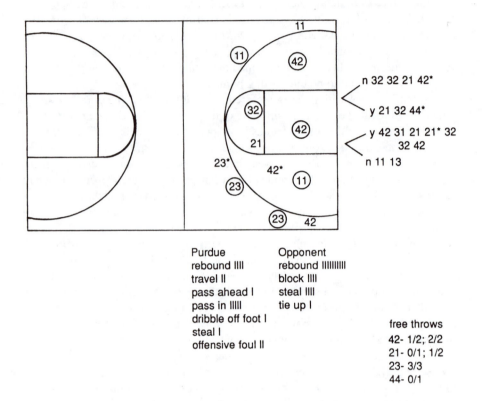

FIGURE 1.1.   Basketball shot chart.

conscious of the confusion between space and time: the spatial rendering of a fluid event always skews the time element (*kairos*), and that time skew needs to be acknowledged and pondered.

Our original scenario showed how nine people at the event might take in different components of the game. Pat, who was making a shot chart something like the one above (Figure 1.1) for the first half, and Peter, who was videotaping for the team (he shuttles the signal between two recorders and makes a tape with offense and a tape with defense), were taking notes that were suitable for research or for coaching. As Pat examined her chart at the end of the half, she told Peter that the chart confirmed that the other team was too short to play with Purdue. They were losing the ball on rebounds, and Purdue had more than their average of inside scores. Of course, she added, the early outside shooting of Jacoby (#23) and Erickson (#11) had opened the inside. And that is interesting because her shot

Player	2 pt goals	3pt goals	free throws	steals	assists	rebounds	blocks	fouls	total points	minutes played
11	1/2	1/2	0/0	1	4	1	0	1	5	15
13	0/1	0/0	0/0	0	0	0	0	1	0	2
21	3/5	0/0	1/3	0	1	3	0	2	7	12
23	0/0	2/3	3/3	0	4	0	0	1	9	20
30	0/0	0/0	0/0	0	0	6	2	2	0	11
31	1/1	0/0	0/0	1	0	3	0	1	2	10
32	4/6	0/0	0/0	0	0	4	2	2	8	10
42	4/6	0/0	3/4	2	0	2	0	1	11	15
44	1/1	0/0	0/1	0	0	1	0	0	2	5

FIGURE 1.2.   Basketball box score.

chart is helping her remember that fact, though it would not convey it to a stranger (there is no sequence of shots marked). Pat's notes are obviously a fan-centered object; they don't reveal, for example, how shots became available or whether a shot was taken because the 30-second clock was about to expire. They don't show who was making the turnovers. Nor do they comment on who was playing good post.

Compare Pat's shot chart of Purdue's first half with the statistics generated on the monitor Peter views as he shoots video footage in the crow's nest (Figure 1.2).

These two depictions of what the Purdue team did during the half (with the second closer to what newspaper readers see in a basketball box score) encourage and suppress story lines we may spin to recount and explain the game. The box score calls attention to individual performance, while the shot chart does a better job at revealing shot selection and shot performance (and, indirectly, ball movement). The shot chart gives us some insight into team performance, while the box score does not provide any sort of team perspective. These depictions also speak differently to those who attended the game than to those who did not, to those who know a great deal about the Purdue women's team vs. those who do not (e.g., which players played above their normal games, which not), and to those who know a great deal about basketball versus those who know little.

ʼ The visualizations we offer, while they may aid in our memories of the game, are problematic if we view them as the primary data for the study. First, they do not yet use the videotapes shot of the offense and the defense—the primary visual record of that game. Perhaps because it is not easily reducible to a map that fits on a page, this technological record that could be seen as a key source of analytic data (and is for the coaching staff) is not yet pictured. But the technology enables a type of data analysis, through computerized analysis of marked game tape, that was not possible ten years ago. It has already revolutionized coaching in football and is poised to do the same in basketball. This approach will reduce reliance on shot charts, and it is worthy of note because it shows how technology can enter into a process and remake it—even if that process is analysis.

Second, even if we ignore the computer analysis and focus on the shot chart and the box score, they are not complete, and do not speak to everyone in the same way, nor do they tell us much about the milieu surrounding those results. Further, we see them as modernist maps—that is, they represent the event in ways that stabilize the story of the game—that push the interpretation toward one truth about the game. Each one of them, taken as the one and only record, points out why we need multiple mappings of events if we are to allow our interpretations to move about among the competing truths about the game. Thus, only when we see them as participating in the construction of multiple views of that basketball game do we begin to find them useful. The good coach uses stat sheets as a guide, but is wary about letting such depictions determine judgment about the game or about performance.

By now it should be clear that our example of a basketball game could also be a writing class in a computer environment or even an electronic discussion. What may be a bit less clear is that this event can be studied empirically, historically, rhetorically, philosophically, and politically. Though empirical studies seem to make the discussion of practices and methods more straightforward by including them in a summary of the procedures of research, all modes of research and scholarship involve research practices. Our goal is to surface the workings of those practices, to examine them, and to call for researchers and scholars to be critical about those research practices. Come clean, in other words.

Stated thus, this project sounds simple. But there are many barriers to its success, barriers that are more obvious in empirical work (perhaps because that work is already open to discussing method).

Why are we researching a basketball game, or studying the use of computers as a tool for teaching writing? When we ask this question we are attempting to get at rationale in terms of ethical and political action: What good are we trying to accomplish in this act of research? Obviously we are trying to make better basketball players and better writers—but what ideal notion(s) of "better" guide our efforts?

Certainly methodological decisions are partly guided by a professional perspective, one that may be partly our own but which is also always coconstructed within the disciplinary communities we inhabit. But our research decisions are also guided by a vision of what constitutes a "good" that we should be striving toward. It is this good, this political and ethical end, that we are trying to surface and critique when we talk about the importance of critical research practices.

When we look at empirical studies in computers and composition—such as are published in *Computers and Composition* or *Written Communication*, as well as in numerous collections—we want to ask how researchers are selecting their sites and subjects, why they are studying what they are studying. Why was it that so many studies in the late 1980s focus on the usefulness of word-processing software to writing, and then in the 1990s everyone seemed to turn to the study of synchronous networks? This shift has one obvious explanation: Teachers finally gained access to network technology and started using it and teaching it. But why did so many of the studies focus on network dynamics within the single writing class? Why have there been so few studies of wide-area network interaction, of cross-class interaction, or network interaction within the corporation? Again, the answer may be obvious. The research is based at a particular site and delimited by the technology that was available and what people were actually doing in their classes. Thus, because very little of the research in computers and composition is underwritten by grant monies (which might allow a research to shape the technological environment somewhat), the research published has been dependent on the technological and social milieu(s) of the researchers who pursued an understanding of writing technologies.

All this seems perfectly reasonable to us: People study what is accessible to study, what is available to them technologically. But why haven't researchers and scholars said so, and, more important, why have they not raised questions about what was not studied? The problem, as we see it, is that researchers and scholars seldom admit up front that their research choices are guided by such factors as local need or accessibility or convenience, and, further, that those factors are guided by political and ethical choices involving institutional bureaucracies, teachers' personal preferences, taxpayer support, and the like. The kind of methodological reflexiveness we are advocating necessarily includes a critical perspective toward one's research practices.

OUR METHODOLOGY

So what about our own practices? Where we are standing as we embark on this journey of articulating critical research practices for computers and composition? How and why are we doing what we do here? We develop our approach in two stages: (a) We examine (and critique) the ideologies informing how theorists and researchers currently study and talk about electronic writing; and (b) we propose a "rhetorical methodology" based on viewing computer writing as a situated practice. The study of electronic writing as a situated practice requires a particular and pragmatic sensitivity to the particulars of the writing context—for example, to the particular *kairos* of the writing situation, including the types of writers and audiences involved, the forms of technology being used, and the type of heuristic methods being applied to the study.

Our critical practices perspective sees methodology for the study of writing not as a rigid set of structures to be applied without question to a set of writing phenomena. Rather, we see methodology as heuristic—and we see research generating situated knowledge—or rather a kind of pragmatic know-how (vs. know-that) kind of knowledge (Sullivan & Porter, 1993a). Too much research in rhetoric and composition aims to produce epistemic knowledge, but because we view writing as a kind of practical knowledge, we believe that a different kind of methodological approach is necessary. (We discuss this approach further in later chapters, especially Chapter 3.)

Our theoretical position sees critical practice (or praxis) as key to the development of knowledge. Rather than granting abstract Theory or Knowledge the privileged position, this research perspective sees knowledge as local, as contingent, and as grounded not in universal structures but in local, situated practices. Attention to the distinctive nature of writing as a situated practice is essential, then, to the methodological philosophy we are developing.

Our view of methodology is not a typical one in computers and composition or in professional writing. Influenced to some extent by theory and research in writing in the disciplines, which has observed the ways in which methodologies are indeed rhetorical constructions, we think that all researchers and theorists work out of a methodology, whatever form of analysis or observation they use and whatever their object of study, and that their methodology constitutes their mode of rhetorical invention. In our vocabulary, then, the strategies for doing empirical research employed by researchers in computers and composition are a kind of rhetorical invention. In a sense, then, what we are doing is putting methodology into (or back into, if you prefer) rhetoric.

As Figure 1.3 shows, we see rhetoric as comprising three elements: ideology (assumptions about what human relations should be and about how people should use symbol systems); practice (how people actually do constitute their relations through regularized symbolic or discursive activity); and method (tactics, procedures, heuristics, or tools that people use for inquiry). The diagram highlights different research emphases within the field of rhetoric/composition. Theorists typically focus on ideology, empirical researchers more typically on method, and

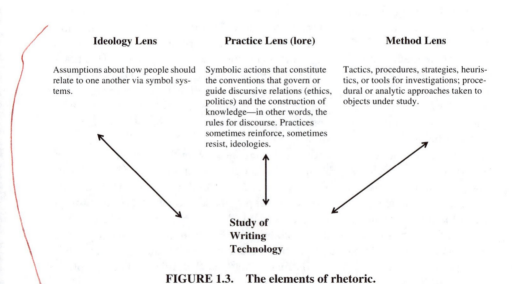

Ideology Lens

Assumptions about how people should relate to one another via symbol systems.

Practice Lens (lore)

Symbolic actions that constitute the conventions that govern or guide discursive relations (ethics, politics) and the construction of knowledge—in other words, the rules for discourse. Practices sometimes reinforce, sometimes resist, ideologies.

Method Lens

Tactics, procedures, strategies, heuristics, or tools for investigations; procedural or analytic approaches taken to objects under study.

Study of Writing Technology

FIGURE 1.3.   The elements of rhetoric.

teachers typically focus on practice (or as Harkin, 1991; North, 1987; and others have labeled it, lore). This diagram attempts not only to create a space for practice as distinct from ideology and method (two things with which it is often confused), but to centralize practice, or situated use.

In rhetoric/composition and in computers and composition, the word *methodology* often means what we are calling method—that is, methodology is equated with particular observational procedures or data-collection strategies and with specific data analysis techniques. Our revision of methodology is intended to call particular attention to its rhetorical nature: all methodology is rhetorical, an explicit or implicit theory of human relations which guides the operation of methods. We do not view the presence of rhetoric as problematic for method, but as empowering—but either way, it's inevitable. Drawing such distinctions is particularly important for our arguments against several of the binaries that incapacitate our field: theory vs. practice, theoretical research vs. empirical research, and workplace vs. classroom (or corporation vs. university). We see the same distinction in Stanley and Wise (1993; was in original 1983 version and later in Harding, 1987b). They view method as "techniques or specific sets of research practices" like a survey or ethnography, while *methodology* refers to "broad, theoretically informed frameworks" (p. 26).

To instantiate these distinctions in this book, we examine researchers' and teachers' study and use of computers as writing tools, as reported in the published literature. We draw freely on the evidence supplied by research in the fields of computers and composition, rhetoric/composition, and professional writing. We consider several different technologies—word processing and electronic-aided publishing; e-mail, electronic networking and synchronous conferencing; and hypertext—though the technologies themselves are not our primary focus. We classify and configure the published research according to its rhetoric, by which we mean its ideology(ies), its practices, and its method(s). We make use of some of our own empirical work, mostly usability studies. We also rely on our experiences consulting for the usability group of a large computer software company; teaching in computer classrooms; mentoring other writing teachers in computer classrooms; directing Ph.D. dissertations in rhetoric/composition and computers and writing; and administering programs that make extensive use of computers to teach writing.

The perspective we have developed and which we apply is one that locates critical research practices in the activity of situated practice. Our terminology is influenced by Lucy Suchman's work *Plans and Situated Actions* (1987) and by a number of pragmatic theorists, both in and outside of composition studies (e.g., Bourdieu, 1977, 1988; Lave & Wenger, 1991; Miller, 1989; Phelps, 1988, 1991; Winograd & Flores, 1986). We have developed some of the theory for this methodological approach in a series of articles (see Sullivan & Porter, 1993a, 1993b). We make use of our previously published material in several chapters, but we develop and reshape this material for the issues important to computers and composition.

This theory also borrows much from emerging developments in feminist methodology (Lather, 1991; Roman, 1992; Smith, 1987, 1990; Stanley, 1990a) and in Scandinavian participatory design (e.g., Bødker, 1989, 1991; Ehn, 1988; Greenbaum & Kyng, 1991). Both movements, one in theorizing about knowledge-making and one in product development in engineering, show places where research methodology intersects with politics: Critical practice is also a political philosophy that views the material conditions (of work, especially) as vital to the understanding of a social activity. Understanding those material conditions is key to changing those conditions.

How do we make space for our positioning of research practices as critical ones? We expect that there are many ways to punch out space for self- and outer-reflection, one of which is the multiple mapping we employ in Chapter 4 (and that we have briefly demonstrated in this chapter with our basketball shot chart). There we fashion the postmodern mapping methods described by Pierre Bourdieu in *Homo Academicus* (1988) and Edward Soja in *Postmodern Geographies* (1989) into a strategy for thinking about some of our own work with computers and usability, both in a classroom and in a workplace setting.

We've decided that nobody much enjoys methodology. Too often methodology is treated as the means by which we get to something else, and it's when that something else is the focus of interest that we run the risk of unreflective practices. Say we unreflectively ask: Is the electronic network hostile to women? There's the interesting question; now how do we answer it? Well, maybe we'll do a survey or a case study. Maybe we'll collect 4,000 email messages and discover through hundreds of hours of painstaking encoding and statistical analysis that men use "aggressive language" more often than do women. (We might have reached the same conclusion by measuring their levels of testosterone, but never mind.) Using some method—and the word connotes "tediousness"—we might arrive at some answer to generate some knowledge for some field of inquiry. In this depiction of the research process, method is the a hairshirt we wear, the penance we pay for new knowledge. We acquire method through a painful initiation akin to hazing (that is, graduate school). We practice method faithfully to achieve academic credentials. Through the aggregate of our collective methodical plodding, we herd together, citing each other's research, to slowly and patiently build a research field, gain power, prestige, promotion. We retire, and then we die, passing the mantle of method on to the next generation. But, we contend, this approach is all wrong, in large part because it travels to its truth unreflectively, because it accepts research questions and methods as ideologically innocent tools to be wielded in the construction of knowledge.

But we see methodology as more than merely a means to something else. The asking of the research question itself and the design of a way to address the question (i.e., the inquiry procedures) constitute a rhetorical activity: a rhetorical inter-action with research participants. At this point of placing methodology inside rhetoric, we can begin to ask questions like, What is our rhetorical aim vis-à-vis these participants? To what end, vis-à-vis those participants, are we aspiring? We see methodology as invention, as the construction of a rhetorical design that contributes to an understanding but that also effects some kind of positive action through a rhetorical practice. Methodology is not merely a means to something else, it is itself an intervening social action and a participation in human events. It is itself an act of rhetoric, both with our participants in research studies and with our colleagues in a given research field.

2

Positions and Perimeters: A Hypertextual Glossary

The position we are advancing in this project could be summarized as follows: We advocate a view of research as a set of **critical practices** (**praxis**) that acknowledge the **rhetorical situatedness** of **participants**, **writing technologies**, and **technology design** and that recognize research as a form of **political and ethical action**. This view is **postmodern** in a certain way.

There are numerous troubling terms here: *critical*? *praxis*? *rhetorical situatedness*? *writing technologies*? *political and ethical action*? Not to mention *postmodern*—the most troubling term of all. These terms and phrases have long and unhappy histories and well-established ambiguities; they deserve some unpacking. Because there are various potential meanings attending these terms, we think it makes sense to establish the perimeters of our thinking about such concepts.

Thus, in this chapter, we situate these terms in the context of their uses in fields as diverse as philosophy, human-computer interaction, and empirical methodology, and also in the context of our use of them in a critical practices approach to research. We adopt a modular, hypertextual approach: The bolded phrases in the first paragraph are defined and discussed below. Point and click on any of the bold terms, then turn the page to find the corresponding discussion. Not electronic hypertext, but close.

CRITICAL

Don't expect us to equate critical with negative criticism, as has been done in much popular usage. We connect critical more with the efforts of researchers to keep themselves alert to those elements in their practices that adopt positions or attitudes or actions without reflection. In our view, a researcher who studies a workplace for several months and then issues a report about writing practices, but does not ever give special notice to the computers because the researcher thinks the office has outdated word-processing software, or because that researcher holds a view that computers are so instrumental in the production of writing that they are not worth noticing—for us, that researcher is missing an opportunity to reflect on the uses of computers in the writing process. His inattention to the tools of production constitutes an unreflectiveness, an uncriticalness.

Correspondingly, a researcher who approaches a study of computers in a classroom environment and establishes a pool of subjects (students) and informants (teachers) as the sources of information about the circulation of power in that classroom without consideration of her own position of power in this study, or without consideration of the power of the physical layout of the particular classroom used, or without consideration of how the classroom is connected to other sites—that researcher is missing a consideration of some of the important elements of power. Her inattention to the valences of power in the site under scrutiny constitutes uncriticalness. In our view, a researcher who presents the results of a case study without interrogating his motivation to do that study, who routinely follows the guidelines for completing such a study without questioning those guidelines, who does not consider the historical dimensions of the findings or the ways in which current theory and literature make certain topics inherently more interesting, who does not reveal his position vis-à-vis the other elements of the study—that researcher is acting unreflectively, uncritically.

We see critical actions taken by researchers, then, as manifestation of the ability to act in the production of knowledge at the same time as they are vigilant about the ways in which our circumstances, abilities, values, and beliefs encourage us to act in certain ways. When we are researching critically, we are presenting our results and the frames out of which our results take shape—historically, theoretically, politically, ethically. When "we" obscure those frames, we risk our critical practices; when we ignore those frames, we resist our critical practices. Yet, practically, we must admit that when we expose those frames—and the tentativeness of findings they imbue—we risk our positions as conveyors of empirical knowledge. Yes, we undercut our authority. Yes, we are/can be accused of not knowing "how" to really do research.

As we see it, we really have no choice but to subject our research action to the constant scrutiny of the reflective and critical eye(s).

Our use of the term *critical* invokes the Critical Theory of the Frankfurt School, which "attempts to promote the project of emancipation by furthering what it understands as the theoretical effort of the critique of domination begun by the Enlightenment and continued by Karl Marx" (Poster, 1989, p. 1; see also Fay, 1987, pp. 4–5; Geuss, 1981). Proponents of the Frankfurt School (Adorno, Habermas, Horkheimer, Marcuse) attempted a reconstruction of Marxist theory in light of twentieth-century philosophies and historical developments, focusing on the role of power in social settings and pushing toward the possibility of changing the world by serving as a "counterforce" (Poster, 1989, p. 3) to hegemonic social practices, and by using critique as a tool to further the possibility of reducing human suffering and enabling greater human freedoms in the face of oppressive systems and discursive practices. The principle behind the aims of the critical movement might be best summed up in Marx's Eleventh Thesis on Feuerbach: "Heretofore, the philosophers have only interpreted the world, in various ways; the point, however, is to change it" (Warry, 1992).

Critical Theory should not be equated with traditional Marxism. According to Walter Nord and John Jermier (1992), the Critical Theory movement in its current form is more eclectic: It draws its focus on communication and liberation from the Frankfurt School; its focus on economics, class, labor, and production from Marx's theory of capitalism; and its focus on domination in gender from feminist critiques of classical Marxist theory.

Our construction of critical resembles, though is not the same as, Max Horkheimer's notion of "critical theory." Like Horkheimer (1972), we use the term *critical* to distinguish an approach to methodology that is different from traditional approaches. Horkheimer criticizes the traditional approach to theory and methodology, which he locates in Descartes's scientific method, as operating in an "isolated sphere" (p. 197), where the scientific activity studies a phenomenon without acknowledging the division of labor involved in its operation, the historical reasons for its existence, or the relation of the object to human life. In other words, traditional theory decontextualizes (Feenberg, 1991), separating knowledge and action and identifying the pursuit of knowledge for its own sake as its goal. In traditional theory, "the object with which the scientific specialist deals is not affected at all by his own theory. Subject and object are kept strictly apart" (p. 229).

Critical in this context means, first, questioning the split between scientific knowledge and values (politics and ethics). Critical theory challenges the presumption of traditional methodology that certain methods of observation and data collection can proceed neutrally to generate certain knowledge. Rather, critical theory begins by noticing the political and ethical situatedness of the methods themselves, as well as the political and ethical implications of determining what counts as "knowledge" in any given instance. A significant concern of such an enterprise is recognizing the power relations in given settings.

Second, critical theory challenges whether the aim of methodology should be knowledge at all. Whose good does knowledge serve? Why have knowledge? Critical theory questions the presumed authority of knowledge constructed on the basis of instrumental reason (i.e., the observation and analysis by an observing, fully conscious researcher of a cause–effect chain operating within a mechanistic universe), and it views the appropriate aim of research or scholarly activity as resisting oppression, liberating those who are enslaved, and improving the conditions of those who are dominated by others. According to Horkheimer, critical theory aims for "man's [sic] emancipation from slavery" (p. 246). It establishes action, in the sense of constructive change, as the appropriate aim of research activity.

Critical theory contextualizes, considering the relationship of the individual to the society in terms of a situated web of relations, including historical factors, the system of labor and production involved, and the class implications of such relations. Our conception of critical is by no means as materialist in its assumptions as Horkheimer's, nor do we privilege the economic to the extent that he does. In the broader terms that we prefer, critical theory is situated in human relations, it acknowledges power relations (including but by no means limited to the variables of class, economics, and labor status), and it aims for the betterment of participants. Mark Poster (1989), more than nearly every other theorist, recognizes that: (a) Critical theory alone is inadequate because it ends up, typically, not self-reflexive or skeptical enough about its own grounding; (b) critical theory needs poststructuralism (e.g., Foucault, Baudrillard) to recognize the limits of its operation; and (c) theory relies on contextual language use. Also, because Poster has a strong sense of the medium for communication, or at least relatively strong for a theorist, he recognizes how computers can impact communication:

> At the ontological level metaphysical dualists may argue that nothing has changed with the introduction of the computer. The world may still be thought by some to be composed of material and mental things. But at the phenomenological level at which the subject experiences itself and the world, the computer changes everything. …Like the other domains of the mode of information, the computer draws attention to the subject as a constituted phenomenon, undermining the illusory assurance of the fixed, defined individual. (pp. 138–139)

Andrew Feenberg has developed Critical Theory specifically as a means of critiquing and constructing uses of technology, and we find his categories useful to our analysis. In *Critical Theory of Technology* (1991), he argues for a critical view that offers an alternative to the two established theories of technology, instrumental and substantive. The instrumental view (the dominant model) treats technology as a neutral collection of tools, "without valuative content" (p. 5), that are adapted to users' purposes. Feenberg identifies four features of this view: (a) Technology is indifferent to the ends of its users; (b) it is indifferent to politics; (c) it is rational; and (d) it can be measured by universal standards (pp. 5–6). In the instrumental view, there is no such thing as bad technology; the good or bad use of technology is determined by its human use. Such a view leads the social sciences, Feenberg claims, to use technology to account for "tensions between tradition, ideology, and efficiency which arise from socio-technical change" (pp. 6–7). The substantive view (the minority model), which is best known in the writings of Martin Heidegger (1977) and Jacques Ellul (and perhaps secondarily in Michel Foucault), contends that new technology "constitutes a new type of cultural system that restructures the entire social world as an object of control…there is no escape other than retreat" (p. 7). The substantive view leads to a radical distrust of technology and, often, to an urge to return to the simplicity of non-technological life.

Feenberg points out that these two positions share a take-it-or-leave-it attitude about technology. If technology is instrumental, it is "indifferent to values" and political debate, focused instead on "efficiency of application" (p. 8). If, instead, technology substantively transmits "cultural domination," we are stuck with choosing either technological progress or more primitive life (p. 8). Feenberg argues that "in neither case can we change it: in both theories, *technology is destiny*" (p. 8). Feenberg turns instead to the task of characterizing a critical theory, one which "charts a difficult course between resignation and utopia" (p. 13). This critical theory, he argues, contends that:

> Technology is not a thing in the ordinary sense of the term, but an "ambivalent" process of development suspended between different possibilities. This "ambivalence" of technology is distinguished from neutrality by the role it attributes to social values in the design, and not merely the use, of technical systems. On this view, technology is not a destiny but a scene of struggle. It is a social battlefield, or perhaps a better metaphor would be a *parliament of things* on which civilizational alternatives are debated and decided. (p. 14)

For Feenberg, a critical perspective toward technology must begin by analyzing "the new forms of oppression associated with modern industrialism" and then "explain how modern technology can be redesigned to adapt it to the needs of a freer society" (p. 13). The critical axiology depends, then, on the ability to critique in two senses. One sense is the popular, negative sense of critique: we must be able to discern the ways in which technology oppresses—what Feenberg considers "postmodern critique" (p. 18). But Feenberg's "critical theory" also has a constructive, proactive aim: to redesign and readapt technologies. In *Alternative Modernity* (1995), Feenberg further explores the technical and social dimensions of technological design using case studies (the Minitel case is the prime computing example, with others focused on medical technology), arguing that technical systems, "cannot be considered finished until they have withstood social tests that expose them to a wide range of public influences and concerns excluded in the design phase" (p. 7). In the cases he describes, the technical systems underwent important changes after the public deemed the systems flawed. In the case of Minitel he points to hackers who introduced new communication applications as humanizers of the Minitel, a reading of that technology which stands in sharp contrast to Marc Augé's (1995) reading of the Minitel as an agent of supermodernity. Feenberg aims, then, to show the ways in which the social and the technical dimensions of design need to work together to democratize design.

Feenberg's discussion of critical theory for technology is useful in describing why we are interested in critical research practices. In his work he is trying to expose the timbers of the structure called technology in ways that people can see a building, and remember a process of building, and a plan for the building, and recall the reason why the building was wanted in the first place. We, too, want to expose the timbers and the construction process—this time the building is research practices—in order to discuss the critical nature of knowledge-making and action in the field of computers and composition. We do this not simply for a negative purpose, but for the constructive purpose of redesigning technologies, and research practices, to suit diverse human needs.

Critical Theory has given rise to what is commonly known as the Critical Social Science (or CSS) movement, which according to Nord and Jermier (1992), "offers an intellectual framework for resisting domination by traditional science and technology, institutionally distorted communication, owners of capital, and patriarchal forces" (p. 203). Brian Fay's book *Critical Social Science* (1987) is perhaps the key defining work of this movement. Fay recognizes that "a theory of how to understand the social world necessarily invokes conceptions both of what humans are and of what they might become" (p. 1). In other words, Fay argues that social science has to entertain questions of identity, politics, and ethics. Fay's approach to this is fairly rationalistic, however. He wants to develop a scientific basis for Critical Social Science: he wants to avoid the charge of idealism and ideology, and thinks there's a way to be "scientific" in the traditional sense (accepting the authority of research/researcher). His notion of liberation is a priori and patriarchal. He wants the masses to understand "the true nature of their existence" (p. 68) and to move beyond false consciousness. Good research frees them, in other words. It is this sort of research that we are decidedly not advocating.

In invoking the term *critical* we are establishing social change as the appropriate aim of research praxis. Determining what kind of social change is needed, and how it should come about, is an issue that we will take up in detail as the book unfolds. However the change can be of various sorts: liberation of the oppressed (Freire), improved communicative relations (Habermas), increased power for computer users, improvement of social conditions, improvement of work conditions (Zuboff), and, in academic contexts, the improvement of learning conditions and the empowerment of students. Though we are invoking Critical Theory, our construction of the idea of critical research practices goes beyond what is conventionally circumscribed as Critical Theory. We are moving toward a version of *critical* that picks up the central themes of traditional Critical Theory but merges them with several other areas: especially the cultural postmodernism of Foucault, postmodern geography (e.g., Soja, 1989), and feminist theory, especially as regards methodology (e.g., Lather, 1991; Luke & Gore, 1992; Stanley, 1990a) and ethics (e.g., Benhabib, 1992; Young, 1990). Our use of the term *critical* is not Marxist in a traditional sense; it does not focus primarily on issues of labor and production; it does not simply connote attack, negative commentary, undermining, or ludic deconstruction. Rather, our notion of critical pushes more toward the sense of critical reflection, challenge, and then positive action. It is closer to what Patti Lather (1992), Teresa Ebert (1991), and others have referred to as "resistance postmodernism," and it might in fact be more appropriately described as postcritical (see discussion of *postmodern*).

PRACTICES

Numerous theorists have extolled the virtues of practice, as we do, but they sometimes do so while holding to a diminished view of practice.

Alasdair MacIntyre (1984), for instance, sees practice as important to the development of the virtue ethic he advocates. Whether an activity or action is excellent (or right or true or just) in any given situation is partly determined by the particular professional practice involved in the activity or action. Thus, for MacIntyre, practice plays a crucial role in the development of an ethical self—and we agree.

Though MacIntyre is praising practice, we have to closely examine what he means by practice:

> By a "practice" I am going to mean any coherent and complex form of socially established cooperative human activity through which goods internal to that form of activity are realized in the course of trying to achieve those standards of excellence which are appropriate to, and partially definitive of, that form of activity, with the result that human powers to achieve excellence, and human conceptions of the ends and goods involved, are systematically extended. (p. 187)

We have no problems with this definition in the abstract, but what MacIntyre means by a "coherent and complex form of socially established cooperative human activity" becomes clear only when we look at his examples. For MacIntyre, bricklaying is not a practice, but architecture is. Planting turnips is not a practice; farming is. In each case, MacIntyre distinguishes between "mere" technical skills and a general field of knowledge. Thus, he reinvents the theory-practice binary in the arena of action, holding up theory (in the form of general knowledge) as the superior term in the pair—except that he calls it "practice." We want to insist that planting turnips and bricklaying—and writing and researching, too—are all practices in the sense that all require a reflectiveness and critical awareness to be done well.

It is useful to examine the dissonance between Donald Schön's and MacIntyre's notions of practice. Actually, what MacIntyre means by practice is closer to what Schön (1983) means by reflective practice. But what is important about MacIntyre's view is that he holds a diminished view of technical skill. Very much unlike Schön, MacIntyre celebrates formal and abstract knowledge as true practice—the philosophical move to formal abstraction, which we will talk about later, in Chapter 5—and creates a strong binary between technical skill and such knowledge. Schön (and postmodernists like Bourdieu and Geertz) denounce such a binary. Schön's view of "reflective practice" insists on the integration of technical and reflective.

Practice is a slippery word, and perhaps the slipperiest in the whole bag of slippery terms we use. In some uses (like MacIntyre's) the term can take on a meaning completely the opposite from how we are using it. Stephen Turner's and Pierre Bourdieu's discussions of practice are both helpful to our understanding and use of the term.

Turner (1994) starts out by recognizing that *practice* is a diverse and slippery term in philosophy and social history. On the one hand it refers to deductive theories, "shared presuppositions," ideologies, traditions, paradigms, or frameworks (where MacIntyre locates his sense of "practice"). At other times it refers to skills, habits, customs, or local activities. Turner sees a difference between these two groups of concepts—one is conceptual, theoretical, and abstract, the latter is physical, concrete, and local—but the difference does not always hold up, and many notions of practice "fall into neither group" (p. 3).

Our notion of theory lies in the first group, and our notion of practice in the second. A practice is not just any action that anyone performs at any time, but rather stylized or customized action: that is, action that through a certain amount of repetition and experiential testing has become a habit or strategy that works and that is or can be passed on to others (like bricklaying, planting turnips, and writing) and that meets some standard for human excellence. We can talk about the practice of teaching composition in these terms: the strategies, types of assignments, and approaches to material that are passed along in the field from teachers to students and to other teachers. The term *practice* denotes repeatability and transferability, custom, and habit. Research, thus, is a kind of practice, and research practices can vary between, and even within, disciplinary communities.

We are talking about this theory-practice binary only momentarily in order to dismantle it, and we have considered how the binary operates counterproductively in fields like professional writing (Sullivan & Porter, 1993a; see Lobkowicz, 1967). Like Turner, we believe that this binary does not always hold up, and in fact we believe that it shouldn't, and that we shouldn't believe in it. We are pushing toward a notion of research and teaching as a praxis: that is, a reflective, thoughtful practice that has critique and questioning built into its operation, an activity that merges theory and practice, and that adds to repeatability and transferability a further notion: revision. We would call such an activity an art.

So why do we foreground the term *practice* in this study? Because we are argu-ing with the academic and scholarly tendency to subordinate practice, either to the God of Theory or to the God of Method. Many (MacIntyre, for example) say that practice is important, but we see few giving it the recognition it deserves when they perform their critiques or set up their research studies. Few are willing to refer to their theories or their research as a kind of practice, though we see it as such. Thus, we want to elevate the status of practice, though we by no means want to create a false God of Practice. We also want to be clear about how we are using the term: We do not mean practices merely as any research actions, but as critical praxis. (By which we mean what? Read on, read on.)

Turner sees the term *practice* as problematic, a flimsy background for building philosophical knowledge. *Practices* (plural) is slightly better because it acknowl-edges the individuality of practices and does not make an unjustified (to Turner) leap to assumptions about commonality (p. 93). However, Turner has difficulties with the notion of "shared practice" because, he wonders, how do we know to what extent habits are really shared? Everything is fundamentally different to Turner, because nothing can be definitively shown to be "the same."

If we were to apply Turner's brand of deconstructive philosophy to our own work, we would be able to use few terms at all in a positive sense. As Turner points out, his critique is mostly a negative one, showing us why something will not work (p. 13) and what we cannot possibly know. With Turner's brand of *dis-soi logoi* it is easy to say what something is not, harder to say what something is.

Because Turner embraces a paradigm with a strictly epistemic notion of knowledge, with its insistence on discovering the "really real," and because he does not have a rhetorical orientation that might help him accept the validity of probable knowledge or shared belief, his criteria for knowledge are limiting in a crippling way. (Turner's epistemology has no special place for probable knowl-edge, which to him is no kind of knowledge.) What he ends up essentializing is "individual habitualizations," a move we find no less problematic than the social or postmodern moves that Turner argues against. You can't get to any valid notion of the social with Turner's analytic procedure, because, he says, "there are no col-lective objects to be accounted for … but only individual habits" (p. 116). In cri-tiquing the social, Turner's critique ends up denying the validity or significance of notions of ideologies of power, both the Marxist and postmodern varieties.

What Turner's discussion does, however, is make us conscious of the danger of essentializing practice and of oversimplifying it. We want to avoid that trap. Using the plural form of the word—*practices*—is a helpful reminder (though it does not ultimately satisfy Turner's critique). We see practices as diverse, yet at the same capable of being repeated and transferred; that is, of being communal-ized. We do not see a necessary incompatibility between the notions of "same" and "different."

In *Outline of a Theory of Practice* (1977) and *The Logic of Practice* (1990), Pierre Bourdieu presents an argument on behalf of practice and questions the presumed superiority of theory. Bourdieu warns in *The Logic of Practice* of the danger of scientific models:

> [Models] are only valid so long as they are taken for what they are, logical models giving an account of the observed facts in the most coherent and most economical way; ... they become false and dangerous as soon as they are treated as the real principles of practices, which amount to simultaneously overestimating the logic of practices and losing sight of what constitutes their real principle. (p. 11)

Bourdieu wants to foreground cultural practices, or what he calls "habitus." Habitus represents the repeated rituals of a culture: that which is done repeatedly, perhaps for no "reason" (in the theoretical sense of *logos*) other than that it is that which is done. The attempt to provide some kind of exterior or legal reason for the activity is the arrogance of the objectivist tradition of methodology.

Bourdieu is arguing for a view of logic from within cultures, rather than a transcultural or universal logic. Scholars must acknowledge "the uncertainties of the uses that the agents may themselves make practically of a symbol so overdetermined that it becomes indeterminate even in terms of the schemes that determine it. The error would here lie in trying to decide the undecidable" (p. 264). Though at times Bourdieu seems to be promoting a methodology that renders human action radically indeterminate, and that at times seems to render research knowledge impossible, his position is simply to call into radical question the assumptions of the objectivist paradigm. Things cannot all be assigned a single, clear position in the structuralist master plan. Rather, the sign of a sound plan is that it recognizes the indeterminacies, gaps, undecidables. And yet we can have plans and we can arrive at understandings about other cultures. Some things happen that do not make sense in the world of "logical logic." Nonetheless they can be seen as a kind of "practical logic."

Our effort is aimed at freeing research practices from the mantle of the objectivist paradigm, where theorists like Alan Gross (1994) seem intent on situating them. The sound research project avoids two kinds of traps: One is the trap of the objectivist paradigm, which Bourdieu warns against. The other trap is the kind of radical individuation and skepticism which Turner falls into, which renders any attempt at collective or social knowledge impossible. Postmodern empirical research is possible, and Bourdieu points the way to it.

A number of researchers from a variety of fields have noticed the dominant tendency in academic scholarship to privilege theory (often portrayed as structure or method) over practice and have begun to challenge this presumed superiority, arguing for the significance of practice. Bourdieu's analysis (1977) of the theory-practice dynamic represents his break from what he refers to as the "positionality of the objectivist stance" he associates with traditional social science research. Bourdieu points out that to understand an activity, such as the gift-giving ritual of Kabyle culture, one must understand the timing of that activity. The static structuralist paradigm does not account for the timing, the situatedness of the ritual, what rhetoric terms *kairos* (see Kinneavy, 1986; Phelps, 1988, pp. 230–231). Theory, in this instance understood to be an all-encompassing structure or framework of understanding, does not account for the positionality of the ritual.

Situated practice is investigated within technology by Lucy Suchman (1987), as she explores the relationship between plans (which function as theory or structure) and the situated actions or practices of the users of a copying machine. She notes that "European navigators" (her analogy for the Western rationalist) tend to view plans as abstract and prior structures, as determining or at least guiding behavior. Her observations of office workers learning to use new copying machines indicate that users proceed more like "Trukese navigators": they know where they want to go, but they do not have any prior navigational plan for getting there. They proceed in an ad hoc fashion, letting the unfolding events of the situation (rather than the preconceived plan) determine what they will do next. The problem, according to Suchman, is that researchers seldom distinguish between the plan (as intention) and the explanatory structure. Her point is that as researchers, we must begin to understand structure as "an emergent product of situated action, rather than its foundation" (p. 67). Our discussion of emerging research (in Chapter 6) provides an example of this form of research navigation.

What these and other researchers are recognizing is that theory, in the common and various ways it is perceived and employed, is by itself inadequate to account for the particular, what we know as practice.

One reason that we find the field of computers and composition an interesting site for critical investigation is that its members have always displayed a keen sensitivity toward practice, both the practice of teaching writing in computer-based environments and the situated uses of technology. Computers and composition is a field that arose, like composition, out of a curricular emphasis on practice. And yet, as such a field grows and develops, and as it becomes invested with research status in the university hierarchy, it can move in directions that put the focus on practices at risk. So we see an interesting tension being played out in the field: a field whose members are practice-oriented yet who are also attracted, maybe seduced by the enhanced status that accrues from objectifying practices (if you are working in the modernist paradigm which emphasizes knowledge production) or from ideologizing them (if you are working in the postmodernist paradigm of critique).

PRAXIS

Rhetoric/composition theory uses praxis in ways that see it as definitely something different from practice. The way Carolyn Miller and Louise Phelps have used praxis might be loosely translated as "reflective action," after Schön's discussion: "reflective action" refers to a thoughtful procedure that is neither "theory" (in the sense of *theoria*, or epistemic/scientific knowledge) nor mere "practice" (in the sense of merely repetitive behaviors, what people do). The major discussions of praxis in rhetoric/composition—for example, Garver (1987), Miller (1989), Phelps (1988)—view praxis as a type of thought/action that questions the validity and usefulness of the theory-practice distinction. Praxis, which occupies the realm of the probable, is connected by Miller, Garver, and others to Aristotle's notion of procedural or productive knowledge, a type of knowledge that has not been well understood in the modern era, and that Descartes dismissed as no knowledge at all. The standard for knowledge since the Enlightenment has been scientific knowledge. Those trying to revive praxis for composition are trying to carve out a space of productive knowledge within the framework of rhetorical invention.

Miller (1989) tries to bridge the theory-practice binary by identifying praxis as a higher form of practice, an "informed or conscious practice." For Miller, praxis is something more than a simple addition of or compromise between theory and practice; it represents a new kind of critical positioning. It is a practice conscious of itself that calls upon "prudential reasoning" (p. 22) for the sake not only of production but for "right conduct" as well. It is informed and politically conscious action, that in its functioning represents an overlap between both practical and productive knowledge (see Herndl, 1993).

Praxis is more than merely high-level practice (i.e., doing rote well-defined tasks). The way Schön describes it, certain kinds of professional areas are defined by the activity of praxis: a kind of thinking that does not start with theoretical knowledge or abstract models, which are then applied to situations, but that begins with immersion in local situations, and then uses epistemic theory as heuristic rather than as explanatory or determining. Ethicists who stress praxis fall into the contextualist or situational camp (e.g., Jonsen & Toulmin, 1988), claiming that one should begin ethical inquiry not by invoking as authoritative metaphysics or general law, but through a case approach that begins with situated instances, which are then critiqued heuristically by various "tools" (such as, perhaps, metaphysics) to reveal a way to respond to a problem. In discussions like these praxis is a way of defining professional expertise in areas where the model of philosophical/epistemic knowledge just does not work very well—for example, urban planning, ethics, and document design.

Praxis, then, is a "practical rhetoric," focused on local writing activities (practice), informed by as well as informing general principles (theory), and calling upon "prudential reasoning." Praxis recognizes the "inseparable relation between reflection and action" (see Phelps, 1988, p. 211, on Freire; Schön, 1983, on professional action as reflection-in-action). The judgment that enables this dynamic is referred to as "practical judgment," that is, *phronesis* (sometimes translated as "prudence"). According to Eugene Garver (1987), this kind of reasoning recognizes the "inferential relation between rules and cases, precepts and examples" (p. 12). It inserts itself into that gap "between apprehending a rule [*episteme*] and applying it [*techne*]" (p. 16). Prudence "requires that the writer [or researcher, we would say] find some middle ground between too much universality—the super-fluous... proclamation of moralizing principles—and too much particularity" (p. 39). The art here requires a fine, balancing judgment that is inescapable and unavoidable (see Phelps, 1988, p. 228), what in *Nichomachean Ethics* Aristotle calls *phronesis*.

What would such a praxis look like when enacted by a writer? Floreak's description (1989) of his own composing process provides an example of a pro-fessional writer engaged in "reflective action" (or praxis) during composing. In his discussion of his work on "Project First Steps," Floreak intertwines theory and practice, not treating them as separate compartments but discussing his project from a kind of theory-in-practice perspective. He calls upon theories of audience and usability methods for assistance and advice, but his commitment is to "trans-lating" this theory in terms of the situations out of which he writes: producing a way to help poor and often illiterate or semiliterate adults provide better care for their children.

As it applies to research activity, praxis refers to a kind of triangulation: not the kind by which you check results by using a variety of empirical or theoretical methods, or by collecting data through a variety of media, but a conceptual one that leads to research that privileges neither the theoretical foundation nor the observed practice. It is a research perspective willing to critique both theory and practice by placing both in dialectical tension, which can then allow either to change. In Chapters 3 and 4, we further elaborate and demonstrate what this crit-ical praxis is and how it works.

RHETORICAL SITUATEDNESS

We certainly will not be defining rhetoric in the popular sense as misleading and deceptive uses of language, usually for political gain, but we also do not view it in any of the more traditional (and limited) senses as "style" or "argument" or "per-suasion." Our view of rhetoric is defined principally by its focus on "situation" and by its concerns about how rhetorical situation guides production. That is to say, we are interested primarily in rhetorical invention—which, to us, includes what researchers term method. But rather than viewing method in a modern, Enlightenment sense as the scientific inquiry that precedes the rhetorical act of informing or persuading readers, we view method itself as rhetorically situated; that is, as part of the rhetorical act and so as subject to *kairos*.

As a productive art, rhetoric is concerned with how a discourse can be con-structed to achieve a certain effect. Other forms of textual analysis—say, linguis-tic or literary—describe discourse with the aim of building general theories or models of language use (as in communication theory or linguistics) or in deter-mining the meaning or intention of a particular text (as in traditional literary analysis). To some extent, rhetoric does the same thing, but with an additional end in mind: Rhetoric applies such descriptions to the end of practice, and so complicates discourse studies. We can do a post hoc empirical analysis to determine what effect the letter we wrote yesterday had on its readers, but how will the knowledge gained from that analysis help us write another letter to a different reader today? Obviously writers call upon prior experience, upon rhetorical principles and compositional practices, to guide their efforts, but since writers are always in new situations, they must select and interpret prior experience to build new writing plans. Rhetoric and composition is interested in how writers build plans, or "representations of situated actions" (Suchman, 1987, p. 50).

Because rhetoric is a situated and applied art, a kairotic art, it generates principles, not rules. The difference is significant: Principles are always interpreted and adjusted for situations and rarely survive in pure form. Rules circumscribe absolute boundaries. "Rather than actions being determined by rules, actors effectively use the normative rules of conduct that are available to produce significant actions" (Suchman, 1987, p. 66). This situational premise is stated in different ways by different theorists—for example, knowledge is local (Geertz, 1983); the significant level of inquiry is practice (Bourdieu, 1977; Phelps, 1988)—but the position is generally that:

> The significance of a linguistic expression on some actual occasion ... lies in its relationship to circumstances that are presupposed or indicated by, but not actually captured in, the expression itself. ...The communicative significance of a linguistic expression is always dependent upon the circumstances of its use. (Suchman, 1987, pp. 58, 60)

The object of analysis for those in computers and composition is not only the composed text, but the writer-in-the-act-of-composing, the audience, and also the computer as aid or as environment. Researchers in computers and composition who work from rhetorical premises examine the text not merely as an autonomous structure but also as a stage in an overall process of action involving the writer and the audience, as well as numerous other discourses. Rhetoric complicates discourse study in computers and composition by involving matters related to situation and process—the setting for discourse as well as the means by which it is produced and received.

Our focus on the term *situated* acknowledges that practices are always exercised at particular moments, at a particular time and place in a culture, society, or group. Rhetoric is the art of applying general strategies to a particular condition, which always involves a modification of the general strategies. It is not enough in rhetoric merely to know the strategies; one must also have developed the critical judgment necessary to make decisions about which ones apply, and how and when to use them, in any particular case. In this sense, rhetoric is a situational and sophistic art.

It was the New Rhetoric of the 1950s and 1960s that revived, for rhetoric, the focus on the situational ground of discourse—especially theorists such as Wayne Booth, Lloyd Bitzer, and James Kinneavy (see Porter, 1992a, p. 53). It was the deconstructionists and poststructuralists of the 1970s and 1980s who questioned the move to make situation (or context in the modernist, static sense) the foundation for rhetorical theory. Rhetoric theorists are familiar with the debate in the journal *Philosophy and Rhetoric* between Lloyd Bitzer (1968), Richard Vatz (1973), and Scott Consigny (1974) over the issue of to what extent situations are "rhetorically constructed" (Vatz's view) or "located in reality" (Bitzer's view). Derrida's deconstruction of context in "Signature Event Context" (1977) and his subsequent debate with John Searle in "Limited Inc ABC … " (1977) raised a serious challenge to the possibility of using context or situation as a trustworthy foundation for discursive relations.

We, too, are wary of essentializing rhetorical situation or context, or any of the constitutive elements of situation, the so-called unities of discourse—writer, reader, text. (Add a fourth: computer.) We are sympathetic to Derrida's deconstruction of context (in "Signature Event Context"). We acknowledge, after the reader-response critics of the 1970s and 1980s, the complexities of the notions of "reader" and "audience" (Porter, 1992a). We accept, after Barthes (1977) and Foucault (1984b), the instability of the notion of writer as "author." We have to be willing to admit the instability of such constructs, to recognize them as themselves rhetorically constructed entities and to not accept them uncritically as the a priori fixed matter of rhetoric.

However, we do not reject such concepts uncritically. We think it is important to interrogate rhetorical setting, but not abandon it. *Kairos* may be elusive and indefinite, but in order for there to be any rhetoric, we must dare some descriptions of it. So warning ourselves, we proceed.

In the next two subsections—on participants and writing technologies—we examine in more detail the complexity of two often foundational notions in empirical research on computers and composition and examine how researchers might acknowledge the complexity of these terms (and so enrich their use in studies), without jettisoning the constructs altogether. In the final subsection, in which we discuss rhetorical situatedness, we consider some product design movements in the computer industry that also emphasize the contextuality of the research situation.

Participants (Researchers and Researched)

Important to our understanding of rhetorical situatedness is the consideration of those who participate in each situation: those who populate a situation and those who enter that situation to study it. The names we give to inquirers is fairly standard in research in computers and composition research: They are the researchers. Interestingly, those who are studied are named differently by the various paradigms that broadly comprise computers and composition: Traditional research (excepting some types of qualitative research) labels them "subjects"; feminist, postmodernist, and much qualitative inquiry involves them as "participants"; and industrial research into the usability of computer systems refers to them as "users." Those differences in labels are not benign; they indicate that those who are studied are positioned differently by those paradigms.

This suggests to us our central point about participants: They are not fixed or stable or determinant of a rhetorical situation. Rather, their subjectivities are constructed both by each of the paradigms in which they live and also by each individual study that addresses their lives and activities. Yes, if we were to study the online lives of basic writers, and to select a particular classroom as our source for people to study, the identities of those same people would differ according to the ways we paradigmatically framed our encounters with them: From a traditional vantage we would see them as subjects whose choice for inclusion had to be matched or randomly selected or justified in some way; from a feminist vantage we would see them as participants (with the researchers) in a study who would need understanding, voice, and power; and from a usability vantage we would see them as potential buyers and would require that they were connected with the product's target market in some way.

These approaches to research entertain at least five positionings of the people who are studied:

1. Disconnection of person and individual identity (e.g., "N = 30 randomly selected subjects").
2. Recognition of demographic identity (e.g., "N = 150 males of high and low socio-economic station and mixed ethnic heritages").
3. Recognition of personal identity (i.e., those studied are studied intensely; they may not be chosen for group representation; they may be sorted demographically at times).
4. Questioning of the stereotypes used to construct #3 and #4 (see, for example, that dividing by gender does not insure even-handed treatment of women but rather labels the ones who are studied the representatives of their gender).
5. Recognition that a person can take on more than one persona (see, for example, a person using one technology instrumentally and another technology critically).

In part these subjectivities are dictated by the research paradigm's position on generalizability. The #1 to #5 choices represent a continuum of views of the self (from those comprised of generalizable features to those entertaining multiple subjectivities) that roughly coincide with the paradigmatic shifts from traditional positivists to traditional naturalists to postmoderns (see Chapter 3 for a discussion of research paradigms). Those paradigms which are studying a particular situation for the purpose of uncovering how this type of situation operates (or how people act in this situation or how certain types of people act in this situation), are likely

to position the people they study in #1 or #2 (with #3 a possibility). Those paradigms which concentrate on the identities of the people as unique are likely to
position those they study as #3 or #4. We see option #5 infrequently, though we
think it an obvious possibility in research that investigates how people deal with a
range of technologies (see Lopez, 1995).

In part the subjectivities are influenced by the amount and types of information
being collected. A survey involving the opinions of several hundred people is not
likely to establish close contact with those people because of the time required to
undertake such an investigation. Instead, it is the case study of a writing team, just
to offer one example, involving four people over a period of 18 months, that
invites close contact and leads naturally to more complex positionings of the people who are studied. While we know of studies that started as surveys and led to
closer contact (see Hawisher & Sullivan, in press), usually the closeness of contact with the people being studied is in some way influenced by the type of information available.

In part the subjectivities are built out of the goals of the investigation. If the primary goal of an inquiry, for example, is to expose the problems that African-
American students have in online forums as a way to challenge egalitarian claims
that online discussion enhances participation of minorities, then the African-
American students who are studied are likely to be seen first as people who
embody and speak for their race and only secondarily as students or as unique or
even multiple personalities. Romano's (1993) recounting of her perceptions of the
subjectivities of her Mexican-American students exposes some of the problems
that accompany such a study: Those people resisted speaking for their race, which
she came to understood as related (in part) to their goal of using the composition
class as a means of assimilation into college, and more basically because it is one
more way for them to lose their identities. Romano's discussion is helpful in highlighting how one teacher/researcher came to an understanding of the gaps
between her original conception of those minority students as representatives of
their race and her eventual sense of them as members of her writing class. Her
study underscores the changing identities of participants over time.

Overall we find rhetorical situatedness complicated by participants (and the
researchers who relate them to us) in at least three important ways: (a) The paradigm accepted by the researchers goes some of the way toward constructing what
the research/ers mean/s by "participants"; (b) the type of data being collected goes
some of the way toward constructing what the research/ers mean/s by "participants"; and (c) identities of "participants" (and "researchers") are not stable over
time. They may change as they interrelate (see Romano, 1993). Their identities
also may change depending on the medium, or writing technology (see Lopez,
1995). So, finally, we do not wish to essentialize or staticize "participants" (or
"researchers" or "rhetorical situatedness"). Instead we hold that research methodologies must recognize and account for the roles that participants are assigned
(and play) in the course of a particular research study, just as they should account

rchers' positionings and even technologies. We further recognize that identities of participants and researchers are paradigmatically complex, interrelated, and temporal.

Writing Technologies

Another part of rhetorical situatedness involves the writing technologies upon which any study in computers and composition centers. The phrase *writing technologies* contains a fundamental ambiguity: are we referring to the act of constructing technologies through writing or to the technologies associated with the act of writing? We obviously choose to focus on the latter in this book.

We considered, but rejected as too limited, other enframements—specifically, computer-mediated communication (CMC). *CMC*, a term popularized by research in organizational communication, places computers in limited roles. They are one medium (out of many) for the transmission of communication messages. As it has developed in communication, CMC typically focuses on the computer as instrumental—a neutral machine view. Further, CMC, along with electronic writing, focuses our research gaze away from print output, which not only is the mainstay of most composition research; it is the only way that most English teachers conceive of writing. We see an important disciplinary distinction between research that views the computer as a writing technology and research that views the computer as a communication medium—in other words, CMC research (see Allen & Hauptman, 1987; Hartman et al., 1991; Keen, 1987; Komsky, 1991; Mackay, 1988; Papa, 1990; Rice & Shook, 1988; Steinfield, 1992). The former sort of research focuses on writing in or with the medium, while the latter research focuses on general usage of the medium. CMC researchers typically focus on patterns of usage (e.g., frequency of use, attitude toward use, types of interactions), usually in terms of a general communication theory and sometimes based on instrumentalist (DiMatteo, 1991) and/or management assumptions about the communication dynamic. While that research provides information about user habits, it does not predominantly address writing issues (our focus): How is the medium used as a writing tool? What happens to writers and writing within the medium? How is the writing process changed by the medium (Porter, 1992b; Porter, 1993)? That's why we prefer the term *writing technologies*.

We need to entertain a further description of the term *writing technologies*, though, particularly if we accept Ong's, McLuhan's, and Innis's contentions that writing itself is a technology (see Ong, 1982). Ong (1977) has argued that the achievements of making spoken words into written text and later into print has called for "massive technological interventions which separate the word from man and man from the word" (p. 22). The spoken word is primary ("simply a datum of life"), with writing being a means of separating the speaker speaking and the speech that is spoken, a device for freezing and storing the word for a period of time, and a technology. Thus, he connects writing with an alienation between speaker and spoken so profound that "only some six thousand years ago, with the invention of the first script around 3500 B.C., did man begin to commit the spoken word to a visually perceived surface set off from himself. There are still millions of men and women who cannot do so" (p. 22).

This disconnection is of particular importance to those in computers and composition who study the (writing of) digitized texts that come into being and remain online.

Writing could conceivably refer to a wide list of symbolic actions (e.g., graffiti, films, flag burning, letters to the editor, paintings, customized menus, and so on); or it could be tied more closely to an identity as a language if we thought of writing as the systematic making of meaning as linguist Geoffrey Sampson (1985) did when he defined writing as a means "to communicate relatively specific ideas by means of permanent, visible marks" (p. 26). Sampson's more restrictive definition for writing is reasonable for the consideration of writing as it connects with speaking, as a frozen kind of speaking.

But we live electronic lives—that is, lives that are porous to enormous amounts of digital information (both verbal and graphic), which forever needs (re)arranging, an activity that we want to fall within the province of writing—and Sampson's definition falls short of describing those evolving realities of electronic writing. Further, we are experiencing electronic environments that are encouraging us to respond/communicate out of rhetorical situations that only vaguely simulate some patterns of speaking. Lest you worry that we envision a brave new world, remember that while these new electronic lives are encouraging new forums and conventions for communication, (a) they are not erasing print culture, and (b) they are providing these emerging forums almost exclusively for those who can pay for them. If anything, print is even more pervasive than ever before; we have millions of laser printers producing printed communications, and how many of us save printed versions of our electronic mail?

The way we see these technologies infecting the definitions we hold for writing is simply described: We see them blurring the boundaries. We are not unique in this position. Both Heim (1987) and Bolter (1991) have examined the impact of technology on the printed book, with Heim worrying that word-processing practices threaten aspects of book-oriented literacy and Bolter celebrating the challenges that electronic writing poses to print culture by proclaiming that we live in the late age of print. Bolter's definition of writing as the "creative play of signs...[with the computer offering] a new field for that play...a new writing space" (p. 10), shows his enthusiasm for the new media of digitized communication and announces an excitement that many who study and theorize hypertext share.

In many ways we are excited as well. A research proposal in chemistry is not necessarily typed today; it may well be developed on a supercomputer and dumped into an agency's customized formatting program, with the budgetary information linked to (and formatted in) a spreadsheet program, with methodology illustrated by an animated module inserted into the file containing the proposal, and on-screen text displaying in multiple colors (see Olsen, 1989). Further, the technology is developing new forms as well as new processes. Is the arrangement of spreadsheet data writing? After some of the convincing work of Barbara Mirel (1996b), we think so. Is an animation module that depicts a process and that anchors the discussion of methods in a technical report writing? We think so. The online layout of pages and the use of color to draw attention during online reading—are those decisions writing? We think so. Ten years ago we would not have posed these questions; the technologies did not exist in ways that allowed such documents to be easily constructed. Ten years (even five years) hence we expect to see new niggles at the boundaries for our meaning of writing. For this book, then, we focus on writing—verbal, graphic, static, dynamic—as it is produced to exist in print or electronically.

Turning our attention to technologies, we might begin by saying that the plural is not accidental. Most critiques of technology in composition studies, communication, and literary studies have included the many types of technology as a collective. This has had some interesting side effects: Proponents of each new technology can look to those critiques and dismiss them as being too general to pertain to this particular technology and also as being irrelevant because they were written before this new technology was invented/popularized. Opponents, on the other hand, have seen key critiques, for example Ohmann's (1985) *College English* article, as debunking the entire effort to teach writing with computers or to study writing that is produced with/for computers. Of course, we doubt that all communication technologies behave so similarly that a singular critique (no matter how powerful the speaker nor eloquent the delivery) can speak with enough richness to effectively dismiss them. But then we have enough experience using these technologies to see them as diverse, while others who do not rely on technology may not see such diversity.

If asked to illustrate that diversity of technologies, we would construct a list of those technologies that are (or have been) involved with the production of writing:

- Styluses (i.e., quills, pens, pencils, chalk, crayons, paintbrushes, typewriters, keyboards, touch screens, electronic pens, digitized pads, electronic mice, etc.).
- Storage (i.e., papyrus, codex, paper, printing plates, paper files, books, electronic files, paths to Internet resources, etc.).
- Production environment (i.e., word processing, MOO/MUD, E-mail, development packages for hypertext or hypermedia or cyberspaces, digital video).
- Production/delivery (i.e., paper, copiers, electronic files, electronic mail, fax, television, films, hypertext, hypertext, hypermedia presentations, etc.).

Although we accept that papyrus, to name one example, is a technology that could be linked with writing, in this book we are interested in the electronic technologies associated with writing. Thus, though the pen is mightier than the sword, it is not as interesting to us in this discussion as the keyboard; nor is snail mail as interesting as email. We are mindful that earlier technologies of writing do not disappear as new ones find favor (most people use word-processing software even though most researchers no longer study it, to name a very recent example), and that often the processes of older technologies are reproduced in newer technologies (see Howard, 1992, for a case study illustrating this in a LISTSERV discussion).

We are not focusing on all electronic technologies, just on those associated with writing. Hence the telephone (which supports communication primarily as an oral medium, though voice mail is an interesting anomaly connected with the phone) is not vital to our discussion while synchronous communication online (a mostly textual medium, which is beginning to include graphical dimensions) is. In a sense, we are interested in the production and delivery of the writing dimensions of electronic communication and with the uses of electronic technology in the production and delivery of printed (or digitized) communication, and we see these interests as the emerging interests of computers and writing research.

"Situated" Technology Design in the Computer Industry

Our position bears a resemblance to, but is not the same as, certain movements and research schools located in the computer industry. We see special promise in participatory design (see Muller & Kuhn, 1993), a movement theorized in Scandinavia (see Ehn, 1988), which approaches the design of computer systems that are automating work activities by declaring workers the experts and building from there. Workers participate in deciding which of the activities they perform could be assisted by automation and which of those activities resist automation. These workers also describe how they work and how their work fits with the work of others in order to develop a worker-centered view of the worksite.

Automation in the work-oriented design view is positioned more as a worker's tool that is part of the process of work and crafted to be an ideal tool to aid that worker than as a replacement worker (as automation fears and realities have publicly positioned work automation in the United States). Pelle Ehn acknowledges that how work is organized in Scandinavia has an impact on this conception—that traditional production issues and work organization patterns there have an impact on the work-oriented design projects he describes as paradigmatic examples. But as he links the design of computer artifacts (i.e., interfaces) with "a concerned social, historical, creative, and planned activity in which we try to anticipate computer artifacts and their use" (p. 171), Ehn argues that work-oriented design is needed because the rational system of design focuses too much on formal analysis of complex systems and too little on the actual situations of work and communication.

In contrast to participatory design, much of the design of computing systems in the United States has proceeded from a system-centered approach that Ehn labels the rational system and that Andrew Feenberg (1991) terms, from the philosophical standpoint, systems rationalism. In a system-centered approach, engineers build a system that assists in the performance of some task—say, the manipulation and storage of student records. That system is built by interviewing experts in student records and by analyzing the actions performed on student records, articulating the steps in the ideal performance of such actions, and programming a system that allows for such manipulations to be done electronically. People are then trained to use the system. Though the original knowledge of what needs to be done (and how) is taken from people, this process has been seen as de-skilling (see Winner, 1991; Zuboff, 1988) the workforce because the resulting system is the authority for how to handle student records, and its users (the original experts) make "mistakes" in their use of the system built from their knowledge. Connected to the Taylorism that deskilled much factory work in the early twentieth century (see Johnson, 1991) and also to artificial intelligence moves to simulate human reasoning (see Simon, 1969), this approach to computer system development has moved human action from the center of the workplace (replacing the human with the tasks that need to be completed). It has also resulted in much public animosity toward mechanization, automation, and computerization (even in composition studies), and with good reason. It must be difficult to be told that a machine you provided with information on how to perform now outperforms you—has replaced you and rendered you unemployable.

However, more social and situated approaches to design have been voiced by prominent U.S. computer scientists. Terry Winograd and Fernando Flores (1986), for example, argue that computer designs grow "out of our already-existent ways of being in the world, and deeply affecting the kinds of beings we are…. Through the emergence of new tools, we come to a changing awareness of human nature and human action, which in turn leads to new technological development. The designing process is part of this 'dance' in which our structure of possibilities is generated" (p. 163). They see humans and machines as involved in a dance of design that focuses more on the possibilities for action than on how correctly and efficiently the particular system components operate.

User-centered design is another social approach to design that includes users as participants in the design of computer products. As it has been popularized by Donald Norman (1988), user-centered design recognizes three components to the design equation—the user, the system, and the designer—positing that each has a model of how their interactions will work. It is interesting that in these depictions the system is almost always in the middle, acting as a go-between for designer and user. In practice, the user-centered design movement has often aimed to develop user (or usability) specifications for projects that can be met by systems without extensive contact with users (see Nielsen, 1993). At interface design conferences, it is not uncommon to hear elaborate discussions of how to develop computer algorithms that can be used to measure system usability without involving humans. Jakob Nielsen, for example, has researched the cost effectiveness of using expert heuristic tests of the interfaces to identify user problems, finding them useful for identifying certain types of problems. Throughout the discussions of usability, *problems* and *errors* are words attached to users, and even in user-centered design the users are watched and coded for errors in their uses of the system under study.

Because system-centered design drives many of the development processes for computing-related products in this country, such critics as Thomas Landauer (1995) contend that techniques already used in user-centered design and usability can turn around the trends of useless products. Landauer argues that successful user-centered design engages in two or three basic activities: analysis, idea evaluation, and testing. Since these are standard product design activities, what makes the activities user-centered is the fact that analysis involves talking to users about what they are trying to accomplish, that idea evaluation involves trying out possibilities on prospective users, and that testing involves having users use the product to do their normal work tasks (p. 274). These design ideas seem more situated until they are linked with the specific practices Landauer suggests. Much of the discussion about implementation focuses on whether heuristics can be substituted for people, on how many user sessions are necessary to locate what percentage of the interface problems, and so on. Although Landauer values user input, and we think his support will enhance the status of social design approaches, we do not see him taking a view of computing that is more complex than Norman's identification of system, designer, and user. Nor do we see him embracing the inevitability of social conditions of design as Winograd and Flores do or adopting a human-centered design approach described by the Scandinavians.

The marginalization, almost commodification, of the user in user-centered design is less a problem in the work of those who study the computing situation from vantages other than system (or interface) design. Suchman (1987), for example, in her work as an anthropologist for Xerox-PARC, has developed a view of human-computer interaction that does not include the designer and hence moves the system from the middle of the picture to one side of a binary (user and system). Her observation of office workers using programmable copy machines leads her to develop a much more culturally complete portrait of technology use. It also leads to an identification of the contested area (between system and user) as the interface: The interface rather than the user becomes the center of problems, errors, and controversy. Brenda Laurel (1991), another anthropologist studying computing activities, sees the activities of computing as focused on human action—a view much closer to the Scandinavian views such as Bødker's (1991), human activity approach to interface design—using theater as the metaphor for capturing the actions in ways that can be translated into interfaces. In addition, because Thomas Malone (1983) roamed the offices of Xerox-PARC looking for inspiration for the interface to NOTECARDS (a hypertextual memory for workers) so that the program would work for more than one type of worker and work task, human activity has had a place in the development of or critique of some computing systems.

We can look more closely at usability practices and see in contextual inquiry a situated approach to gathering user information that was developed out of usability engineering efforts at Digital Equipment Corporation (Whiteside, Bennett, & Holtzblatt, 1988), one example of how social and system blur. Contextual inquiry, in keeping with the design process requirements Landauer proposes, requires programmers, systems analysts, and information designers to observe the uses of their products at the actual site of customer use (Beabes & Flanders, 1995; Holtzblatt & Jones, 1993) before and during the design phase. Unfortunately, getting out in the field per se does not guarantee that the engagement with users or the procedure for data collection will be sufficiently contextualized. Contextual inquiry as described (e.g., Beabes & Flanders, 1995) is user-based, and it intends to contrast its approach with lab-based observation of users performing tasks (see Dieli, 1988; Duin, 1993; Nielsen, 1990). In practice, however, we have seen how contextual inquiry can often remain product-based: that is, the programmer or designer goes out in the field to discover problems in the product as designed, rather than to discover what the user needs to do (in order to design better products to begin with). We saw in our study of Max (see Chapter 4) how designers can sometimes take a quick-fix, product-based approach in the field. Rather than engaging with users in order to design better products, designers can all too easily fall into the trap of accepting the design as is and using the fieldwork to tweak the product into some kind of minimal acceptability.

While we think any attempt to study the situated uses of computer technology is better than no attempt at all, we caution that contextual inquiry per se does not guarantee user-focused design because those entering the users' workplaces go there with a system idea already in mind. Such an approach of system before user may not deliver either diversity of perspective or the kind of participant or user advocacy we are promoting. The kind of inquiry strategy we are promoting is contextual, to be sure, but it is based more on ethnographic approaches to research (e.g., Suchman, 1987), which involve some depth of engagement with the user's culture, more than simply a problem-seeking "visit" to the user's site. We have also seen how in practice researchers can become slaves to the method of contextual inquiry, putting devotion to methodological rigor ahead of users and context.

Usability practices such as contextual inquiry, and even the less contextualized and more widely used observation of users in labs, serve the positive purpose of exposing programmers and systems designers to customers, and such an exposure can only be beneficial, as programmers and designers learn more about how users work. As with any tool, its usefulness depends on the way it is used. We do not see that contextual inquiry as currently practiced meets the criteria we are developing for critical research. Critical research requires a degree of reflexivity on the part of the researcher, an attempt to understand the disciplinary ethical and political bias that influences any research observation. Critical research requires one to be flexible in terms of methodological design. Though Beabes & Flanders (1995) stress the importance of reflection and situated design of critical inquiry (pp. 417–

418), we do not see that reflection and flexibility have yet become standard practice in contextual inquiry.

It is also important to point out that the usability industry has a different aim for research than does the field of computers and composition. Research in computers and composition has various aims—to understand the nature of writing with computers, to build knowledge in a research field, to improve teaching practices in computer classrooms, to learn about the effects of new writing technology—but all of those aims serve the general goal of better writing. The usability industry aims, as Mary Dieli (1988) argues, to "deliver information about users to product developers in a timely fashion" (p. 2). It uses research and method in the service of product development (Sullivan, 1989a). Our immodest view is that the usability industry might focus less on the product and more on the users of the product; that is, after all, what usability is supposed to represent (understanding and concern for user).

POLITICAL AND ETHICAL ACTION

We view rhetoric as a productive art that is imbricated with the practical arts of politics and ethics (see Porter, in press, Chapter 3). Thus we view rhetorical acts, in which we include research acts, as a manner of doing something as well as saying something (Porter, 1995). In other words, research activities are practical actions that, as such, have political and ethical implications. Methodology is always both political and ethical.

Research is political in the sense that it always has to do with power relations, particularly in two respects: (a) between the researcher and the researched, and (b) between the researcher and the professional or disciplinary paradigm within which she works (and with which she at least partly contends). The disciplinary paradigm is also situated in an academic tradition and mode of production, which exert a powerful political influence. The phrase *power relations* signifies the darker side of human relations, usually involving larger institutional practices that dominate or control individuals. We might also refer to relations in a more benign sense simply to "footing" (Dillon, 1986), that is, to the relational footing or basis of connectivity between any people.

Research is ethical in two senses: First, it has to do with constructing identity, that is, with subjectivity. The activity of research constitutes roles for individuals, for researchers and for researched, as well as for the communities of researchers that collect themselves around certain themes, topics, and problems and thus define themselves as fields or disciplines or interest areas. It is a self-defining activity. Second, methodology has to do with determining a "should" for a "we" (Lyotard & Thébaud, 1985). Despite the claims of some research to be descriptive rather than evaluative, all research rests on an assumption of a norm, a standard of measure. All research presupposes some kind of utopian ideal state, which serves

..... is yardstick for measuring what is happening at the moment and as the *telos* for research activity. All research activity is motivated by a current problem, inadequacy, gap, or question, and thus aims at some ideal state of potential resolution. In the sense that it imagines a should and strives toward one, all research activity has ethical implications. Critical research practice makes its ideals manifest.

In Chapter 5 we examine in more detail the senses in which methodology is both political and ethical, and consider issues that such an argument has for researchers who study writing with computers. The theoretical framework we develop for approaching this topic is at the same time postmodern, rhetorical, and feminist. Chiefly, we argue that the activity of research has to stop overlooking and start admitting its political and ethical situatedness.

POSTMODERN

As we see it, each of the concepts we have treated in this chapter could be a book in itself. (In fact, one is: Turner's *The Social Theory of Practices*.) We have tried to model in this chapter one feature of critical research practice: the step of acknowledging the complexity (approaching instability) of terminology. We have tried to situate our use of key terms in the frame of critical discussions that surround them. We have by no means been comprehensive in our treatment, but we have admitted that the terms we use are sites of struggles (aren't all terms?), and to some extent we have shown what the struggle is about.

Is our project postmodern? *Postmodern* is another hotly contested term, and we are sorry to have to use it. Postmodernism is by its nature resistant to definition (Faigley, 1992, pp. 3–5), though we can dare some general descriptions: As a philosophical movement, as opposed to its aesthetic and sociohistorical aspects (p. 6), postmodernism:

- Involves the loss of faith in rational design (p. 5).
- Challenges the faith in the unity of the subject and the authority of individual consciousness (Smith, 1988).
- Expresses "incredulity toward meta-narratives" (Lyotard, 1984) and suspicion toward totalizing Theories, grand schemes, a priori notions of good, grand narratives of freedom, justice, liberation, or truth.
- Recognizes, at times even celebrates, "the fragmentary, the ephemeral, the contingent" (Faigley, 1992, p. 4) and the indeterminate (Hassan, 1993, p. 282), while it courts contradiction and irony.
- Focuses on the working of power in institutions and rhetorical settings.
- In terms of rhetoric, examines how acts of rhetoric are acts of power which exclude and include, giving some bodies definitions and obscuring others (Foucault, 1983, 1984a).

Of course, postmodernism is centrally defined by its argument with modernism and with traditionalism. Key characters of postmodernism—Derrida, Lyotard, Baudrillard, Foucault, Lacan, Irigaray—begin by challenging the logocentrism of the Western philosophical tradition and move from there to question the presumptions and methods of a variety of disciplines (Lacan and Irigaray in psychology, for instance; Foucault in the social sciences).

The term *postmodern* is frequently misunderstood or reduced to absurdity. Arthur Walzer and Alan Gross (1994), for instance, equate *postmodern* with *social constructionist*—a conflation that is particularly puzzling given the numerous critiques of social constructionism by postmodern theorists of various sorts (especially by feminists and by cultural studies theorists). (See Porter, 1992a, for example, on the distinction between postmodern and social constructionist views of community.) Walzer and Gross criticize the ethical relativism of what they term postmodernism, without recognizing differences between various postmodern positions. The postmodernism they abhor might be seen as the most extreme sort of deconstruction, what Ebert (1991) refers to as ludic postmodernism, which views all language as mere gaming and all meaning, facts, truth, knowledge as radically indeterminate. Walzer and Gross do not acknowledge the variety of forms of postmodernism: for example, cultural studies, critical theory, feminist, "resistance postmodernism" (in Ebert's sense). Nor do they acknowledge a postmodern ethics; their view sees postmodernism as incapable of ethical construction. Since our position on research involves ethical action and aims to improve the lot of participants in that research (both people being studied and the researchers), and would also be classified by Lather as a postmodern approach to research, we take issue with their contention that postmodernism is incapable of ethical construction (see Chapter 5 for further discussion).

In addition to ethics, postmodern research must also consider its relationship to the knowledge generated in research. Too much traditional research proceeds in awe of the model of scientific knowledge. Too many researchers feel that the standard by which their work should be judged is scientific/epistemic knowledge, and so their work attempts to achieve that standard of certainty. The result is research that ends with overgeneralized conclusions or with insignificant ones; the research might generate knowledge in a static sense, but the form of knowledge produced cannot be readily deployed in the service of any kind of rhetorical action. It ends up being information, but without any context of use. (Certainly the information can be used, and no doubt is, but the research itself cannot extend to comment on how the information can be used. Its methods do not validate such advice.)

Don't confuse our position with a kind of exaggerated and radical deconstruction, which ends up being a kind of antimetaphysical metaphysics of the word. It denounces conventional metaphysical philosophy, but does so using the methods of metaphysical philosophy—and so ends up reinscribing it. Other researchers do recognize the situated and rhetorical nature of research, recognize that research is always situated in some community of believers, and that knowledge is a socially generated product (e.g., Doheny-Farina, 1989; Feyerabend, 1988; Kuhn, 1970). Still, belief that knowledge is socially constructed does not necessarily lead to a manipulative cynicism about it. (That is, knowledge becomes whatever you can get your community to believe; "method is what you make it.")

Our view gives weight to prior knowledge (without assigning to it the status of certain knowledge) but assigns equal weight to the mandates of situation. Our view says that community belief is important, but not all-determining. It is not then what is typically held to be a social constructionist view (or maybe the stereotyped notion of that view). We see precedents to this situated view in critical legal theory, situation ethics (e.g., Jonsen and Toulmin, 1988), and feminist methodology (in which an absolute form of deconstruction has to be rejected, because it ends up being uncommitted, accepting a stance that leaves the status quo—the presumption of masculine defining personhood—in place).

The position we advocate could be said to be postmodern, but in a very particular way that is closer, in Ebert's (1991) terms, to resistance postmodernism, or, in Lather's (1991) terms, to an aim to emancipate rather than to deconstruct, or to Porter's (in press) sense of "committed postmodernism," rather than to ludic postmodernism. We are working toward a description of a postmodern research methodology, which we see as defined mainly by a focus on situated practice, a focus we see developing in several strands of research, including that of feminist methodologists such as Michelle Fine, Liz Stanley, Sue Wise, Patti Lather, Leslie Roman, and others. What we are doing might be more accurately termed "postcritical," in Lather's (1992) sense. That is, it stresses a liberatory aim, but has a critical consciousness of its own position (at least insofar as that is possible). This position, as Lather frames it, arises out of the feminist critique of Marxist critical theory, that is, out of the understanding that even though it stressed a liberatory theme, the Marxist position was critically unaware of its own implicit collusion with the patriarchal tradition.

There are two key characteristics of a postcritical methodology: First, postcritical research does not have an a priori aim in mind. The vision of the desired end state is not established at the beginning of the process; rather, it develops and arises through the process, in dialogic concert with research participants. (See the discussion, in Chapter 5, of the principle "liberate the oppressed through empowerment of participants.") Second, postcritical research problematizes agency. It presumes neither the death of the subject nor the unified being of the subject; rather, it proceeds on the basis of multiple and shifting subjectivities that enable opportunities for change, at least at local levels.

For us, critical practice is key to the development of knowledge. Rather than granting abstract Theory, Knowledge, or Method the privileged position, this research perspective sees knowledge as local, as contingent, and as grounded not in universal structures but in local situated practices. Attention to the distinctive nature of writing-as-situated practice is essential, then, to the methodological philosophy we are developing.

Ultimately, we are proposing a rhetorical methodology based on viewing computer writing as critical practice. A critical study of electronic writing as situated—whether we study it in the classroom or the academy, in the workplace or usability lab—requires the development of a particular and pragmatic sensitivity to the particulars of writing context—for example, to the *kairos* of a particular writing situation, including the types of writers and audiences involved, the forms of technology being used, and the type of heuristic methods being applied to the study. It requires, too, a political sensitivity to the multiple perspectives at work in a writing situation and an ethical resolve to work for the betterment of participants. In the remainder of this book we try to describe, practically and procedurally, how this point of view works.

3

Articulating Methodology as Praxis

All manner of research and scholarship deploys methodology. We are interested here in the relationship between researchers' conceptions of methodology and their actual research practices. How critically do researchers in computers and writing view their methodologies? Do they accept and apply precut methods to their research? Do they critique and revise methods as they apply/make them? Do they develop new methods, or do they mix methods? Most reports of research do not help us decide much about the practices of method because they tend to be conventionalized, asking us to think that the researchers selected and applied methods appropriate for the study. These reports use the conventional rules of methodology as criteria that they use to argue for the quality of their research design rather than to invoke the electronic site (in the case of naturalistic field studies) or to problematize the vocabulary of the researchers (in the case of surveys and interviews).

We contend that research practices in computers and composition research are of necessity a praxis, though write-ups of such practices sometimes mask the heuristic nature of researchers' methods in practice. Specific research practices, though, are situated in and through their methodologies; indeed their meaning derives, to a certain extent, from their enactments of those methodologies. Of course, this position could be interpreted as a privileging of theory over practice because we suggest here that methodology has theoretical dimensions (Sullivan & Porter, 1993a). But, to our way of thinking, treating methodology as a set of anti-

septically applied rules that govern research practices strips the knowledge-making ("ology") possibilities out of method and limits the potential of such research
to effect productive change.

We focus on research as praxis—a concept that we hope, after the discussion
in Chapter 2, will not be confused with unreflective practice because it refers to a
type of conduct that negotiates between positions rather than grounding itself in
any particular position. We call upon discussions of the research process from
several approaches to methodology, as we advance a notion of research methodology as heuristic, a notion we feel will provide a more useful and flexible model
for critical research practices. Our position is that methodology as used in computers and composition studies represents different types of socially constructed
argumentative warrants. As such, it should be seen as heuristic, rather than foundational, in nature, and therefore as dynamic and negotiable.

To note that methodology is socially constructed is hardly novel or surprising
(see Latour, 1987; in composition see Berkenkotter & Huckin, 1993, 1995; Lauer
& Sullivan, 1993). We suspect that most researchers in computers and composition, whether they do qualitative or quantitative studies, will even agree in the
abstract. However, the implications of this view for researchers' methodologies
may be more controversial. This view leads to the conclusion that research methodology should not be something we apply or select so much as something we
construct out of particular situations and then argue for in the write-ups of our
studies. This notion sees methodology as heuristic rather than a priori determining; in this view methodology intersects with and is perhaps changed by practice;
it is more than simply a formula used in the course of reporting on practice.

We begin, then, to articulate methodology as praxis with these contentions:

1. We need to acknowledge several points about methodology in computers and
    writing:
    —Theory is already in the electronic writing site (even if it is implicit).
    —The technology of a site impacts on the events that researchers observe.
    —Interaction in cyberspace is computer-mediated as well as filtered
     through traditional screens of researcher, participants, observation tools,
     and so on.
    —Computers add possibilities for the collection of classroom data (e.g., key-
     stroke capture) and change the dynamics of some traditional collection
     approaches (e.g., some interactions are online and not spoken).
    —Researchers bring theory to their studies of computers and writing, but they
     also bring their experiences as users of technology and their experiences as
     teachers. That mix results in a commitment to the study.
    —Methodology is built out of a particular site (not simply selected from
     options outside the research context).
    —The knowledge of and interests of the community impinge on what is stud-
     ied and how it is addressed.

2.   We can't just uncritically accept research methods as given to us in a suppos-
     edly valid form by the social sciences, or, God forbid, the sciences (for an
     opposing view, see Gross, 1994).
3.   We can't assume, as some do, that simply opposing positivism is enough to
     protect methods from the charge of being unreflective.
4.   We do believe that research proceeds through a process of self-reflection and
     critical inquiry.
5.   Our ultimate aim is the betterment of research participants (including
     researchers).

In this chapter, we pay special attention to the difference between considering
methodology as a collection of rules and guidelines that dictate research practice
vs. heuristics that aid the researcher in the situated and criticial practice of
research. We find this distinction important because it affects researchers' abilities to voice the kinds of special considerations that are added when the research
involves online components and ultimately to engage in the critical practices we
see as essential to praxis.

We proceed by examining several general accounts of research processes in
order to argue for a view of process as negotiated through the activities of research
practice. We will talk of traditional research processes, feminist research processes, and our own version of critical praxis as enframements for the work of
research—its praxis. Much of the discussion focuses on positioning our views in
relation to dominant approaches to methodology.

The constructions of methodology that we label *traditional* view methodology
as theory in the sense of rules governing practice. To traditionalists, methodology
is somehow (and that somehow is mysterious) embodied in methods that are
themselves a collective of rules or guidelines for research practice, making the
constructing and regulating of methods the province of methodology. They are
sanctioned and given validity by community consensus about their identity and
use; they are licensed, in other words. How the "correct" methods are selected (or
made self-evident) is handled either by attaching thcm to the nature of the questions (e.g., Robert Yin, 1994, contends that case study designs answer how and
why questions, while surveys answer what questions) or by identifying methods
with theoretical stances (e.g., composition studies has identified protocol analysis
with cognitive studies of writing).

Traditional views of methodology often consider theory a belief system and
methods the neutral tools that are shared by various systems of belief. That word
neutrality fronts quite a thorny concept, as it implies an innocence of political and
ethical involvement we are not willing to accept. (In Chapter 5 we take up the
problem of neutrality.) For example, cultural ethnography is widely divergent
from quantitative ethnography in its understanding of what ethnography is, what
its purposes are, and what kinds of knowledge it generates. Both rely on interviewing informants, and in neither is interviewing treated as a volatile component

of the research practice; indeed this and other data collection tools often are invisible (or at least exempt from ideological scrutiny), except from the perspective of establishing a proper or reliable procedure for their use. Procedural texts address such questions as: "How do I conduct interviews?" not "In what ways do interviews encourage me to like some participants and give their views more weight than others I dislike?" How can the primary data collection tool be invisible? neutral? not open to critique? Further, certain traditionalist guidebooks for ethnographic research offer both qualitative and quantitative tools for analysis as neutral options in a cultural ethnography (see for example, Russell Bernard's *Research Methods in Cultural Anthropology,* 1988, which has analysis chapters entitled "Qualitative Analysis," "Coding and Codebooks for Quantitative Data," "Univariate Statistics: Describing a Variable," "Bivariate Analysis: Testing Relationships," and "Multivariate Analysis"). How is it that treatments of method can place such divergent methodological perspectives side by side?

We think the tacit agreement within traditional methodology not to question the common data collection methods allows such a move. Certainly it allows Martyn Hammersley (1992) to bridge the qualitative-quantitative gap and link case studies, surveys, and experiments under the umbrella of "selection of cases" (p. 184). Hammersley claims that these three methods are related in their handling of all methodological issues, and that they differ along axes of how many cases are handled, amount of detail, degree of likely accuracy, degree of control, and degree of reactivity. By asserting continuums instead of gaps, he links qualitative and quantitative research under the traditionalist umbrella—a move we agree with. Key to his ability to maneuver in this way is the sameness he projects for methods of data collection: They are invisible.

Thus, we see this traditionalist distinction between methodology-as-theory-codifying and method-as-application-of-methodology as allowing for a view of the methods used in research as neutral, as solid, as delivering reliable results when employed properly, as existing outside of their use, as mere instruments. Such a view of methods isolates the procedures of research from methodological discussions (and therefore from methodological critique) and thus exists in contradistinction to a critical practices position.

We see this distinction as dangerous for several reasons: First, if an approach to research is attacked as theoretically unsound, researchers will often continue to use its methods as if they were not implicated in the attack; second, if a particular method is attacked as problematic or invalid, that criticism is often framed acontextually and universally as a way to debunk all research employing that method; third, once a method has been attacked, procedural fixes (e.g., matching subjects to deal with subject problems in a quasi-experiment) are instantiated and seen as fixing the methodological problems of the method; fourth, if the results of some research are under attack, the methods used can be attacked as the wrong ones to be used acontextually and universally.

We see the tidy separation of method and methodology as comforting to researchers who are taking up the complex tasks of research, and perhaps to some extent necessary during the learning phase, yet dangerous in its possibilities for easy answers and non-critical practice.

TRADITIONALIST DEPICTIONS OF PROCESS: POSITIVIST TO NATURALIST

We do not think there is one traditional position to which all traditional researchers ascribe. We see traditional positions as comprising a continuum from unreflective positivism to a more situationally aware naturalism. Our characterization is doomed to be somewhat oversimplified, yet we persist because we want to characterize research that is not self-critical, since self-critique is a key component to critical practice.

We can locate a number of positivist blueprints for the research process. Fred Kerlinger (1973), for example, sees the province of research as answering the research questions it poses while maintaining the strictest control possible over the variation that might occur. The design, which is completed before the study begins, contains: (a) a plan: "The *plan* is the overall scheme or program of the research. It includes an outline of what the investigator will do from writing the hypotheses and their operational implications to the final analysis of the data" (p. 300); (b) a structure: "the outline, the scheme, the paradigm for the operation of the variables...and their relation and juxtaposition, we build structural schemes for accomplishing operational research purposes" (p. 300); and (c) a strategy: "more specific than the plan. It includes the methods to be used to gather and analyze the the data. In other words, strategy implies *how* the research objectives will be reached and *how* the problems encountered in the research will be tackled" (p. 300).

Such an approach to the research process is not limited to experimental design, however. Bernard (1988) offers an ideal research process for ethnographic research that reminds us of Kerlinger's:

1. first, a theoretical problem is formulated;
2. next, an appropriate site and method are selected;
3. then, data are collected and analyzed;
4. and finally, the theoretical proposition with which the research was launched is either challenged or supported. (p. 110)

He goes on to discuss a real research process that is much messier and involves struggling for a research question, a site, and methods, doing a literature search, collecting data, and analyzing it. His depiction is still linear, and it is focused on making decisions directing the practice of research before that practice begins.

We can also look to Donald Campbell and Julian Stanley's (1966) monograph as naming and describing many of the accepted methods in educational research. Although updated by Thomas Cook and Donald Campbell (1979), by Eugene Webb, et al. (1981), and later by Campbell (1988), *Experimental and Quasi-experimental Designs for Research* has encapsulated the design advice given generations of researchers who study learning and classrooms. Campbell and Stanley (1966) articulate design templates and threats to validity for each and all designs. Their classification scheme implies that designs improve as more researcher control is possible—that, for example, a "true experiment" (for which at least a treatment and a control are developed and subjects are randomly assigned into groups) is more desirable than a "pre-experiment" (for which one treatment is developed for one group and thus there is no control)—and thus the researcher would assess the research situation and plan the best design possible in that situation. If the researcher were doing classroom research for computers and writing in two secondary schools, only one of which had a computer classroom, for example, she probably would not be able to randomize students into treatment (those working in computer labs) and control (those working in traditional rooms) conditions. Thus, the strongest design she could use would be a "quasi-experiment," because she could not manipulate which subjects received what curriculum. Campbell and Stanley also present a list of threats to internal and external validity for research designs and state that certain kinds of threats are inherently more liable for certain types of design.

Traditional research also requires considerable preplanning of research that locks the procedures of that research into place. Yvonna Lincoln and Egon Guba (1985), as prelude to their critique of conventional design approaches, describe what they see as the influence of Campbell and Stanley (and other traditionalist luminaries) on the approach traditional researchers take to establishing a design before they begin a study. Lincoln and Guba contend that the traditional process requires that all these steps be followed before research can be begun:

1. The statement of a problem, an evaluand, or policy option,
2. The statement of a theoretical perspective,
3. The statement of procedures that will be employed which specifies how
   a. sampling
   b. instrumentation
   c. data-analytic procedures are tied to 1 and 2,
4. The establishment of a time schedule,
5. The designation of agents,
6. The projection of budget, and
7. The statement of the expected end product(s). (pp. 222–223)

While we certainly think preplanning is necessary to research (we certainly would not allow a graduate student to begin a dissertation without a plan for the research she/he was undertaking) to the extent that all process decisions are determined before any data is collected, we find the traditional position of prethinking the practice of research robs that process of its knowledge-making power.

In Sullivan and Porter (1993a), we picture several approaches to methodology in professional writing as method-driven or problem-driven. (Note: We did not, as Nancy Blyler, 1995, reported, advocate method-driven research; instead we described and critiqued it and several other approaches in our efforts to establish a heuristic approach.) We would contend that these depictions apply in computers and composition and in composition research as well. We argue that in a methods-driven approach (a) methods are given procedures, well-established and trustworthy bases for observing practice, and (b) applying method to practice properly can help us verify or generate models and theories. We saw a method-driven tactic as what apprentice researchers often perceive as the proper use of methodology: that is, they see their research design task as finding a new application for a tried-and-true method. But we also noted that most discussions of methodology instruct researchers to start with topics and questions, and let the inquiry into the topic guide the choice of method (see Kothenbeutel, 1988; Miles & Huberman, 1994; Yin, 1994). They suggest that a researcher start by noticing a problem or question in computers and writing practice or theory, then select the method appropriate for inquiry into that question, and then apply the method to practice to verify old theory or to generate new theory. Arguments about methodology within this framework typically focus on method as a static construct that one applies to a setting in order to reveal its principles of operation and to investigate which method yields a better answer to particular questions. This approach does not see method as something that is continuously shaped by the practice of research or by the situation.

A synoptic view of the traditional approach to the process of research projected by traditional researchers who are positivists might look something like Figure 3.1, below.

No guidebook depicts the traditional approach in one drawing as we have in Figure 3.1, though the positions we outlined above are fairly consonant with the drawing. Some, like Bernard, would see theory as existing above design rather than neutrally preceding it and interacting with design decisions. Others, like Campbell and Stanley, would see choice of method as very cut-and-dried, and not mysterious. Traditionalists would also disagree on the finer points of how to conduct research. What we are interested in, and try to depict in Figure 3.1, is that these traditional positivist approaches to research tend to recognize the influence of theory on design (What you believe shapes what you see as important to study), but also present it as holding little sway over the implementation of a particular study's design. Such views maintain a theory-practice division in methodology by implying that the theory helps to formulate research action that is then carried out through the application of methods and the analysis of the data those methods collect. They maintain the superiority of theory over action, but also enslave action

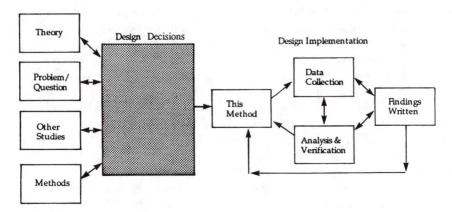

FIGURE 3.1.   A traditional (positivist) approach to the empirical research process.

to predetermined method (at least in theory). The aim of such a practice is the objectivity or neutrality that traditional positivist research craves; the methods are unaffected by the situation under study (or at least in theory). Such a depiction of the theory-practice dispute organizes various practices into methods that are then selected and applied. The key here, what we see as the main problem with this model, is that it does not allow practice to suggest a new method. Though one might contend that the arrows sending one back through the process (because of some sort of problem) constitute practice's source of power, and we agree, that source is a mysterious and blunted one. Furthermore, nobody takes it seriously.

We recognize, however, that a significant number of qualitative researchers stress the importance of questions arising out of the natural settings of the participants, and thus diverge from Figure 3.1 in their depiction of the research process. They generally claim, and we agree, that the collection of data and the analysis of data should be involved in the emergence of the design because what happens in the field impacts on the questions and design; that is, things that the participants say and do can change the focus of the research (see Lincoln & Guba, 1985). They are further aware of the ways in which a researcher interacts with the participants and the situation and is implicated in the results.

Lincoln and Guba describe their process of naturalistic inquiry as one that must be described paradigmatically rather than by its methods:

> It is not crucial that naturalistic inquiry be carried out using qualitative methods exclusively, or at all (although mounting a naturalistic inquiry by purely quantitative means stretches the imagination). Conversely, it is quite possible to carry out a conventional inquiry using qualitative methods exclusively (although to do so would seem incredible to some). But the inquirer who does not adopt, however provisionally, the *axioms* of the naturalistic paradigm cannot be said to be *doing* naturalistic inquiry. (p. 250).

They also claim that such inquiry presumes to rely on the human instrument, and assumes that humans will commit themselves to learn and "continue to hone the skills needed in order to operate as an effective instrument" (p. 250). They further claim that naturalistic inquiry begins with a design statement which acts as a "springboard" that assures a good start and a "benchmark" against which changes can be measured (p. 251). That initial design should: (a) determine a focus for the inquiry; (b) determine the fit of the paradigm to the focus; (c) determine the fit of the inquiry paradigm to the substantive theory guiding the inquiry; (d) determine where and from whom data will be collected; (e) determine the successive stages of the inquiry; (f) determine the instrumentation; (g) plan data collection and recording modes; (h) plan data analysis procedures; (i) plan logistics; and (j) plan for trustworthiness (Chapter 9). Finally, they claim that the inquirer must become familiar with the site before starting.

Lincoln and Guba are adamant about the tentative nature of the preliminary design, stressing the fact that the research emerges out of the natural setting that is being studied and underscoring that conviction by discussing how each of the ten elements of the initial design can change as the study unfolds. But their connection of the term *benchmark* with the start of the study undercuts that tentativeness, as it renders a stable initial picture of the site against which to measure changes at the site over time. If they really wanted to be tentative, Lincoln and Guba would be reluctant to benchmark a site and its people before they understand the actions and values important to that group. We see their early benchmarking not so much as a naturalistic maneuver as it is a traditional move to establish a before-and-after comparison (a pre- and post-test).

Leslie Roman and Michael Apple (1990) have argued that naturalistic research is not the break with traditional research that its proponents seek, and we agree. While naturalistic research makes important modifications by attending to the social subjects inside their contexts, it does not totally break with the traditional paradigm. Roman and Apple point out that naturalistic ethnography's obsession with maintaining and relating the natural (as opposed to the artificial) leads to minimizing the researcher's interaction with subjects in order to minimize the distortions that may be caused by that person's intrusion into social relations behind the natural actions they witness; and even after taking extra precautions they still may be witnessing behavior that would not occur were they not present (pp. 48–52).

We do not claim that traditionalists are not thoughtful or careful about doing research. Practitioners of traditionalist methods, particularly the naturalists, may well appreciate the importance of scrutinizing practice. They may even, for instance, notice the ways in which practice can influence changes in methodology. They may accept that research methods are socially constructed. Most researchers certainly accept that the research observer brings theory to the research setting. Naturalists further contend that the design emerges over time spent collecting data. And yet researchers can hold these views and still not practice research as praxis, at least not in the sense we are describing. A key feature of praxis is the move to problematize method—part of which requires overthrowing the neat compartmentalization offered by traditional methods, part of which requires a self-reflectiveness about process that is incompatible with traditional attempts to understand, undisturbed by the researcher, the cultures/phenomena they study.

SOCIALIZED METHOD TO PROBLEMATIZED METHOD

Our depiction of traditional research processes suggests that method is a social-ized concept that needs to be problematized from at least two perspectives, one of methodological choice and one of the judgment of methodological quality. We hold that too easy and unreflective a reliance on the stability of a method poses the danger of making foundational categories, which is a modernist move. Relegating method to choice fails to recognize that methodological rules are socially con-structed as well as situationally adjusted—and we would also add critically enacted—as they are invoked.

We can see problematized method emerging in these discussions of the social-ization of/into method. Eliot Eisner and Alan Peshkin (1990), for example, detail how "choice" among methods can mask a complex set of decisions, at times even from the researchers, when those researchers use "problem-driven" to move past "method-driven" research design and say, that "[o]nce the problem has been ade-quately conceptualized, the question or method can be easily answered" (p. 9). Eisner and Peshkin argue:

> While such advice is comforting, it is too simple. *First, what constitutes a problem is not independent of the methods one knows how to use.* Few of us seek problems we have no skill in addressing. What we know how to do is what we usually try to do. But the problem is still more complex. The methods into which we have been socialized provide powerful filters through which we view the world. ...Complexi-ties do not stop here. Being socialized into method also means being socialized into a set of norms that define acceptable scholarship. (p. 9, emphasis ours)

Eisner and Peshkin's discussion of socialization into method raises a second needed perspective on problematizing method, the question of methodological quality, which is often reduced to concepts such as "rigor." Rigor is frequently discussed in disputes between those with qualitative and quantitative approaches to empirical research. Qualitative research aims to achieve its rigor through its dense and detailed scrutiny of one or more cases, while quantitative research aims to achieve its rigor through careful application of measures and statistical checks. Thus, when researchers try to merge their studies of a phenomenon, problem, the-ory, or issue, they stumble over the problem of how to connect such disparate research activities. Eisner and Peshkin identify four ways that advocates try to reconcile or respond to this disparity: (a) that there are no differences between qualitative and conventional research (by which they mean experimental research, surveys, and other investigations aiming to uncover principles and trends they might generalize to explain or predict the behavior of a population, and that are different from our notion of traditional research processes, because Eisner and Peshkin aim to explain the qualitative-quantitative categorization while we focus on research practices) because they are both liable for the same criteria; (b) that conventional and qualitative methods complement each other, with each type suitable for different types of questions; (c) that qualitative research is "soft" and less trustworthy than conventional research, and therefore can only be used for exploratory work; and (d) that conventional methods are suspect because they try to apply a natural science paradigm to human behavior. Eisner and Peshkin explain that they use variant notions of rigor to cooperate, or that they deny the possibility of cooperation. Rigor, then, is complex enough in its meanings that it is not a criterion that can be applied as a recipe, nor does it mean the same thing to all researchers in every research situation. Thus, a general requirement that research be rigorous does not lead to consistent action, and the more completely some external sense of rigor (i.e., drawn from the conventions of another discipline) is applied to the judgment of computers and writing research, the less likely that research is to acknowledge the ways in which the situation of the research affects the researcher's ability to invoke a textbook notion of rigorous method, as the Halio debate (below) shows.

We find both perspectives on the socialization of method—methodological choice and the judgment of methodological quality—important to research methodology for computers and writing. Certainly the debate that sprang up over Marcia Halio's (1990a) study of the relative value of teaching writing with Macintosh or DOS machines helps us to understand how and why judgments about methodological quality enter into our published discussions of research. Halio's article reported a descriptive study she conducted at the University of Delaware that contrasted the impact of teaching writing using Macintosh and DOS-based platforms. The article triggered considerable electronic debate, inspired conference sessions, and packed the "Computers and Controversy" section of *Computers and Composition.*

Interestingly enough, though the article entered the debate over the relative merits of Macintosh and DOS platforms that has been alive since 1983, and claimed that DOS machines led to better student papers (which could have effectively ended a debate that many of us enjoy), the printed criticism of the article focused on methodological problems (a rarity in computers and composition discussions). Would the article have attracted as much attention if it decided that Macintoshes were better platforms than DOS machines? We think so. Deans and important engineering faculty would still have sent the article to all their colleagues in writing suggesting they purchase the machines that make a difference. Therein lies the key. What ruffled so many feathers was the conclusion that the machines made the difference—that differences in writing quality could be abstracted from the activity of writing and attributed to the machine being used for that activity. The proponents of computers in writing classes were not ready to concede the power for causing writing improvement to the machines (as opposed to human factors of curriculum, environment, student motivation, institutional culture, and so on).

The criticism of Halio's work, however, pointed out flaws in her methodology. These methodological critiques included:

- Objections about the participants
  —sample groups were not randomly assembled (Youra, 1990)
  —sample size was inadequate (Youra)
  —two groups were not established as equal at the start (Kaplan & Moulthrop, 1990)
  —no knowledge of students' writing abilities before class (Kaplan & Moulthrop)
  —no knowledge of the culture surrounding them (Kaplan & Moulthrop; Slatin et al., 1990)
- Objections about instruction
  —did not take software into account (Slatin et al.; Youra)
  —did not explain computer instruction or curricula (Kaplan & Moulthrop; Slatin et al.; Youra)
- Objections about performance measures
  —measures inadequate to support interpretation (Slatin et al.)
  —papers evaluated by Writer's Workbench rather than teachers (Kaplan & Moulthrop; Youra)
  —no texts from both sides used (Slatin et al.)
  —poorer readability scores equated with better writing (Kaplan & Moulthrop; Slatin, et al.)
- Objections about the interpretation
  —overgeneralized from descriptive data (Kaplan & Moulthrop; Slatin et al.)
  —validity of observations questioned (Kaplan & Moulthrop)
  —isolation on user and machine to exclusion of other factors considered technocentric (Kaplan & Moulthrop)
  —criticism of student topics questioned (Kaplan & Moulthrop; Slatin, et al.)

Halio's (1990b) response to these criticisms began by noting that cognitive psychologists and human-computer interaction specialists were lending heavy support to her position but that composition teachers were offering steady criticism. (It is ironic that she was invoking the authority of "scientists" as she faced stern-faced methodological critiques that were fashioned out of the traditional methods those scientists used.) The bulk of her response focused on answering micro-method questions about using Writer's Workbench, selection of student essays, characteristics of students in the study, self-selection into sections, teaching methods, computer training, and qualitative judgments about writing. When she spoke in general of research design, Halio contended, "My published essay, however, never claimed to be a tightly structured study. It certainly is 'descriptive' research. But I think it is important for teachers to report what they see happening to writing in their computer classrooms" (p. 106).

Her comments about research design make it clear to us that she was not operating out of the same constraints about design that her critics were. Yet it also seems clear that Halio's research breached the boundaries of socialized method, even though its critics varied in their notions of rigor, and it invited the computers and writing community to demonstrate that this research violated its methodological expectations. Why was it discussed so vigorously? In large part, it was because of the subject matter it addressed and the conclusions it reached. The answer Halio put forward provided easy answers for deans who were preparing to buy equipment, or not. What was the implication of the response on method for future studies? We think that Halio's mixing of teaching observations and research reporting form contributed mightily to the response. The conclusions she reached would have been far more acceptable if they had been comments made after an anecdotal account of experiences in writing classes—it would have been classified, by Stephen North (1987), as teaching lore—and indeed Halio (1990b) tried to retreat to the lore position. But because Halio framed her essay as a research report, she invoked a differing set of expectations about design and evidence and claimed a greater generalizable force for her conclusions—it would have been characterized as experimental knowledge by North.

What is most interesting in this saga, however, is that while critics did not agree (with Halio or each other) about the types of methodological judgments to render, they all used a big methodological stick to beat the study into submission. Steven Youra invoked experimental criticisms, while Nancy Kaplan and Stuart Moulthrop invoked descriptive ones, and John Slatin et al. used micro-method objections. More interesting to us, none of the discussions problematized method; they treated it traditionally, as a set of rules that had been applied injudiciously (which to some extent is reasonable because of the presentation of the original study). They assumed that a method existed that would be the right one, even though they disagreed about which method that would be. Their senses of how methodological guidelines had been broken were varied, making it almost impossible for Halio to issue a coherent methodological response to her critics. Halio's response was to retreat from the label of research, into calling the piece a teacher's observations.

As teachers of new researchers, we too are troubled by the discussion. We think episodes such as this one potentially intimidate new researchers who want to conduct research that breaks with traditional rules but who now are likely to be more apprehensive than usual about challenging the rules of research, which everyone must know and agree with since they produce them to critique a study.

One of our goals in this book is to help new postmodern researchers develop a critical praxis that they can use to combat traditional methodological rules/guidelines. To do so, we seek to legitimize the problematizing of method, which falls outside the research process actions of traditional approaches to research.

If traditional approaches to the process of research do not adequately problematize method, where then do we turn? Who is doing work that might model all (or part) of the kinds of research processes we advocate?

FEMINIST DEPICTIONS OF PROCESS:
ESSENTIALIST AND MATERIALIST

Feminist approaches to the research process problematize the practice of research because they challenge the core of scientific knowledge-making on the basis that it does not accommodate gender in its construction of knowledge categories—and thus is fundamentally masculinist in both its conclusions and its day-to-day actions (see Harding, 1986; Keller, 1985; and Lather, 1991). That challenge to the core processes of scientific activity is what makes us interested in feminist methods. We find that very often the research principles feminists espouse lead them to conduct research that is radically situated, which we find a component of critical practice. Their principles, too, lead to positions that view knowledge as productive rather than epistemic, that is, for feminist researchers knowing only counts when it improves the lot of the researchers and the women participants. We actually hold many points in common with those who espouse postmodern and feminist methodologies in feminist sociology, anthropology, and education (e.g., Bell, 1993; Lather, 1991; Roman, 1992; Stanley & Wise, 1990, 1993), as we all focus on differences and are sensitive to the particular kairotic (and at times in their cases, erotic) features of situated action. Rather than privileging abstracted and so-called objective principles and procedures at the same time as the research methods are endenturing research practices by making those practices work in the service of abstract principles (as traditional approaches to research so often do), we agree with feminist researchers who consider particular human action as significant and researcher activity as an element that must be foregrounded and problematized in the doing and the telling of the research. Thus, researchers and participants develop a dynamic and relational focus rather than a static one. We also agree that ethical and political dimensions are always already embedded in the research we conduct; we do not pretend that neutrality is a viable concept. Though we strive for fair and even-handed accounts, we also begin from a position that is acutely aware of the barriers to fair and even-handed representation. We are suggesting that fair-and even-handedness of representation is achieved through research practices that acknowledge the diversity and complexity of each research design—not through practices that attempt to hide that diversity and complexity behind socialized method.

We do not presume that feminist research is a monolithic, postmodern construct. Just as traditionalist positions span a continuum, so do feminist ones, from essentialist to postmodern and materialist. Essentialist feminist researchers (e.g., Reinharz, 1992a, 1992b; Westkott, 1977) ascribe to the belief that feminist research is done *on*, *for*, and *by* women, while postmodern researchers (e.g., Harding, 1987a; Hollingsworth, 1994) interested in emancipation add *with* women, and materialists (e.g., Lather, 1991; Roman, 1992) focus on how emancipation reflects and is reflected in politics and power.

Some feminists are traditionalists who disagree with the tradition in the area of the status of and treatment of gender. Certainly one could argue that Shulamit Reinharz's inclusion of all methods used to study women without a situated critique of those methods is a universal move that is consonant with traditionalist approaches. *Feminist Methods in Social Research* (1992a) includes the work of many women researchers who theoretically and/or politically disagree, it organizes discussions according to the method being used in the study, and it includes little self-critique. Reinharz's criteria for feminist research seems to be that it is exclusively *on* and *for* women. Ann Oakley (1974) has further argued that sociology is sexist because it focuses on men and their activities, because it builds artificial constructs that distort human experience and make women's "sociological visibility" low, because it is a field with founding fathers, because it is populated by men, and because it uses the ideology of gender to perpetuate stereotyped views of the world (p. 27). Liz Stanley and Sue Wise (1993) agree with Oakley and others: "This feminist criticism has cogently argued the point that much social science work quite simply ignores women's presence within vast areas of social reality. But also where women's presence isn't ignored it is viewed and presented in distorted and sexist ways" (p. 27).

This feminist criticism of masculinist institutions of knowledge-making has allowed for a common bond among researchers of differing theoretical affiliations and has separated even traditional feminist researchers from other traditionalists who are not feminists. Although they have not evolved a single view, many feminists in the social sciences and education hold that the researchers and the subjects of the research are coinvolved in the research and that the experience of the research should not be separated from the analysis/findings (this separation, they claim, perpetuates the male mystification of research and science). All these researchers are further aware that "one implication of feminist criticisms of sexism within the social sciences is that future research ought to be *on* and *for* women, and should be carried out *by* women" (Stanley & Wise, 1993, p. 30). Kleiber and Light (1978) present these three points as the cornerstones of interactive methodology, rejecting traditional notions of objectivity. Though their methods remain traditional, their emphasis that the research is *for* women places an emphasis on the researched.

Stanley and Wise (1990) disagree, arguing that feminist method must flow from the relationships of feminist theory, experience, and research. This break with traditionalist approaches is further extended by materialist feminist researchers such as Patti Lather (1992) and Leslie Roman (1992) in education. Both Lather and Roman argue that an emphasis on the researched cannot mean that those who are researched are objectified; instead, the researchers and researched enter into a relationship that exists for the purpose of emancipation—to empower the researched, to educate the researcher. In this relationship, the notion of analytical distance is breached and the guidelines for non-interference in subjects' lives are suspended in favor of helping participants better their lives.

Stanley and Wise specifically address research practices when they argue that feminist method must flow from the relationships of feminist theory, experience, and research. Not willing to embrace a theory-first (deductive) view of science or an experience-first (inductive) view of science, they hold that there must be a relationship between theory and practice, "which not only sees these as inextricably interwoven, but which sees experience and practice as the basis of theory, and theory as the means of changing practice" (p. 58).

Stanley and Wise (1990) further talk of research practice when they articulate the sites where knowledge-making is contested and constructed:

- In the researcher-researched relationship.
- In emotion as a research experience.
- In the intellectual autobiography of the researchers.
- In how to manage differing 'realities' and understandings of researchers and researched.
- In the complex question of power in research and writing. (p. 23)

By foregrounding as constructed some of the sites that are traditionally used to distance the researcher from the research (or site or data collection), the participants (or subjects), and the findings, Stanley and Wise argue for a nature of research that is at least self-interested and perhaps partisan. More importantly, they find a concrete way to insist that neutrality is not neutral, and it is not neutral in at least the above five ways. This contribution is key to feminists' assault on traditionalists' unproblematic notions of concepts such as rigor. No longer, to extend this example, can rigor be measured by the distance (read: objectivity) achieved between researchers and those they research because the traditional relationships of researcher observing subjects (at a site but) from a distance in order to explain their behavior vis-à-vis some important problem/issue/theory has already been framed by the community of researchers (or at least this researcher) before any observation begins.

Though they address the components of research, few feminist researchers address process directly. Usually they speak of where and how they differ from the traditional—be that subject matter, theory, purpose, or stance. This does not mean they are insensitive to the nuances of research practices. When Sandra Hollingsworth (1994) charted the changes in her own teaching of feminist methods to graduate students in education, to offer just one example, she offered a contrast of traditional and feminist methods that illuminates the differences between traditional classroom research in education and feminist classroom research. Through a recounting of how the class operated over four semesters, of student projects and responses, of her own attempts to bring the course more into line with feminist teacher research, and of the milieu in which these courses took place, Hollingsworth instantiated a number of claims that feminists make about research. Namely, she articulated her own struggle to break out of a traditional mode of teaching a research methods class to Ph.D. students in education (i.e., which research questions are derived in an ideal setting and applied to the "real world," where students' projects are publishable texts or well-ordered prospectuses for research, where progress is made in some sort of linear fashion) and to move toward a feminist brand of teacher research (i.e., one where the students begin in conversation, in reflection of and observation of their own experiences, and work toward transformation, at the very least of themselves). Consider her comparison of traditional research practices in education with feminist practices:

Traditional	Feminist
—begins in isolation	—begins in conversation
—begins with questions from others' theories	—begins with observation of own experience
	—discovers own voice, theory
—reproduces others' methods to collect data	—notice where personal theory and standard classroom image clash
	—clarify differences by gathering info
—use others' analysis schemes to reduce data	—create tentative new classroom image to incorporate focused data
	—suspend image; allow it to shift dialectically
	—listen to alternative theories, images, examples
	—data coded by incorporating personal and alternative theories
	—data interpreted within school, social, and political contexts
—summarize at end	—continuous re-imaging and summarizing
—results take standard format	—results are tentative an non-prescriptive
—only significant results reported	—results help clarify personal voice and others in multiple form
—change in researcher not reported (p. 63)	—personal transformation is important result

Although Hollingsworth focuses on finding ways to develop feminist approaches that are useful for teacher research, the contrast between her approach and the approach she labels *traditional* is stark. The traditional approach operates within the closed framework of the acceptable research practices we discussed earlier, while the feminist version of the teacher researcher operates from the dis-

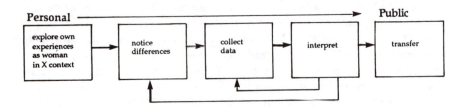

FIGURE 3.2.   A feminist approach to the empirical research process.

junctures between stated positions and lived experience. This does not fully articulate the researcher-researched relationship discussed by Lather (1986, 1991,
1992) or by Stanley and Wise (1990) because the researcher and the researched
are conflated in teacher research. But it does expose the differences between traditional and feminist processes, and it begins to show the dialectical relationships
between theory and practice, between method and data, and between researcher
and researched that operate in postmodern feminist research.

As Figure 3.2 shows, feminist research processes are instigated by and
grounded in the personal experiences of the researcher (and feminist researchers
admit that they are), they use observation and analysis to investigate the differences (and problems) surfacing through an exploration of that experience, and
they have as their goal improvement of the lot of the participants (including the
researcher). The three middle boxes could be traditionalist, if they did not come
after a consciousness-raising about "women" and "my status as a woman" that
focuses and filters the inquiry. The final box of transfer is a transformation (an
improvement in society) that is hoped for in all feminist research. This transfer is
the critical (in the constructive sense) element in postmodern and materialist feminist methodologies, but it is important to all feminist researchers, and it is this
interestedness that compels us to respect their work.

In general, we find several aspects of the feminists' process attractive: (a) The
goal of improvement of the lot of the participants is consonant with our own goal
of improving the lot of the oppressed (however *oppressed* might be defined and
established); (b) the focus on the researcher as part of the process and as a legitimate speaker positions the researcher as a situated speaker; and (c) the insistence
on the contextualization of research dovetails with our insistence that research be
rhetorically situated.

Interestingly enough, we share these characteristics with many feminist methodologists who aim to forge a feminist praxis (Lather, 1991; Stanley & Wise,
1990). We see rhetoric (as discipline) and feminism (as research methodology) as
highly compatible: Both proceed focused on differences, and both are sensitive to
the particular kairotic (and erotic) features of situated action. Rather than privileging abstracted and objective principles and procedures, they consider particular

human action as significant. They develop a dynamic and relational focus rather than a static one. True, feminist research has lenses that focus it on the relationships of feminist theory, experience, and research; some even limit its scope by saying future research "ought to be *on* and *for* women, and should be carried out *by* women" (quoted in Stanley & Wise, 1993, p. 30).

Feminist researchers' insistences—yes, their insistences—on localizing, humanizing, politicizing, theorizing, and even self-criticizing, make their work a powerful influence on our thinking. These insistences lead to such research actions as attaching the researcher to the researched, foregrounding the emotions of the researchers and participants as integral to the fabric of the study, telling the intellectual biography of the researchers to the study, disclosing the differing realities of researchers and participants, and questioning how the researcher has used the power he/she has over the participants. While these categories or insistences are named in Stanley and Wise (1990), they are widely evident (see Hollingsworth, 1994; Kirsch, 1993; Lather, 1991; Maher & Tetreault, 1994; Sullivan, 1992). Mary Margaret Fonow and Judith Cook (1991) take a similar view on these positions as they review feminist research from many disciplines and argue that four themes run throughout the work: reflexivity, action orientation, attention to the affective, and use of the situation at hand. The research solidarity that is emerging in this era is labeled by Fonow and Cook as the second wave of feminist epistemology and methodology.

But we do not always find feminist research self-critical or ironic, both key components to our notion of praxis. Those feminists who focus exclusively (and straightforwardly) on gender as the subject of research, for example, have already been taken to task as potentially ignoring other important factors of oppression such as class, race, age, sexual orientation, and so on. Audre Lorde (1984) and bell hooks (1981, 1989), for example, have both argued that difference, more generally than gender, should be central to feminist theory because it better captures the positionalities of women who have overlapping experiences of oppression. (Our discussion of the oppressed in Chapter 5 is related to this point.) And their point is well taken. We think that some feminist methodologists are so involved with the seemingly never-ending task of combatting the oppression of masculinist methods that they can overlook the potential for oppression in their own characterizations of research and its methods.

We also do not find feminist researchers continuously critical of their methods. This is not a universal comment. Michelle Fine (1992) ably critiques the way feminists situate themselves into the research texts they create, as she argues that too many researchers do not reach activism as a stance because they get caught up in trying to give voice to the participants in their studies. These researchers, she claims, try very hard to inject their research with critical comments about institutions that have come from the researched, but still select and arrange the quotes to use and run the risk of romanticizing the poor (pp. 215–219). Certainly Fine is conducting the kind of reflective critique that we see as needed, but we think it has little force among those practicing feminist research, as a common strategy for meeting the criteria of giving voice to the participants' views is to quote them (often without contextualizing the quotes). We see that certain feminist antimethods (such as injecting quotes from participants) have been accepted as methods—almost beyond critique—because they were embraced as answers that correct masculinist decontextualizing of method found in traditionalist approaches.

PROBLEMATIZING METHODS: MOVING INTO CRITICAL PRAXIS

We turn now to our own version of problematizing method, keeping in mind a key question for our stance that insists on continuous critical perspective on research: How can research proceed if the very methods used are always open to scrutiny? Or, to put it more colloquially, Won't our research be disabled by too much navel gazing?

Our answer is that methodology, in addition to becoming problematized and to becoming an element of a study that must be argued for, can usefully become heuristic. We further think that by becoming aware of the need for critique of method inside the methodology of research and scholarship, we can develop a set of methodologies for computers and composition studies that creatively contributes to computers and composition research.

Does our view of methodology as heuristic disable methodology? Alan Gross (1994) thinks so. He believes that in our view "no research enterprise can get off the ground" because with our view "theory cannot really explain [or predict] practices" (p. 830). Gross wants to maintain clear and separate divisions between acts of theory, practice, and method, with *theory* as the predictive and explanatory power term. Thus, he sees our work as potentially threatening to that clean division of power.

The bottom line is that Gross doesn't think much of workplace studies (the topic we were discussing in the article he critiqued—see Sullivan & Porter, 1993a). Gross's idea of the ultimate goal for workplace writing research is to "win the attention and lasting respect of its disciplinary neighbors in Speech Communication, literary studies, and the human sciences" (p. 839). This is in sharp contrast to workplace researchers' attempts to, as Jeanne Halpern (1988) says, "get in deep" into the interdisciplinary problems that find their academic boundaries erased in work settings. For Gross, workplace writing research is a stepchild moving between disciplines, and, by implication, along with other situated work such as computers and composition research, it is inferior: it does not have, nor can it ever achieve, the methodological rigor of the sciences, nor does it have the broad and ethical vision of the humanities. Like other interdisciplinary and applied efforts, it will constantly be caught between these two standards of excellence. It has to balance both, yet is doomed, ultimately, to secondary status.

Our argument is that the standards are wrong and that in fact there is a realm in which workplace writing research, computers and writing research, and other interdisciplinary research are far superior to the models Gross holds up. For example, workplace writing research as currently practiced is more sensitive to local writing conditions and modes of production than any body of research of which Gross approves. Computers and composition research is much more attuned to the changing nature of writing. Unfortunately, Gross's ideas are disabling in their own way: to the possibility of transdisciplinary or cross-methodological inquiry, maybe even to the possibility of research on writing. In his view we should stick to the clearly established disciplinary frames, because those provide the only standards for methodological judgment.

As you might expect, we disagree. We think that real methodological power and productive inquiry exist beyond and between the conventional boundaries, in transdisciplinarity, and that the best research (re)defines methodological standards (while remaining conscious of and, to a degree, respectful of them).

Once we accept that the methods we use provide powerful filters through which we view the world, we can adjust to a position of using those filters with at least a relative consciousness. Our methodological concepts influence our perception (see Van Maanen, 1988); our task as researchers is to be aware of that influence (as far as possible) and to use it heuristically to help shape our research. Now we think that most computers and composition researchers recognize this premise, at least privately and in the abstract, and view it as that part of research that is behind the scenes. Most, however, have still not dared to articulate this as explicit praxis.

The power of methodology lies in the boundaries and frameworks it invokes, and, yes, these boundaries are ideological and socially constituted. However, what gives them their knowledge-generating power is that they are community frameworks, constituted and agreed upon by researchers (see Berkenkotter, 1989; Berkenkotter & Huckin, 1993; Huckin, 1987). We can accept these frameworks as given by the community, or we can argue to the community that one or more particular framework(s), justifiably reshaped by this situation, provide helpful filters/guides for this, and perhaps other, computers and composition research. Our preferred approach is the second, which we call *methodology as praxis* (see Figure 3.3). This approach incorporates the feminist processes depicted in Figure 3.2 by highlighting the middle of that process and problematizing it.

As we have shown, many traditionalists work from a select-and-then-apply-a-method approach to methodology. They do not typically explore how the question changes as differing methodologies embrace it, or how the method changes as the constraints of a particular research situation unfold. This can be particularly problematic in computers and composition research because of the rapidly changing environments that interest us and the constraints on (and technological opportunities for) collecting data. We do not hesitate to attest that the situation exerts powerful constraints on the design of the research. We want to recognize the potential

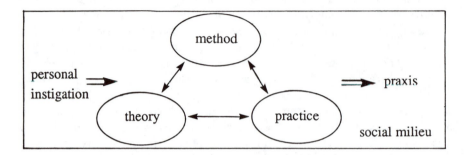

FIGURE 3.3.   Problematized method (praxis).

of practice to change theory and method (what we try to represent in Figure 3.3). We want to highlight the problematics from a positive light.

Consider some typical situational constraints based on our firsthand experiences with colleagues' and students' research projects. A person studying the use of online discussions in a multicultural classroom was able to collect considerable data in one semester, but when the teacher changed to someone who was not as comfortable with technology, the class virtually abandoned the online discussions. Another person who wanted to study how online discussion supported the development of computer books had to switch to studying revision because the most relevant book was in revision at the time of his research. A person who was studying teachers' responses to email recruited a multiethnic pool of participants but had to shift emphasis away from diversity claims when many participants dropped out during the study. A person who planned to study the uses of email to support community in a documentation company had to shift focus to studying personal home pages because of the volume of email involved. A person who planned to study the ways that offline communities in high schools affected the online discussions across high schools could not locate enough positive sites within driving distance to support the offline-online contrasts.

In all of these studies, the methodology (and in part the research questions) shifted as the situation affected the unfolding plan over time. We do not think this uncommon in qualitative studies; not only is it common, it's unavoidable. But researchers who do not acknowledge the impact of the situation, and who do not use the heuristic quality of method to aid them in dealing with shifts over time, run the risk of writing research reports that reaffirm the social norms of methodology, even when their own methods have deviated from those norms in reasonable, defensible, even laudable ways. Methodology that is portrayed as a set of immutable principles, rather than as heuristic guidelines, masks the impact of the situation—of the practice—on the study in ways that could unconsciously reinscribe theory's dominance over practice. It seems to us that the real contribution of many computer and composition studies is to challenge the sanctities of method. They need to acknowledge the fact that they are praxis—and, we would argue further, technologically situated praxis—in order to succeed.

If you see study of computers and composition as the activity of going "out there" and bringing information back to support or enhance your curriculum, you run the risk of accepting uncritically the methodologies associated with social sciences. You decide to survey writing teachers about their international uses of the Internet, follow given survey methodology—and that methodology remains "pure." Research in this scenario is simply information collection. The setting loses power to affect the theory or the method; the theory loses power to affect the method or the setting. If, rather, you see the activity as at least in part "constructing methodology," you become critical of methodology. You do not simply transport methodology, you adjust methodology to setting and the theory—and your explanation of this adjustment becomes a significant feature of your write-up of that study.

A CRITICAL PRACTICES DEPICTION OF PROCESS

A critical practices approach, as we see it, involves continuous critical framing of research practices: it is not something to be done early and then forgotten. It is an ever-present activity; it is critical practicing. We might depict it as we did in Chapter 1, where ideology, method, and practice were in constant contact during research, but that picture is meant to introduce concepts for a theoretical positioning. It's too easy to say "OK" to that picture and yet not change how you practice research. We mostly want critical practices to have heuristic force in the activity of research, to identify with the everyday research activities of continuously and critically framing, focusing, gathering, and analyzing the major components of a study (researchers, participants, societies, and events). In addition to problematizing the actions of a study, as Figure 3.3 does, we see the critical practices approach working within a social milieu (this includes for us the political and ethical dimensions of that space) and engaged in problematizing the instigation of research as well as the praxical action flowing out of that research. Thus, Figure 3.4 depicts how critical practices draw wider communities into the critical practices approach.

Although research may be written about in a way that describes the question/problem/theory instigating research, the methods used, the data collected, and the analysis done (as we suggest in Figure 3.1), research that is conducted as a group of critical practices tries to understand how key research interacts with and is shaped by the actors and contexts of action that make up the events of the research.

With our crude rendering we are trying to suggest several arenas of actions, relationships, and concerns that may well change over time as a study unfolds. For

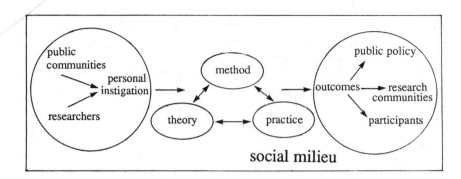

FIGURE 3.4. A critical practices approach to empirical research.

example, personal instigation is not a straightforward event—say, Saul being struck down by the word of God as he traveled to Damascus—that leads inevitably to a particular study. Instigation arises out of the tensions among the public communities, communities of researchers, and the researcher who is beginning a particular investigation in a particular place. Thus, personal instigation is not a simple event. Instead, the revelation of what to study is always already embedded in many discourses, communities, and events. To be unreflective of that instigation—say, to insist on one particular and literal interpretation of the Saul-Paul story—is to neglect the tensions that allow certain revelations to be foregrounded at the same time as they deny others.

So, too, the action components flowing from the experiences of research are not self-evident or unproblematized. Not every study results in the same type of action (some examples are change in policy, heightened awareness by participants of their positions in society, publicizing the problems faced by participants, etc.), and there are often tensions related to the types of action that researchers can/ought/should take as a consequence of their investigations.

We are trying to suggest that as actions happen the critical process accommodates the repositioning of elements such as researcher-researched relationships, institutional involvement, societal pressures, key events, and so on. The governing idea is that the research process is a continuous (and often dialectical) reshaping of its own picture vis-à-vis the ideal the researcher holds in her/his mind's eye. Critical practices are the actions researchers take and the responses of critique to research actions that they take as they come into contact with people (researchers and participants) and events (instigated by researchers, participants, society, and so on) inside an environment (and attitude) of self-reflective and critical inquiry.

Overall in this book we are promoting methodological reflectiveness and methodological flexibility. We doubt that anyone will object, at least in the abstract, to reflectiveness, as it fits in with the sentiment toward critical positioning of theorizing in computers and composition. But we are not advocating this position in the abstract. Instead, we are urging a critical reflectiveness that makes explicit the biases, intrusions, doubts, and mistakes that characterize any research activity, as much as we are ourselves aware of them. 'Fess up, in other words, and include that confession in your write-up.

Methodological flexibility may be more controversial, as it directly opposes the limited view of methodological rigor as strict adherence to a preset list of methodological rules and regulations as the basis for deciding the quality of the research (we recognize that not everyone takes this limited view and refer you to Eisner and Peshkin, 1990, for an in-depth discussion of the range of meanings possible for rigor). *Flexibility* may suggest to some a sloppy or imprecise approach to methodology. (It may even bring to mind approaches to pluralism in the academy that were used to cover up the fact that university power remained/s in the same hands that wielded it before the concept was developed.)

We are not advocating sloppy or imprecise work: quite the opposite. We are arguing that method is not distributed from on high, carried out to the letter, and in that carrying out judged to be quality research. The situations that surround the researchers, the researched, their goals and questions, and ultimately the inquiry itself, require researchers to use and critique and adjust and defend their processes (methods) to see those processes as heuristic aids in the search for understanding, albeit very powerful ones, for they have been used by past researchers in some-what analogous situations. For researchers, it is much less comforting to hold this position (than it is to hold the position that X methods are applied in Y situations) because methodological flexibility requires the researcher to argue the suitability of the various steps of the process and to admit that other methods might have worked as well—or better.

We suspect that the community fears that such an argument carried on in print might devalue the results of the inquiry. Will it disable methodology, as Gross predicts?

A vivid example comes to mind. In the late 1980s Stephen Doheny-Farina (1989) studied a graduate student in two settings, a corporate internship and a graduate literature class. His intent was to contrast the cultures and the kinds of socialization into communication these cultures encouraged of this student. After he published an account of this study, Gregory Clark suggested a different approach to understanding this data, so Clark and Doheny-Farina (1990) revisited the study from a different angle. Their new interpretation (was it a "study"?), which was published in *Written Communication*, caused such a dialogue among its reviewers and the authors that three other people were invited to comment on the article. Further, Doheny-Farina talked at the 1992 Conference on College Composition and Communication in Boston about the ways in which the review-ers' comments had pushed the authors to abandon their original discussion—an interpretation that had offered more than one set of findings—in favor of a single, consistent reading of the data. Tremendous pressure was put on Clark and Doheny-Farina to conform to the sense that an article should produce a unified view for its analysis: to reach an answer. Of course, since Clark and Doheny-Farina's answer in *Written Communication* was different from Doheny-Farina's answer in 1989, already there was more than one answer. Yet, the journal persisted in urging a definitive reading, and in the end the authors chose a reading (although they also gave numerous pointers to other readings). Approaching the data from a different perspective, deploying analytic flexibility, yielded different questions and different answers. It also yielded uncertainty and much discussion among researchers about the methodological advisability of such a public show of this reflectiveness and flexibility. Was it opening a door for some air or opening Pandora's box?

A NEGATIVE EXAMPLE FROM CMC RESEARCH IN ORGANIZATIONAL COMMUNICATION

What does this critical research praxis look like in computers and composition research? One computers and communication research tradition that can serve as a negative example is the computer-mediated research done in organizational communication. Much of that research is (and has always been) experimental (see, for example, Komsky, 1991; Papa, 1990; Rice, 1982; Schmitz & Fulk, 1991; Steinfield, 1985). But the experimental approach is not per se problematic as much as are the unreflective methods and questionable theory accompanying much of this work. Computers and composition knows of that research through the work of Sara Kiesler and her colleagues at Carnegie Mellon (for overview, see Sproull & Kiesler, 1991a, 1991b) and through several reviews of computer-mediated research (Hawisher, 1992a, 1992b; Eldred & Hawisher, 1995). Focused on discovering the differences in the nature of and effectiveness of communication that is conducted or received from online, face-to-face, paper, phone, or television, vigorous lines of research are under way. We find this research driven by comparing how new technologies upset (or reinforce) theories of organizational communication. Typically, it will involve an experiment that has some subjects grouped into conditions that perform the same tasks using differing technologies. In this way, hypotheses about how these technologies will operate are tested.

We find this theory-first approach unreflective and derivative and certainly not directed at the betterment of research participants. True, people in organizational communication need to make decisions (or to justify their decisions) about the uses of technologies in their organizations. This is particularly important in light of critiques such as Thomas Landauer's (1995), which details how computers are not making organizations more productive even though businesses have invested massive amounts of capital computerizing their work. But the simplicity of the theory about computers and communication that underlies this contrastive technologies approach used by organizational communication astounds us. We begin by expecting that a new technology may lead to a different notion of communication. For someone to think that a new technology presents merely a different co.. duit for communication and that it will result only in some varying features or procedures or responses, strikes us as naive. It's almost as if they are running *Consumer Reports*–style product comparisons, and never considering the premise that new kinds of communication may result from new technologies of communication.

Often the technologies are not carefully described either. When people are using email to communicate, are they using a primitive setup (e.g., Mail-X with a line editor) or are they using their primary word processing software with a mailer attached (e.g., MS-Word and MS-Mail)? If two studies of email, done with these differing setups, reach differing conclusions about the usefulness of email for interoffice memos is the basis of difference in their findings attributable to the participants involved, or to the corporate cultures of the sites they studied, or to the differences in the technologies? Given the thin or nonexistent description normally devoted to the technologies invoked, we cannot venture an opinion. Further, if the studies were done with students rather than with workers, and they often are, we are not so sure we would trust the findings as the basis for a business decision, because we think the cultures of college differ from the cultures of various workplaces.

The point this hypothetical discussion raises is that communication theory is not something belonging to preexisting models of organizational communication and then applied to investigations that use preset methods to measure the effects of new technologies as workplace practices. Nor do new technologies simply add a possible channel that can be used for communication (how would we explain the phenomenon of the fax machine if that were the case?). Emerging workplace communication technologies participate in the theorizing of communication, as do the cultures (school, organizational, business, public) surrounding and being built by communication. Studies that ignore this set of relationships in their framing of CMC inquiry risk the kind of understanding we hope critical inquiry fosters.

RESEARCH REPORTS AND THE TRACES OF POSITIVE EXAMPLES OF CRITICIAL PRAXIS

We wish that we had a comprehensive positive example of the type of research praxis we advocate, but we are not surprised that it does not yet exist. It takes time for challenges to established methodology to be codified into the texts that represent research. The write-ups evolve more slowly than the methodologies.

Currently, there is no established genre for reporting such self-criticism inside a research report at the same time as there is a strong genre supporting the traditional approach to research. The standard reporting format—problem statement, previous literature, methods, findings, and discussion—invites the argument of the research to focus on establishing the research questions (How does this problem fit into the previous inquiries of the research community?) and defending the results (Which of the findings needs to be shored up by argument in order to withstand the objections of those who are not like-minded?). In fact, work such as that by John Swales and Hazem Najjar (1987) identifies criteria for introductions that ask each study to frame its problem as a problem of significance for the research community. To our way of thinking, the long-accepted approach focuses on getting the community to listen to (or better yet, to accept) your framing of the research problem, describing the acceptable methods you followed, presenting your findings, and arguing for those interpretations you think are important (and usually subtle).

But there is evidence that such a snapshot of the research report is a historically situated one. Carol Berkenkotter and Thomas Huckin (1993; see also Berkenkotter & Huckin, 1995) argue that genres are "dynamic rhetorical forms that develop from responses to recurrent situations and serve to stabilize experience and give it coherence and meaning" (p. 478). They also argue that genres are situated activities that involve form and content in conventions that both signal and reproduce a community's "norms, epistemology, ideology, and social ontology" (p. 478). Their primary evidence for generic dynamism is Huckin's (1987) study of form in scientific journals from World War II to the present. That study found changes in even the most conservative of journals. Thus, they argue, and we agree, that research reports reflect the changes in community thinking (rather than stopping change from occurring).

But change is understandably slow. Hence, the ways in which the researcher has acted in self-reflective and critical ways are not yet presented systematically and openly in research reports. We can return to our earlier example of self-reflexive discussion in composition and professional writing, Clark and Doheny-Farina (1990). In that study, the authors devoted an article to reinterpreting their understanding of Anna's (a writing major) writing in two different settings (interning in a local health care office and taking a graduate literature class). Doheny-Farina (1989) had already presented the case traditionally, so they did not explain the study's methods; they focused, instead, on the ways in which their interpretations changed as they focused on the difference between their own values and the participant's. Clark and Doheny-Farina recognized that "through the process of writing and revising it [this essay], we recognized that the focus of our study had shifted away from Anna's experience to our own experience of making sense out of Anna's experience….We believe that the practice of exchanging and examining the diverse interpretations and arguments that an experience such as hers can provoke is the way we best build the theory that guides the teaching of writing" (pp. 479–480). We might add two observations: First, the Clark and Doheny-Farina article was not the initial presentation of Anna's case and we do not think there would be room for such extensive elaboration of interpretation in an article that also had to report the study; and second, the article voiced several other interpretations beyond its own without arguing them down, an approach we find unusual and refreshing. While articles such as these do exist, extended critical discussions of the researcher or the methods or the participants are not yet included in the initial articles presenting research. Of course we recognize that it would be easier to say there should be two write-ups—a straightforward one and a self-reflexive one—for reasons of space alone, if we could not articulate any other reasons. But we think that stance is only possible for established researchers, and instead we advocate write-ups that include more of both of Clark and Doheny-Farina's articles.

Thus, as we search for examples of critical praxis in computers and writing research, we engage in the search for those traces of critical research practices that remain within the conventions of the research write-up.

One trace can be seen in Nick Carbone et al.'s (1993) report of their joint investigation into teachers' online voices. The teacher-researchers, as they discuss the origins of this study, relate that the differences in their online voices on Daedalus Interchange sessions became more pronounced as they worked together and, at the same time, more problematic to them. They decided to focus on those differences in voice because they seemed to have as powerful an effect as the technology, and to their way of thinking (and published thinking), the voice differences should not have been so powerful. In this discussion, we can see traces of the careful noticing and personal commitment that is needed to drive critical research practices, and the group approach reflects the thoughtful teacher-centered research into computer classes emanating from Amherst (see also Curtis & Klem, 1992; Klem & Moran, 1992, 1995; Moran, 1992).

Another trace can be seen in Sibylle Gruber's (1995) situated evaluation of online discussion in a graduate seminar. Gruber, herself a graduate student, approached the question of egalitarian online discourse in a classroom from the perspectives of situating the talk; but more importantly, she herself was an insider. She identified with the positions of the participants more fully than most researchers can because she was a researcher who emerged out of the position that traditionally is reserved for participants. Because of this unique positioning—as a true insider—she may have gotten more candid remarks. Thus, in Gruber's study we see the kind of situatedness we need to see in more studies.

Glenda Conway's (1995) ethnographic study of collaboration among high school basic writers in a computer lab offers a third article with traces of the critical praxis we desire. Her detailing of her data collection process and of the stances of the major figures in the research includes commentary about goals and doubts: "I found myself worrying about the sociological, economic, and personal consequences of James' behavior and thought patterns. I began to find myself hoping he would 'come around' during the time I was observing him. He didn't, as my results show" (p. 87). Though she did not extend the discussion to other possibilities she did not choose, the traces of her self-questioning are present.

An example of the complexity of situating technology can be found in Elizabeth Lopez's (1995) study of the geographies of computer classrooms for professional writing classes. She shows how variation in physical design and curricular use of computers accounts for different events that happen in theoretically similar classes. By focusing on particular classes and sorting out the technologies used by each class, rather than by focusing on technologies and selecting classes that use the key ones, Lopez does not ground her study in a particular technology (or cluster of technologies) or set up her study to compare the effects of certain technologies.

Examples such as these encourage us, but make us want more. At the same time, we glimpse too few traces of self-reflectiveness or criticalness about data analysis in articles that label themselves as empirical. It is far more likely to see those traces in articles that claim to be theoretical or critical in approach but use empirical cases as part of their inquiry; we're thinking here of Lester Faigley's (1992) chapter on synchronous networking in *Fragments of Rationality* or Susan Romano's (1993) discussion of ethnicity in her critique of egalitarian network claims. We hope for more critical work that extends into the analysis of data, in addition to the traces we are beginning to see elsewhere.

Our view of research as an enterprise forged out of critical practices does not intend to undermine the authority of methodology for computers and composition research. Instead we want to bring that authority out of the shadows of neutrality so that we may consider the benefits and limitations of such authority. None of the concepts we have addressed is, alone, sufficient to develop or verify knowledge in computers and composition research—or in any research field, for that matter. Research as critical practice requires that we continuously apply multiple concepts, not just in order to retest with a variety of methods or add triangulation of theory, method, or data, but to bring different epistemologies (or different sorts of warrants) to bear on the same situations. We are calling this activity praxis, which requires balancing and juxtaposing warrants, bringing them into dialectic interaction.

To the extent that methodology is also theory, it becomes problematized and an element of a study that must be argued for in the reporting of the study (yes, we think methodology should always be justified, not just when it departs from accepted practices). By calling method into question, we hope that researchers can develop a set of methodologies for studies that creatively contribute to computers and writing research.

It may sound as though we are undermining the entire basis for any writing or rhetoric research, the very knowledge base of the discipline itself. We think not. What we are trying to do is to expose these terms as social constructs in the midst of an ongoing social process (i.e., the development of a discipline) and award them a new status—as heuristic. This may perhaps undermine the basis of disciplinary knowledge as *episteme*, but in its place we offer *praxis*, our suggestion being that strategic knowledge (and not knowledge in the scientific sense), should perhaps be the aim of a productive field.

Thus, as minimal steps we argue that in order for researchers to problematize their practices, they need to:

- Use more elastic notions of methods so that methodological legacies — "case study," "survey," etc., are not seen as a path to be chosen but instead are adapted to fit the circumstances of studying writing technologies.
- Defend "divergences" (i.e., points where their methodology departs from "socialized method").
- "Reflect back on" the methodology, critique the methodology, and suggest changes. Conclusions might be conclusions about the methodology as well as the practice.
- Admit the role of multiple theories in guiding researchers' and writers' activities and observations.

We further suggest that the praxis we describe asks researchers to:

- Admit that methods accepted by the field are socially constructed, and push at them.
- Articulate the ways in which technological processes clash with research processes in order to complicate the understanding of the research site.
- Place themselves in all studies (no matter how quantitative).
- Map the history of the assumptions, the interpretations, and the critique that inhabit a particular study.
- Show the ways that multiple framings (disciplinary, methodological, researcher–researched relationships, and so on) enter into the inquiry. (Multiple framing is the subject of Chapter 4.)
- Examine the ways in which political and ethical positions are worked out in the research. (Political and ethical advocacy is the subject of Chapter 5.)
- Display the tensions alive in the inquiry at all stages of the work. (Exposing tensions is the subject of Chapter 7.)

In the chapters that follow, we develop several of the critical activities, at least as they have been central to our understanding of critical research practices. Our aim is to begin to demonstrate how we deploy these critical concepts in our own thinking about research for computers and composition.

4

Postmodern Mapping and Methodological Interfaces

> When research comes to study the very realm within which it operates, the results
> which it obtains can be immediately reinvested in scientific work as instruments of
> reflexive knowledge of the conditions and the social limits of this work, which is
> one of the principle weapons of epistemological vigilance.
>
> (Bourdieu, *Homo Academicus*, 1988, p. 15).

In this chapter (see Porter & Sullivan, 1996), we hope to be methodologically reflective and "epistemologically vigilant," as we examine issues in the study of computers in the classroom and in the workplace—that is, as we examine "the very realm" in which computers and composition operates. We are especially interested in considering various methodological frames we use as researchers (and as readers of research), and in noting the strengths and limitations of those frames.

The study of computer use in the workplace or in the classroom can be guided by discussions in several fields. We can call on computers and composition, professional writing, organizational communication, technology transfer in sociology and communication, usability studies in human factors and computing, interface studies in computer support for collaborative work, technology theories in literary and communication studies, and other likely areas. We argue in this chapter that as we read or plan to do research (what we earlier called instigation), we must be aware of (a) the ways that we frame (and are framed in) our specific studies; and (b) the possible disciplinary positions we could take for that research—within frames of ideology, method, theory, and practice.

As Chapter 3 argues, traditional researchers can no longer confidently ground their studies by simply announcing the method used—a "case study" perhaps, or a "survey," or an "ethnography"—in conjunction with a certain unique site. Because we are conscious of multiple disciplines' traditions of method, and because we are aware of the contingency of our findings and the ideology of site selection, we cannot let ourselves be comfortable with merely announcing a particular method or site. We have to critique both methods and sites. We have to situate each investigation: Why undertake this study at this time? How does it contribute to current issues? What frame(s) of understanding are we bringing to the study?

From the previous chapter it is obvious that we see methodology not as Method—that is, not in the modernist sense as rigid structures to be applied without critique to a set of writing phenomena. Rather, we see methodology in a postmodern sense as local, contingent, malleable, and heuristic, and we see research generating situated knowledge—or rather a kind of pragmatic know-how (vs. know-that) kind of knowledge.

We begin the discussion in this chapter with (1) a brief description of the postmodern mapping methodology that is our chief analytic tool for critical framing. We then turn to (2) a discussion of three of our research experiences as illustration of various emframements. In the first experience we were researchers doing a case study; in the second we were corporate consultants doing a qualitative metaanalysis; in the third we were corporate consultants developing a database of research findings. Through the use of research scene maps, we hope to show how our position in each experience—the critical frame we took and the role that was assigned (or that we assigned ourselves)—was both methodologically empowering and methodologically blinding (we must admit). Each of those frames is further critiqued as we then introduce methodological frame maps as a way to (3) consider some of the methodological frames we see as operating in the three fields in which this volume is most directly involved: computers and composition, professional writing, and rhetoric theory.

METHODOLOGY: POSTMODERN MAPPING

First, a word or two about methodology. Our own method in this chapter is a spatial/visual kind of postmodern geography. We use postmodern mapping methods similar to those used by Pierre Bourdieu in *Homo Academicus* (1988) and Edward Soja in *Postmodern Geographies* (1989). Mapping is one tactic for constructing positionings of research that are reflexive—a key to developing postmodern understandings of research (see Barton & Barton, 1993; Foucault, 1984a). We ourselves have used this method of mapping relationships and positions visually and spatially in several works (Sullivan & Porter, 1993a, 1993b). We have a lot of good theoretical reasons to support our mapping, but we also just like to draw pictures. It helps our thinking.

Postmodern geographies recognize the significance of the construction of space. Space provides a frame of reference for the physical world (Werlen, 1993). Some frames of reference become powerful through repeated use and social consensus—for example, ways to measure and position subjects—and then they can become "reified." Their status as frame is forgotten, and they become "natural," or "real," or "things as they are." They affect our rhetoric and our methodology in that whether we like them or not we are forced to deal with these frames. Even in (and maybe especially in) our arguments to reject or revise them, we have to deal with them because they represent common belief systems. A critical methodology is aware of the frame as frame. It may be alert, as David Sibley (1995) is, to zones of ambiguity at the borders of societal groups—borders that are enforced through the use of images of exclusion—and study how "political, social, and socio-spatial relationships" (p. 183) are turned from zones of uncertainty (about the identity of the institution) to zones of security through the policing of boundaries. It may accept or not accept the frame to a more or less extent, but it remains alert to the frame, to its strengths as well as limitations, and to the presence of alternate frames.

Carol Gilligan's critique of the ethical studies of Perry and Kohlberg is an example of the clash of frames. In *A Different Voice* (1982), Gilligan called attention to Kohlberg's (and others') neglect of the gender frame in their studies of moral development. Their assumption was that moral actions could be classified without recourse to a gender frame—in other words, that moral theory was gender neutral and would apply equally to men and women. Gilligan's methodological contribution was to reveal the paucity of such a frame and to argue that, far from being an insignificant or accidental difference, the difference of gender is critical to understanding ethics. Her argument also showed that such claims to ethical neutrality were not ungendered, but were actually disguised arguments for masculine ethics.

We have not noticed others in computers and composition, rhetoric/composition, or professional writing using a comparably postmodern mapping strategy. Several theorists in rhetoric/composition, however, have used a kind of modernist mapping procedure: for example, Louise Phelps (1988) in *Composition as a Human Science* (see also Lyon, 1992; Phelps, 1991) and James Kinneavy (1971) in *A Theory of Discourse*. The assumption of a modernist mapping strategy is that the map represents information about an existing and static reality. Such maps are used more for organizational and representational purposes than for heuristic ones.

Maps may be constructed out of observations that support categories of interest, as Bourdieu did in *Homo Academicus*. In that work he developed comparative mappings of the French faculty (see p. 50, for example) in order to argue that in the social structures of the 1968 French academic world one can find the sources of their professional categories. His maps were critical to teasing out the distinctions made in the study about the varied types of power at work, and they were constructed statistically out of the data supporting oppositions he developed among academic capital, cultural capital, and intellectual capital. These maps became reflexive because the project was centered on Bourdieu's own environment and positioned him within the frame. They helped him establish that turn to the self portrait.

In a sense Bourdieu was anticipating the moves of current cultural geographers, such as Soja, who create geographical renderings of communities that include competing pictures of social and physical space. In his treatment of Los Angeles, for example, Soja builds a space for Los Angeles by treating the space historically, by contrasting cultural factors for the 1960s and 1980s while simultaneously presenting competing maps that depict employment, employment shifts, plant closings, changes in aerospace employment, electronics firms, corporate and banking headquarters, residences for engineers, residences of blue-collar and executive workers, and distribution of ethnic residents. He then undercuts the medley of maps by showing how a totalizing vision of the space is impossible given the various paradoxes at work in the mappings. Although he does not add himself to the picture (even though he is a Los Angeles area resident and urban planner), Soja reasserts the importance, complexity, and fluidity of social space.

We were drawn to Bourdieu's and Soja's uses of maps because they differed in origin, yet both displayed the questioning of framework that brought their maps into focus and kept their focus from becoming too stable. The tension created by not using one single map to "fix" the categories, pictures, generalizations, and so on, allowed varying and sometimes disturbingly dissimilar positions to shimmer in the discussion. (Note: Bourdieu's maps of French faculty in 1968 were gleaned from a statistical clustering of the profiles amassed in his study of their backgrounds, achievements, politics, philosophical stances, and so on. They were made reflexive by his positioning of himself within the frame and his critical focusing on his own environment. Soja's maps of Los Angeles, more diverse, were a demonstration of how differing representations, maps and matrices, dealt with the complex problem of constructing a postmodern geographical account of the social, physical, historical and political lives of the area's residents in the 1960s and 1980s. Soja's series of maps attempted to show how impossible, even misguided, it would be to build a totalizing account of Los Angeles.)

We are fascinated by such mappings and see them as a way to position research studies—both in their locale and in their disciplinary field, and thereby to guide methodological reflections. A map can be judged, we think, on what it allows, what it blocks, what else might be pictured, how it freezes time, and how it allows time to escape.

The mappings that follow depict research scene maps of three experiences from our own work with computers in workplace situations. By describing these situations and by mapping our current reflections on them, we show both how our collective research informs a better understanding of issues surrounding computers and writing in the workplace, and also how it blinds researchers to important considerations. Later, by mapping the participants in the three experiences into disciplinary frames, we can begin to discuss how particular research experiences fit into (and challenge and poke holes in) the collective research we are completing in this area. In our first experience the writer we are studying (Max) plays several roles (writer, designer, usability tester, student) and has trouble negotiating these roles well enough to see the bigger picture; in other words, he is, like us, blind to his frame. In the second and third experiences a number of framing problems emerge: First, the testers in ABC's Usability Department resist seeing their methods as methods. Second, we as the researchers and consultants in the project are not successful in helping the testers see their methodological blind spots. Third, we as the researchers-turned-developers produce too academic a concept for the database. Fourth, we as the developers cannot manage to overcome platform delivery problems inherent in the project.

RESEARCH SCENE MAPS

Research Experience #1: The Max Study

In 1989–1990, we conducted a longitudinal case study of a developing professional writer, who wrote, revised, tested, and then revised again a tutorial for learning Aldus PageMaker 3.01 (for details of this study, see Porter & Sullivan, 1994; Sullivan & Porter, 1990a; 1990b; 1993a). In the first part of the study, we focused particularly on how the writer (Max) responded to the five usability tests he ran, looking at how he interacted with his users (all of them women) and at how he revised his document based on user input. We observed that Max's rhetorical orientation—that is, his implicit theory of rhetoric, in this specific case a theory about how computer documentation is supposed to work—served as a terministic screen influencing what he saw the users doing and also how he responded to user input in a subsequent version of the document.

Max began this project as a student in Jim's advanced technical writing class, and our study of his work spanned several classes. We began gathering information about this document as a part of our study into how students in Jim's class incorporated feedback from readers about instructional texts they were writing (Porter, 1989; Sullivan & Porter, 1990a). But we became more interested in Max as his class experience became more distant, both because his investment in that piece of writing was intense and also because he was intent on testing the usability of the document he was creating.

In our study of Max's usability test we observed that he slotted the users' actions and comments into the framework he already held: "Max's view of documentation and his use of the user test information reflected his systems orientation and his bias toward content and correctness criteria" (Sullivan & Porter, 1990a, p. 34). Max's theory was that content not only mattered most but was also discretely separate from and prior to writing. "'Writing', to Max, is a means of packaging content, for which reason it may be important. But Max did not have anything like a social constructionist notion of writing. To Max, writing did not influence or interact with 'content'; it simply transmitted it. In other words, Max held to an information transfer model (see Driskill, 1989, p. 128)" (Sullivan & Porter, 1993a, p. 227). Max further evidenced values in keeping with an engineering systems orientation: "[G]ood documentation is comprehensive, covering all the necessary material and providing a complete and accurate description of a procedure. Users must be told everything to do; [Max's] tutorial provides lockstep directions for performing the tasks—and either the users get it 'right' or they get it 'wrong'" (Sullivan & Porter, 1990a, p. 34).

We found Max's rhetorical theory consonant with his systems approach, an approach that predictably led him to add to the content or to fix the style whenever he encountered user problems. He did not consider making changes in the presentation of system information (as the system was a given in his orientation), nor did he entertain changes to the design of the document (as the design had been crafted to accommodate a logical presentation of the system). We do not find Max's actions uncommon among documentation writers; his interpretive screen highlighted such problems as missing information, poorly understood terms, and stylistic blunders at the same time as it filtered out such problems as users' needs for other tasks to be included in the tutorial. Our sense of Max's encounters with users was this: "We could say that Max was not 'attuned' enough to practice (see Phelps, 1988, pp. 220–223, on attunement), not sensitive enough to his data, to his observations of users. We could also say that he was not conscious enough of his own theory. We would say that he expressed no awareness of it at all—it was simply a given of the setting" (Sullivan & Porter, 1993a, pp. 227–228).

As we examine this phase of the Max study from our current interest in clarifying the framing of the work, we see two ways the writer could have worked out of the difficulty. Max's blind spot was that he viewed practice—in this case, what users actually did with his tutorial—as simply providing information, or data. The more productive use of practice here would have been to see it as dialectically challenging theory, to regard the data of the user test as resistant to the dominant assumptions Max was bringing to the setting (see de Certeau, 1984, on the resistant nature of practice). The other way Max might have helped himself is by calling upon multiple theories. To admit that there are multiple theories is, in the first instance, to notice the inadequacy of Theory conceived as a single and universal unifying structure.

Figure 4.1 depicts our current understanding of the research scene operating in last phase of the Max study. Max was studying the users of his tutorial as a prelude to making final changes to that document. Simultaneously, we were studying Max studying the users' use of the tutorial.

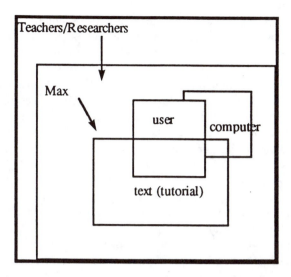

FIGURE 4.1. Teachers/researchers observing Max obtaining user
feedback about tutorial.

The text is made dominant in our map because it dominated Max's concerns.
Although Max could have been focusing primarily on the users or on their interaction with computers, he focused almost exclusively on the text he had produced,
trying to judge its success. Likewise, we could have focused on the users, the
interaction between users and computers, or the text. Further, we could have
focused on Max, on our relationship to this phase of the study, or on the relationship of this picture to the ones we could have drawn of earlier phases in the study.
We chose to focus on Max (Sullivan & Porter, 1990a) and his interaction with the
event of users trying to negotiate a print tutorial and a computer to create a document. We could have put this event in the context of earlier classroom behavior
(Sullivan & Porter, 1990b), in the context of the history of the document's development, or in the context of the users' backgrounds and reasons for cooperating
with the study. We could also have focused on our own reasons for singling out
this event in the history of Max's involvement with this document. We could have
focused on the gender issue: To what degree were Max's responses to the users
responses to them as women? Would he have treated their responses more seriously if the users had been men? In short, the study could support other depictions.

Although our case study of Max and his document (and we have determined
that there is no single "Max study" here) looks at a student usability specialist at
work, we find our study typical of workplace studies of documentation in its
placement of the computer as fixed entity in the frame. Although the document

Max is testing is produced to help students use the computer to learn how to lay out text and graphics in a computer context, the computer is the most remote consideration. Max hardly ever concerns himself with how users and computers work together; he does not focus on computer use habits. When he does focus on the computer, he usually comments that a user doesn't understand some aspect of the operating system. Because he accepts the system as prior and correct and given in his commentary (much like the developers using a rational systems model that we discussed in Chapter 2), the user is labeled as "in error" in such cases. So, the computer has a kind of background force (as tool or as wizard), but no interactive identity (as assistant or partner or servant).

This view of the role of the computer might explain why workplace researchers in professional writing have, for the most part, not much considered the role of technology in defining workplace writing (a point we discuss in more detail in a later section of this chapter): The computer is simply a given, a neutral platform, a necessary infrastructure supporting writing activities but not fundamentally influencing or constituting those activities—and not itself changeable (at least not by writers). This is a blind spot.

Research Experience #2: The Meta-analysis Project

From 1990 to 1993, we conducted two projects as freelance consultants for the usability department of a software development firm (which we'll call ABC). In the first project, which we called the Meta-Analysis Project, we analyzed more than sixty usability reports produced by members of the department over an eighteen-month period, conducted interviews with members of the group, and ran a follow-up survey. In this project, we were situated as reviewers and meta-analysts of the group's collective work.

The aim of the Meta-Analysis Project was to recommend ways the group could better manage and use its research data. We were brought in to help ABC determine what their four years of work in testing the usability of software had accomplished. "What have we learned?" was management's central question. To accomplish this task we read the reports produced over eighteen months, looking for commonalities in their methods, their subjects, their topical concerns, their analytic strategies, their reports' themes, and so on. We also interviewed all the members of the department in order to discern their positions vis-à-vis the work, their opinions of what they had learned, and their needs for codifying that knowledge. After codifying some of our findings (using techniques for qualitative meta-analysis), we followed those interviews with a survey about synthesizing usability findings. Our six months of research yielded a report detailing the reports' common themes and recommending that the department build a database for report findings.

In our research consulting experience, we focused on identifying themes that cut across products, because the usability studies in the department were classified according to products. If you asked the testers about what they did, testers always talked from the perspective of particular products—software applications—and occasionally interface components, but unless specifically prompted they seldom talked about issues that cut across products (e.g., problems users have with online help or problems new users have with computers). We saw our task, in part, as one that identified those cross-product themes as a way to help the testers think more synthetically about the knowledge they were developing. In our report, therefore, we talked about the knowledges the department was displaying in their reports about (a) specific products, (b) product types (themes across particular products), (c) users, and (d) methods for testing usability of computer products. We claimed that the first knowledge was overt and featured, while the second, third, and fourth were present, but buried. Those other knowledges tended to be talked about in the hall—"Inexperienced users tend to have trouble with this type of action"; or "We know X about feedback that users need"; or "Use Y test to get at your question"—but they were not foregrounded in the reports (though they were normally in the reports if we dug for them).

Figure 4.2 depicts the relationships we uncovered as we proceeded through the project. Because we did not use only the reports in our work, but supplemented them with interviews that probed into the way the testers saw the report fitting into the task of improving usability, the way they did their studies, and what they

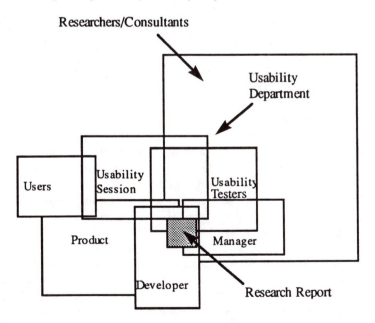

FIGURE 4.2.   Researchers/consultants focus on usability testers, who are focused on the usability test session and the research report.

thought was important about what they were learning, we were able to build a setting for those reports.

As we reflected on the project, and as we learned more from its results and from the people in the department, our mapping of the context for their reports became more complex. As Figure 4.2 tries to illustrate, the reports are a juncture available for the discussion of concerns arising out of the central event of the department, the usability session. These reports are the site for working out questions such as: How do the testers synthesize their knowledge of the product with the responses users have in their usability sessions? How do the usability sessions affect the conceptions developers have of the product?

Thus, we have situated the usability research report as one potential center for Figure 4.2 (the other is the usability session), and foreground it, because we realized that the usability reports were situated in a complex network of relations that revolved around the usability session, but which involved product developers, managers, testers, and the usability participants themselves. The usability sessions provide the events that drive the department, while the reports are tremendously important, then, as a trace of significant events, of a community of previously disparate groups that existed momentarily for a specified purpose, and then disintegrated (though repeated usability studies might make a community that is less transitory even as it remains focused on a particular purpose—i.e., improving the use of product X).

As a result of our study, we claim that the reports are the stability of the department. We acknowledge that other renderings of these relationships are possible. If someone else valued the usability testers as the center—as the embodiment, because of their multiple experiences of usability events, of usability knowledge in the group—a different drawing would emerge. Alternative pictures could also accompany centering the activities on the product being developed or on the usability session.

Interestingly enough, we doubt that anyone in the department would center the knowledge-making action of their work on the users who participate in the usability sessions, even those who believe the session generates product knowledge; those users act primarily as enablers. In other words, even though the ostensible purpose of usability is to focus attention on users (in an industry that has been notorious for its neglect of users in favor of systems design), what happens through the usability process is that the mandates of empirical methodology, or product considerations, or the client's research questions, or the process of writing the usability report itself tend to take precedence. The benefit to participants—that is, the users who participate in the test session, who stand in for future users of the product—gets lost in the complexity of the process and the distractions of methodological "purity." The political setting of the usability test session creates a conflict for usability test specialists: Who are they supposed to be advocates for? What happens in effect is that they end up serving their client's needs first (i.e., product developers within the company who come to the usability group for help), then serving the Holy God of Method (as handed down by the boss, the usability managers). Though the test specialists certainly do intend to serve as advocates for users, and certainly do so relative to the rest of the company, their advocacy for users must compete with other concerns. Of course the same sort of thing happens to researchers and teachers. We always have divided loyalties.

Research Experience #3: The Database Project

A second project we did for ABC, which we called the Database Project, extended from the first. Together with a third consultant, who directed this project, we developed an online usability database for storing significant test findings. Our aim was to help the group consolidate its usability knowledge by making test results more readily accessible to group members working on new projects (and also to other departments in the company seeking usability input). Our role in this project was somewhat different. Rather than serving as reviewers/researchers, we were creating a product for use by the group. In this project, then, we were more writers/designers, who ourselves also had to be usability testers to understand the group's needs.

As a way to get the database started, our consulting team developed the database entries for all past reports, and planned to move the task of constructing new entries to the usability testers as the consulting team's work was completed. Although the database was completed (for a brief moment), the department testers were never convinced to enter their new reports into the database. Thus, after six months, the database was not current enough to justify its day-to-day use; it became an historical artifact in the form we developed it. The central idea of the project—to put findings online—did not die, however; instead it pushed the department to put all reports online internally and to begin to put report excerpts online for the whole company.

Why did this project evolve along different lines after our involvement with it ceased? There are many reasons, some related to the database platform, some to the testers' habits, some to the workload/reward system in the department, some to a difference in conception of its worth/use, and so on. A short answer is that the database as we conceived of it did not automate an action that testers currently did by hand, and so using it was not a comfortable move for them.

In large part the problems with the database can be traced to its platform for delivery. Instead of having the database loaded onto the machines that testers used for their written work (Windows workstations), the database was housed in a special machine (a free-standing Macintosh workstation on a cart). This meant that a person had to go and locate the designated machine (it could be in one of ten or twelve offices), perhaps wait until another person finished using it, push the cart to his/her office, plug it in, and try to remember how to use it. We did some training and provided brief written instructions for use; but most of the researchers had little understanding of searching for material in the ways that librarians (and academics) would, and consequently the instructions (which got separated from the machine very quickly) could not provide the understanding of how to exploit the database's full usefulness. We should have known better than to underestimate the effect of the technological environment on office behaviors, and we should have built better training/documentation into the project.

We had been excited about the prospects of this database because we thought that it could ease a number of difficulties for the testers. It could, for example, help the testers quickly decide whether any previous studies were relevant to a current request for testing; it could help testers link present findings to past findings; it could help researchers locate reports with similar methods to the ones they were contemplating; and so on. Management was excited because the database had a section that tried to track the impact of studies (i.e., how many of the suggested changes were made) and because part of the database could be loaded onto a central server for the company to see (which was a way to advertise the success of the group). A number of the testers were enthusiastic because they wanted an easier way to get at reports, findings, and methods.

All these various sources of excitement contributed to another kind of problem: Too much interest can tend to generate too many focuses. It is true in theory that databases can support alternative focuses (they actually are the best method for flexibly arranging nonnumerical information for future retrieval). But in this case, some of the information required by the database to make it meet some of the needs was not part of the group's established report-writing procedures, and we found that changing those procedures went beyond the scope of the project. The most notable example was tracking the impact of the study by listing how many of a report's recommendations were adopted. That tracking required data which was not in the original report, which could not be gathered until several weeks after the report was published, and which was not gathered consistently by the department for some very good reasons. Understandably, testers were going to resist constructing database entries that could not be completed until they did follow-up several weeks after writing the report. They were more likely to write database entries when those entries could be written simultaneously with the report and could be taken (almost verbatim) from the report, but such entries could not meet the varied goals for the database.

In part because the department head who had initiated the project left the company, and in part because none of the three consultants was actually a member of the department (nor were we able to do the work to adapt the database to the emerging needs over time), the difficulties with the database we designed were never solved, but the project idea did evolve. Today it consists of putting report excerpts online for the company. It now focuses on dissemination of results (one of the department head's goals) rather than helping the testers (as we intended) or tracking department success (one of the department head's goals). A prime departmental goal is to make usability information available instantaneously (and

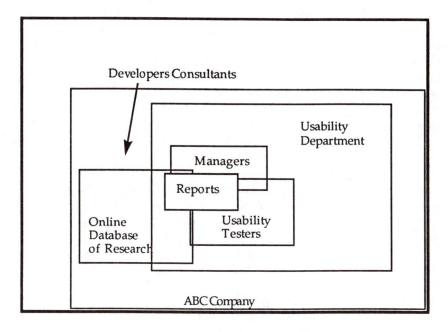

FIGURE 4.3.   Developer-produced database that does not have
close connection to usability testers.

online), which they think particularly helpful to those employees at remote locations.

Figure 4.3 depicts our relationship with ABC in the Database Project as it
unfolded over the year or so we participated in it. We see ourselves as outsiders to
the department and the company, which gave us the distance to do successful
meta-analysis research and also the distance to be out of touch in the database
project. To our way of thinking, the reports continued to dominate the knowledge-
making relationships, with the database seen as having more to do with those outside the department and less to do with the testers and their report-creating processes. As is obvious from our discussion above, Figure 4.3 reflects our
understanding of the ways the project evolved and is not our ideal. Had the project
turned out as we hoped, the testers would have a closer relationship with the
online database, making the database less the province of the company.

If Figure 4.3 were drawn from the perspective of another group touched by the
Database Project, we expect the relationships depicted would change. Few in the
department were interested in using the database to stimulate research; few
thought it important to their mission beyond its ability to make some usability
information available to the company. We recognize that because we could not

a product that integrated itself easily into the testers' writing processes, we could not effect the change we wanted in their writing habits. The computer proved to be a mighty foe in this case. It showed us how technological habits of writing resist changes that are not technologically easy to enact. Early on in the project, we recognized that the platform problem would be an obstacle to the database's having the effect we wanted, but we did not have the power or authority or financial support to change the platform. We suggested the importance of coordinating the database design with training in the use of the database and in rethinking report-writing processes, but the department, for various reasons, was not interested in rethinking their report-writing procedures. Even though we were experienced writing teachers, we did not realize how hard it would be to adjust their writing processes. Perhaps because we didn't provide the package on a platform that would make it easy for them to fit into their current procedures, we could not overcome our positions as consultants (outsiders who are temporarily involved, transients to be survived rather than heeded).

Our experiences point to how important it is for researchers in computers and writing to develop research scene maps (like Figures 4.1, 4.2, and 4.3), which depict the complexities of research setting. In such maps, researchers situate themselves in relation to their own sites of study and reflect on their potential positionings within those sites: in other words, try to understand your standpoint, including the limits of your own field or disciplinary frame.

Two other points we want to make about the research scene mapping strategies we have used above: First, no two maps are alike. When you begin to configure the complexity of relations in any study, and when you position yourself in the study, you see that there are various roles for researchers and participants, multiple alignments, all sorts of preferences and blind spots. It seems like a mess. Second, we do not conclude from the apparent mess that "no two research projects are alike, that all research studies are distinct"—or that critical research is impossible or invalid. Indeed, we think critical mapping adds to the accountability of a study by thoughtful positioning of the research scene. The power of the mapping strategy is in showing that by mapping you can get a better handle on a messy picture. (Chaos theory is, after all, a theory about how chaos works.) Postmodern research may be messy-modal rather than multimodal, but we think there can be such a thing as a postmodern methodology that is not self-contradictory, and that still is capable of generating local knowledge (in Geertz's sense of the term).

METHODOLOGICAL FRAME MAPS

We now want to turn to consider positioning our methodological frames for each of the three experiences in terms of several fields' views of research. By examining these three research experiences in light of a number of research communities' potential interest in the issues they surface—and also those communities' disin-

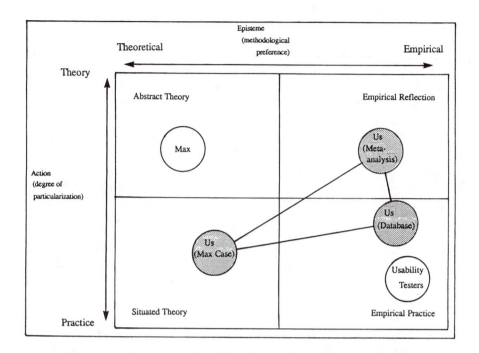

FIGURE 4.4.   Methodological frames for three research experiences.

terest in certain aspects of the experiences—we can depict some of the research boundaries at work in our interdisciplinary field. Figure 4.4 depicts various methodological positions that we see operating in a number of fields interested in the study of computers and writing in the workplace (including computers and composition, rhetoric/composition, and professional writing), and it positions our three research experiences discussed above within its grid. Partly, this grid operates by identifying a range of positions along a theory-practice continuum (an argument we develop in Sullivan & Porter, 1993a).

This map operates on two axes: the theory-to-practice axis (depicted vertically) and the theoretical-to-empirical axis (depicted horizontally). The vertical axis locates knowledge according to degree of particularity: Is general knowledge or Theory possible across situations? If you think so, then you tend toward the abstract or general grid (upper left). The horizontal axis is the one of methodological preference; in rhetoric/composition, we see this as the continuum between those who prefer theoretical approaches and those who prefer empirical approaches to generating knowledge.

Loosely construed, the axes construct four quadrants for characterizing methodology. If we identified the most extreme positions, the four corners of the square, we might distinguish them thus:

- Abstract theory, which focuses on abstract relationships and identities, and does not situate its thoughts in particulars (believed or observed)—the position of ahistorical metanarrative and traditional philosophy.
- Empirical reflection, which focuses on abstract discussions of method and does not situate its thoughts in particulars.
- Situated theory, which focuses on relationships and identities that are grounded in particular situations, but does not suggest those relationships are part of a larger metanarrative.
- Empirical practice, which focuses on observed behavior in particular situations, but does not theorize those observations in any abstract way (i.e., acceptance of methods as established and fixed).

Obviously, the most extreme positions (the corners) are the clearest, cleanest, neatest, and most difficult to locate in the spectre of published research. Nobody actually lives there. Simultaneously, the center of the square is the richest, most contradictory, most contingent, and most difficult to maintain position. (Is this the position of praxis, the point of balance between theory and practice that Carolyn Miller, 1989, talks about?) If we mapped actual scholars, researchers, and writers onto this map, few would fall either in the corners or in the center. Yet we do see tendencies in researchers to privilege certain frames.

As we map the three experiences we discussed earlier onto this grid of theory, practice, and method, we see Max as occupying the "abstract theory" quadrant. He wanted to believe in the importance of observing the particular behaviors of the users he studies. Yet he deflected the data of their "practices" by interpreting all of their actions in terms of an overall Theory of Text, System, and User that he was not willing to surrender or revise. In his theory, the system is a given, and the trick to writing documentation is to produce a piece of documentation that will help the ignorant user understand (notice: not "use") the system. In Max's defense, we have to acknowledge that the role of technical writers in most companies is probably firmly established along these very lines. How often do technical writers actually have the political power to suggest changes in system design? Frequently they are working in a realm in which engineers and systems designers rule absolutely.

We see the members of the usability department at ABC as occupying the "empirical practice" quadrant. For the most part, they do not believe that developing knowledge across tests is part of their mission; they see their job as answering the client's questions now, and quickly. In their frame, knowledge is specific to the product, to the client's needs, and to the particular test. Thus, they see little value in studying findings from other tests, even though they would allow that extending findings across tests would improve the scientific value of their work.

We see ourselves as occupying different positions in the three different studies which leads us to suspect that we are somewhat nomadic in our approach to research. But it may also be true that our position is influenced by, and changes because of, our sense of our coparticipants' needs in each study.

In the Max study, our critique of Max took the form of our wishing he would pay more attention to users. "Listen to these people," we wanted to tell him but we didn't. (In retrospect, in order to exercise a critical approach, we should have done so.) We wanted him to take a situated approach to his theory but instead allowed him to retain his ideal stance. In our work on the Meta-Analysis Project, we took the position of empirically reflective researchers examining the methodological assumptions of a group of research practitioners. To some extent, our problems with the Database Project may have been due to our maintaining this reflective role despite the fact that our assigned role in the second project was fundamentally different. We suspect that our being methodologically overreflective prevented us from designing the database in a more practice-oriented way that the department would have found more palatable.

We are suggesting, too—in case it is not obvious by now—that researchers in computers and composition, rhetoric/composition, and professional writing also have their preferred quadrants. In fact, disciplines and subdisciplines tend to occupy some sectors and not others. Much of the research and the teaching/learning accounts in rhetoric/composition, for example, fit into empirical practice, while much of the theoretical work fits into abstract theory. Workplace research in professional writing locates most of its work in practice, with situated theory and empirical practice gathering most of the work. Computers and composition publishes primarily about practice, with theory of texts/hypertexts fitting into the abstract theory sector. Research into the use of computers in the workplace fits primarily into empirical practice.

We see these methodological preferences linking up with site preferences. Figure 4.5 maps different research sites on the same frame. From left to right, the grid distinguishes between studies that are highly conscious of the role of technology ("technology rich") vs. those that dismiss the role of technology or which do not study environments in which that role is very obvious. (We would, however, contend that technology does inform composition instruction even in the traditional classroom—though because machines aren't actually in the classroom, the presence of the "print paradigm" is not so obvious.) From top to bottom, the grid represents studies that focus on classroom activities vs. research in the workplace.

While we see some complexity in the way we might map researchers on our methodological frames grid (because no one actually occupies the extreme corners), it is striking to us how widely research fields differ in their preferences for site. Computers and composition researchers examine the effects of computer technologies on writing, and hardly anybody else bothers to do so. Between 1990

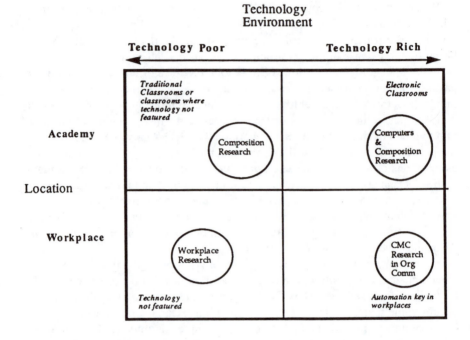

FIGURE 4.5. Methodological frame map for fields studying writing practices.

and 1992, *Computers and Composition,* the primary journal for the computers and composition community, published 52 articles on computers and writing, 100% of its total. No surprise there, but it is surprising that during that same time *College Composition and Communication* published only two articles on computers and writing (2.4% of its total), *College English* published four (3.9%), *Research in the Teaching of English* published three (6.5%), and *Written Communication* nine (17.6%) (Sullivan, 1993a). (We see this same pattern of segregation in published collections, discussed below.) In other words, we find evidence of a fairly exclusive segregation in the matter of who covers what sites. It may well be that these research communities are defining themselves, de facto, according to sites. But if this is true, then we wish to challenge the segregation, especially because there seems to be no research institution taking responsibility as yet for publishing the study of computers and writing in the workplace.

Research in computers and composition by and large occupies the upper right quadrant: it is classroom-based and technology-based, as we see in articles published in *Computers and Composition* and in numerous collections (e.g.,

Hawisher & Selfe, 1991; Selfe & Hilligoss, 1994). This may be due in large part to the fact that many people in the computers and composition community are first-year composition teachers and administrators in charge of computer labs. They tend to have a firmly situated view, methodologically, which fits with their situated view of technology. The strength of this research approach is its situated and thoughtful approach to technology; however, we do not see much evidence of attention to workplace writing practices. The preferred site of study for computers and composition research is the first-year computer classroom. While there is considerable need to study the first-year classroom, exclusive focus on a single dominant site limits the field's potential for effecting change outside the writing classroom. We see it this way: The workplace is the primary writing site our students will inhabit, and the computer is one lingua franca that links the classroom and the workplace. Computers give us a way to cut across the dominant binary in place here—classroom vs. workplace—providing a means for researchers to change workplace writing practice. We think computers and composition researchers' critical and thoughtful approach to writing technologies should extend to all the sites where technology is used in the production of writing.

Professional writing researchers, by contrast, have paid close attention to workplace writing practices—but, interestingly, without much attention to the technologies that support workplace writing. In the several major collections focusing on workplace studies in professional writing, few contributors focus on computers. We identified four major collections of workplace research in professional writing: Blyler and Thralls (1993), Kogen (1989), Odell and Goswami (1985), and Spilka (1993). Of a total of 61 chapters in these four collections, only three chapters focus predominantly on computer technologies in the workplace. Sullivan and Dautermann's collection, *Electronic Literacies in the Workplace* (1996), was conceived precisely to fill this gap.

Workplace studies in professional writing also underestimate the importance of the classroom as a workplace research site. There are frequent discussions of the classroom in professional writing research, but few classroom studies. The distinction here is key. Workplace research too often assumes that knowledge about the workplace should feed classroom practice, but not vice versa. The classroom perhaps is the best site for effecting fundamental changes in the nature of workplace literacy; it certainly provides an opportunity for experimentation, for testing new possibilities (whereas workplace action can be constrained by "the way things have always been done").

Rhetoric theorists/historians and composition researchers have tended either to ignore the workplace as unimportant (from the political right, in an instrumental way: as simply an applied location for rhetoric theory) or to treat it with suspicion (from the political left, in a substantive way: as Big Business or The Capitalist Enterprise). The tendency is to view electronic technologies as neutral or transparent—that is, as not having a significant effect on discursive practices but being, at best, a simple channel for discursive practices. Some who have noticed the technology have cast it in an evil light, seeing computers mainly as tools for a capitalist bureaucracy (Ohmann, 1985). We notice that recent major collections by rhetoric/composition theorists contain no focused discussion of the role of computer writing technology: of a total of 39 chapters in the Enos and Brown (1993), Gere (1993), and Harkin and Schilb (1991) collections, no chapter focuses predominantly on the role of computer technology. Though we feel that computer writing technology is an incredibly important influence on "defining the new rhetorics" of postmodernism, most postmodern rhetoric theorists apparently disagree. Though not a collection, Lester Faigley's *Fragments of Rationality* (1992) is one significant exception that, we hope, signals a change.

A fourth group of researchers not directly in the general composition community provides yet another position on these issues. Researchers like Zuboff (1988) and Sproull and Kiesler (1991a, 1991b) take what we would call a CMC perspective toward the use of computers in the workplace (Porter, 1993). This perspective is defined by its predominant focus on the modes of technology used for communication in business, but its focus is by and large not writing itself. While this research perspective tends to be situated in some respects (especially sensitive to the role of technology, broadly construed), it interprets workplace practices in terms of an overall communication theory applied to specific media choices (e.g., email vs. telephone). CMC research favors oral over print media, and tends not to take a developed rhetorical or critical view that acknowledges writing itself as a distinct kind of technology with its own rhetorical nature.

DESIGN NOTES

Because mapping is key to the critical research practices we are advocating, we will briefly consider how research maps such as those used above are constructed.

Methodological frame maps are tricky to design, as we have discovered through trying to teach such tactics in graduate rhetoric courses. In a methodological frame map, for instance, the researcher has to start by imagining key continuums that may unlock variation in a study (e.g., among positions in the field, or among a set of interconnected fields, or among positions taken by institutions and/or participants in a study). Locating the binaries operative in a study is a useful place to begin (see Chapter 7 for a discussion of the tactic of using multiple binaries). The researcher must position herself/himself/themselves in the scene. The researcher must account in some way for changing stances over time (e.g., see Figure 4.4). And the researcher has to be sure that she is working with a continuum rather than a set of categories, though it is possible to map a continuum against a set of categories (as we do in Figure 4.5).

Forming dual and intersecting continuums into a grid is also tricky. For example, it is better not to map time on the X (horizontal) axis, as that disrupts the notion of the mapping of space. If time is important to your project (and it always should be), then you might consider making two maps at different times. If you need to think through several continuums, coordinate several maps rather than trying to squeeze too many dimensions onto the same map. Other advice: Keep one continuum as the X axis in all the maps. Make sure your Y (vertical) axis continuums are all oriented in the same direction (e.g., all conservative positions at top, all liberal at bottom, etc.).

Of course in applying these mapping procedures, it is important to:

- Frame the research scene for your study, being sure to show shifts over time (e.g., shifts in the focus for the site, shifts in the advocacy role of the researcher).
- Understand philosophical positions.
- Expose mismatches (e.g., contrast expectations and findings).
- Show change across maps.
- Show contrast in views.
- Position your work within a larger field(s) (i.e., a field scene map).
- Articulate what your key terms are and why they matter.
- Use multiple maps to avoid totalizing and freezing "situation."

We are suggesting that researchers ought to employ both research scene (see Chapter 7 for an example of the construction of research scene maps) and methodological frame maps as tactics for identifying the rich and varied possibilities of any study and for exploring the nuances and problematics of the research focus. For us, maps are a theorizing technique. They do not yield an immutable set of categories, but are useful instead as a tool for thinking about what frames might be present and operating in a particular study both inside that study and between that study and the disciplinary communities that are relevant to it. These maps exist in time and can be used as a record of the ways representations are changing. They serve the purpose of particularizing the study to its situation. (For instance, notice that none of the three research scene maps could possibly be used by anyone else, since the depiction is particular to that study: You can imitate the technique, but you can't reuse those maps.)

We view Figures 4.1, 4.2, and 4.3 as research scene maps that view the various components and participants of a study contextually. Based loosely on the conventions of Venn diagrams, such maps, when they are used in a modernist way, aim to clarify complex relationships by mapping them in relationship to one another. Modernist depictions typically do not show the movement or flexibility seen in postmodern mappings (for instance, see Gilles Deleuze and Félix Guattari's depiction of a rhizome in *A Thousand Plateaus,* 1987). Thus, they allow readers to say, "Aha! So this is what it adds up to! The report [to comment on what is happening in Figure 4.2] is the province of the interaction between developers, testers, and managers, but it is never open to the users for comment. Tsk, tsk." But such diagrams are not entirely stable, even for modernists. In qualitative studies such as those described in Figures 4.1, 4.2, and 4.3, maps such as these do work to particularize and situate the relationships in such a way that precludes wild speculation about how such situations generally work.

Figures 4.4 and 4.5 are methodological frame maps. They break with the typical modernist depictions of contextual relationships in a study in several important ways that allow you to see how we use postmodern mapping in the interrogation of methodological framings and in the relationship of study participants and researchers. Instead of taking its conventions of construction and reading from Venn diagrams, these figures connect with the plotting of coordinates on an XY-axis. These diagrams are not, as the earlier ones were, a fabric woven somewhere and placed somewhat arbitrarily on a page. Instead, particular points on the picture take on more meaning because they represent an intersection of two continuums. For example, in Figure 4.4, Max is placed in the upper left section of the frame, which means that we see his beliefs about writing operating in such a way as to privilege theoretical knowledge as it is defined in a modernist paradigm. By contrast, we take up different positions in the three research experiences we depict, while the workers from ABC are clearly positioned within a paradigm that focuses on the particular in all situations without pushing to theorize the research they conduct. Our multiple placements on the map serve to show that we have not developed an ideal position for research methodology (which of course the Ideal Researcher is supposed to occupy). Nor do they show us in close harmony with the other participants. Indeed, this map would not exist if we were developing a picture of harmony.

Figure 4.5 extends the approach taken with these research experiences to the problem of disciplinary framing. Because these studies are connecting the classroom and workplace writing that is involved with technology, Figure 4.5 examines the ways in which work is positioned in the fields that study writing practices. It says: Suppose we look at the research on writing, first from the perspective of location (i.e., is it more focused on writing related to succeeding in the academy, or is it more focused on writing related to communicating successfully in workplace situations?) and then from the perspective of technology environment (i.e., is it more likely to take place in technology poor or technology rich environments?). How will such a sorting position the research on writing? While we could have constructed Figure 4.5 by placing individual studies on that XY-axis (as Bourdieu did in *Homo Academicus*), we simplified the depiction to show that this crossing of perspectives yields different positions for different disciplinary groups. A more careful mapping of this type would next turn to studies that do not fit the framing, for they are the most interesting.

We hope that the methodological mapping strategy we are offering here suggests some fruitful possibilities for researchers who are doing research on computers and writing in the workplace and in the classroom. Clearly, this mapping technique has the heuristic intent of encouraging researchers to "situate" their studies according to two interrelated frames.

First, researchers can use research scene maps to plot the relationships within specific studies (as we do in Figures 4.1, 4.2, and 4.3), situating themselves in relation to participants in the study and to the numerous possible focuses of a given study. As we have discussed, it is often difficult—and maybe impossible—for researchers to do this while they are engaged in data collection. As we noticed in the Database Project, we were not able to understand our situated role in the project until we were well into the project. Such reflection perhaps must necessarily occur sometime later, but that is not to dismiss its value as a practical knowledge that can be deployed in future projects. In addition, the mapping is intended to distinguish a project, to identify the particular roles for participants and researchers, the social elements involved, the textual dynamics—in short, to complicate the usual view that research involves two parties, observer and participant. (This is particularly important to feminist researchers and others who want to draw participants into researcher roles and to draw research into emancipatory frames.)

Second, researchers can use methodological frame maps to plot their research position relative to other researchers in a field, or in several fields (as we do in Figures 4.4 and 4.5). Mapping is a way to identify preferences, tendencies, and of course blind spots. Such a mapping exercise can serve to critique fields' interests and locations ("Perhaps we are doing too much work on X"; "Perhaps we are doing too many studies only situated in the workplace"). It can also serve to suggest places for new researchers to locate: The blind spots and gaps in a research field's work offer an opportunity for the new researcher to make a significant contribution.

How are the two frames interrelated? What makes our approach to mapping postmodern is that the interpretation of findings moves between the two frames, the research scene frame and the methodological frame. One frame identifies the relations within a study, the other frame identifies the relations between a study and other work in a field, and the two frames destabilize each other.

5

The Politics and Ethics of Studying Writing With Computers

> Perhaps the computer is neither good nor evil, but both. By this I
> mean not merely that computers can be used for good or evil purposes, but
> that they can evolve into very different technologies in the framework of strategies
> of domination and democratization. (Feenberg, 1991, p. 91)

In Chapter 2, we claimed that the aim of research should be to pursue some constructive program of political and ethical action. In this chapter, we elaborate that position by talking about the aim of research. Our chief question is this: What is research supposed to accomplish, and for whom?

In this respect, Chapter 5 addresses the back end of our critical practices depiction of the research process (see the shaded portion of Figure 5.1), that is, in this chapter we focus on the telos of research activity—praxis as it operates in some kind of social milieu, but particularly as focused on research participants. In Chapter 6, we will focus more on the front end, the emergence of research.

In the first part of this chapter, we call upon critical postmodern theory to develop a position, and a supporting vocabulary, to help us (a) articulate criteria for distinguishing between uses of the computer that dominate and uses that empower and liberate, and (b) consider what such an argument means for researchers who study writing with computers. This theoretical stance is, at the

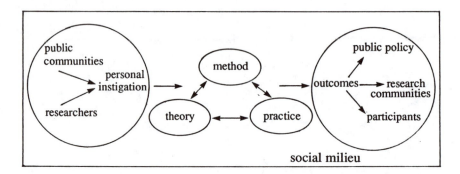

FIGURE 5.1.   A critical practices approach to empirical research (focus on aims).

same time, postmodern, feminist, and rhetorical. We argue against viewing computer technology and research participants in a detached, decontextualized way and in favor of seeing technology from a critical viewpoint as created by, situated in, and constitutive of basic human relations. This critical view of technology is affiliated with the so-called second cybernetic, a philosophical movement in computer theory that "looks at the world [and technology] from the standpoint of the involved subject rather than from that of the external observer" (Feenberg, 1991, p. 106; Winograd, 1995). It sees technology not as abstracted or decontextualized systems—what Rob Kling (1980) calls the theoretical perspective of systems rationalism—but rather as involving real people using human-designed machines for situated purposes. The view is a rhetorical outlook toward technology and computers, one that is suspicious of Theory—that is, the traditional kind that claims universal authorizing status—but acknowledges the importance of theorizing (see Sosnoski, 1991, p. 199)—that is, local, contingent, and situated reflection and analysis that has a status as heuristic rather than as Law.

In the second part of the chapter we instantiate our view by examining the degree to which various studies in computers and composition situate (or could situate) themselves politically, ethically, and technologically. Traces of such situated inquiry are evident in numerous studies, though few existing studies comprehensively enact the kinds of procedures we are advocating.

CRITICAL CONTEXTUALIZATION AND THE
CONFIGURATION OF POLITICS, ETHICS, AND RHETORIC

We are defining politics as having to do with relations of institutional power (a) between the researcher and the researched, and (b) between the researcher and the professional or disciplinary paradigm(s) within which she works (and with which

she at least partly contends). The disciplinary paradigm itself has a sense of purpose (e.g., a tradition of knowledge-making, or of scholarly resuscitation of lost
ideas, or of product development), employs certain preferred modes of production
(e.g., empirical inquiry, rhetorical inquiry, historical inquiry, philosophical
inquiry, or product engineering), and resides in a particular institutional and social
context, and all of these factors exert a powerful political influence.

Our articulation of ethics is not what has traditionally been regarded as ethics,
especially not within research methodology. (Traditional discussions of the ethics
of research tend to focus on issues of right of privacy, confidentiality of information obtained, and the issue of informed consent of research participants; see, for
example, Webb et al., 1981, Chapter 5.) Traditional ethics concerns moral right/
wrong and, especially, issues of justice and fairness (often involving the distribution of property, or what Iris Marion Young, 1990, calls the "distributive paradigm of justice"). But we are viewing ethics, first, in the postmodern sense of
having to do with relations, or intersubjectivity, or, in terms of our methodological focus, as the ways roles are constituted and reconstituted for individuals, for
researchers and for researched, as well as for the communities of researchers that
collect themselves around certain themes, topics, and problems and thus define
themselves as fields, disciplines, or interest areas. Second, and more conventionally, we view ethics as having to do with the process of determining a should for
a we (Lyotard & Thébaud, 1985; Porter, in press). This understanding raises several immediate questions: Who is "we"? Researchers? participants? research
field? society?—or all of the above? For whose benefit does/should research
operate? What changes should it effect? We see these questions as political and
ethical interrogations necessary to the operation of critical research. The process
of establishing value is inevitable in the operation of research (or of rhetoric), and
we see it as important that such value be explicitly articulated.

The first move we object to in traditional methodology is the separation of pol-
itics/ethics from research, from inquiry, or from knowledge, but the second move
we wish to counter is the separation of politics and ethics from each other. We
agree with the position advocated by Nancy Blyler (1995), who urges research to
move more in the direction of "critical interpretation," by which she means a form
of research that recognizes and questions the ethical and political implications of
the research setting. The ethical question of what we should do must stay connected to the issue of power relations (Porter, in press): To what degree does the
determination of a "should" for a "we" represent the oppression of an "other"? By
what mechanisms of power are such decisions made? These are questions that
link power and ethics. Politics links with ethics in the examination of the ways
subjectivities are established (and modified) through relations of power.

These conceptions of politics and ethics coordinate with the the agenda of critical theorists like Andrew Feenberg (1991) and Seyla Benhabib (1992) who criticize philosophy, theory, and rationalist technology whenever those theories
decontextualize or abstract systems from human concerns so that they treat people

as "generalized others." These critical theorists—a certain irony there—promote contextualized inquiry (or decision making that is attentive to particular social settings, distinct forms of technology, and the differences among groups, even individuals).

In Chapter 3, we considered how computers and composition research in the 1980s was based mostly on what Feenberg calls an "instrumental" approach to technology (that is, the view that technology is politically and ethically neutral, that its good or bad use is determined by what people do with technology). Later studies took more of a substantive approach to understanding the relationship between technology and human participants, but that did not blunt Feenberg's critique, which is based on the division (in both approaches) between technology and humans. The instrumental approach views technology as neutral (and innocent): The tool itself can be misused, of course, but the goodness or badness is not in the tool; its goodness or badness is determined by its human use. Used properly, technology can only be positive. The substantive view sees the tool as having an innate influence on human action. The tool is not so innocent, but rather it effects a change on human behavior or consciousness, and in the case of modern technologies, that change is usually dehumanizing.

Feenberg critiques both approaches for failure to be "critical." Neither the instrumental nor the substantive positions allows that technologies are human designs. Neither takes into account the diverse ways that humans can interact with the same technology. Neither considers that human interaction with machines is part of technology, that is, that technology does not equal the hardware and software alone.

Mark Poster (1989) articulates this critique in terms of differing philosophical traditions' views of technology. He points out that:

> At the ontological level metaphysical dualists may argue that nothing has changed with the introduction of the computer. The world may still be thought by some to be composed of material and mental things. But at the phenomenological level at which the subject experiences itself and the world, the computer changes everything. ... Like the other domains of the mode of information, the computer draws attention to the subject as constituted phenomenon, undermining the illusory assurance of the fixed, defined individual. (pp. 138–139)

Both the instrumental and substantive approaches separate technology from human use, and Feenberg argues for an integrated view. Feenberg's critical theory of technology aims to counter the modernist notion of technology which ends up installing in technology "the values and interests of ruling classes and elites" (p. 14). Far from seeing technology as a neutral tool, which the rationalist supposes (e.g., Habermas), or as inherently bad, Feenberg argues for viewing the tool in its context of design and use.

The chief thrust of Feenberg's discussion is to reject the decontextualizi move of Big T Theory and philosophy toward formal abstraction or bias. Th move "reifies technology by abstracting [it] from all contextual considerations" (p. 181). Feenberg cites the decontextualizing practice of formal abstraction for "suppressing the dimensions of contextual relatedness and potentiality" as it "transforms its objects into mere means, an operation that prejudices their status as much as any valuative choice" (p. 170).

Feenberg specifies four "reifying moments of technical practice," ways that this formal approach to technology cuts technology off from its social practices: "decontextualization (the separation of object from context); reductionism (the separation of primary from secondary qualities); autonomization (the separation of subject from object); positioning (the subject situates itself strategically ... 'above' social processes)" (pp. 184, 188).

To counter the rationalistic move toward decontextualization, Feenberg offers the contextualizing move of critical theory, which historicizes, situates, and personalizes technology; that is, critical theory applies technology to particular users in particular places at particular times: "Critical theory shatters the illusion [of neutrality] by recovering the lost contexts and developing a historically concrete understanding of technology" (p. 181). We see such a move as characteristic of rhetoric—at least of the sophistic variety—and of some feminist theories, as well as a move of Feenberg's brand of critical theory.

The critical view does need some criteria for making judgments about the use(s) of technology. If technology is neither inherently good nor inherently bad, by what standards do we make judgments about it? Feenberg identifies four countermoves to the reifying practices mentioned above that can be invoked to resituate technology within the realm of social practices: concretization, vocation, aesthetic investment, and collegiality. Feenberg's description of these countermoves in *Critical Theory of Technology* is disappointingly brief, and he himself is theoretically abstract when it comes to setting a proactive agenda toward technology change. However, we have found his categories helpful to our thinking; we think these strategies can be usefully applied to critical research. In Table 5.1 we represent how these countermoves could be interpreted as criteria for determining critical research.

Table 5.1 also incorporates Shoshana Zuboff's (1988) distinction between uses of technology that "informate" vs. those that "automate," because we see it as a helpful one that dovetails neatly with Feenberg's countermoves. Automation "displaces the human presence" (p. 10) by computerizing activities in a way that either eliminates the human presence altogether or reduces it to a lesser status (cognitively, institutionally) in some production process. Computer technology that "informates," on the other hand, enhances the status of the human presence in the production process, perhaps by engaging people in new ways or by allowing them to collect new types of information or in some cases actually producing a new "quality of information" (p. 10). Informating "sets into motion a series of

**TABLE 5.1.   Feenberg's (and Zuboff's) Categories for
Technological Change as Applied to Critical Research**

Categories	Criteria for Research	Examples in Research
concretization (vs. decontextualization)	Researchers contextualize and situate both technologies and participants. They do not describe them in general terms or treat them as a generic class, but rather are connected to particular differences.	Hawisher & Sullivan (in press) Cushman (1996a)
vocation (vs. reductionism)	Researchers treat participants and technologies holistically, not reducing either simply to constituent elements (variables), but respecting the complexity of their subjectivities.	Romano (1993)
aesthetic investment (vs. autonominization)	Researchers exhibit a concern for overall quality of life/work for participants (and not just for narrow research results, or answers to research questions, or field benefits).	
collegiality (vs. positioning)	Researchers work with participants in "the coordination of effort" (Feenberg, 1991, p. 190) and share responsibility for improving institutional and social conditions and work conditions.	Hawisher & Sullivan (in press)
informating (vs. automating)	Researchers work proactively to promote uses of computers which humanize and democratize, uses which "informate" rather than merely "automate" (Zuboff) or otherwise dehumanize and diminish participants.	Mirel (1996a) Lopez (1995)

dynamics that will ultimately reconfigure the nature of work and the social relationships that organize productive activity" (pp. 10-11). Thus, Zuboff's distinction calls attention to the importance of social relations in the workplace. In a way, she is saying that better relations and enhanced status for workers should be the primary goal of technology applications in the workplace (i.e., as opposed to reducing worker status or eliminating workers altogether). The focus should be on the people affected by technology rather than on the processes of technology or the products it creates.

In her discussion of methodology, Liz Stanley (1990b) provides yet another example of a critical theorist developing criteria for evaluating research practices. Stanley emphasizes modes of production (as does Feenberg), but she looks more at the economic conditions of production and situates the discussion specifically in terms of academic research. Stanley's discussion argues "for taking seriously at an intellectual and analytical level the academic mode of production" (p. 11). By "academic mode of production" she means a complex institutional structure that includes "departments, faculties, and whole institutions ... office staff, cleaners, porters, refectory and cafeteria staff" (p. 5), as well as materials and tools like "blackboards, computers, blank sheets of paper, books, articles and conference papers in the making, but also people: as research subjects/objects, and also as students" (p. 5). She further considers how the academic modes of production interrelate with an academic market, an economy of production and consumption with "overlapping divisions of labor" (p. 6), as well as a system of economic exchange. She develops criteria for evaluating "good research" (p. 13), which should "account for the conditions of its own production" and strive for what she calls an "unalienated knowledge," by which she means situated knowledge that is a form of praxis—useful practical knowledge that is grounded in real settings and directed at actual persons (p. 12). So Stanley's frame of the institution thoroughly contextualizes the material forms of production. She reminds us that those material forms are not merely incidentals to be disregarded, but are signs of a technological system that plays a part in constituting relations.

The move to critical contextualization of technologies, and also research itself, as modes of production is another way of affirming praxis as a form of knowledge—a different sort of knowledge than, but of equal status to, epistemic, scientific knowledge. Acknowledging the legitimacy of praxis involves recognizing that in certain fields of human social action—such as politics, ethics, law, medicine (perhaps), and rhetoric—logical or mathematical certainty is an impossible (and perhaps invalid) goal. To cater to certainty as the norm is to apply an unreasonable and impractical (literally) standard to human social action. Praxis as it applies to methodology means recognizing that the modernist scientific paradigm is an inadequate and illegitimate basis for the study of human social action.

This view derives support from two methodological directions: feminist method in the human sciences (discussed in Chapter 3) and situated approaches to computing design (discussed in Chapter 2). Feminists who are discussing method have made visible many political and ethical choices that are backgrounded in modernist methodologies. Their contributions to postmodern methodology are profound. Like the feminists, we view research as a radically situated activity, bounded by place, circumstance, philosophy, participant actions, researcher experience, and so on. Like the feminists, we see research as dynamic action.

Computer designers who pay attention to users in context (e.g., Bødker, 1989, 1991, Suchman, 1987) are important to our thinking as well because they have managed to break the stranglehold of the machine and of the philosophical privileging of formal abstraction through their emphasis on the situated design of computing environments. While these designers are not postmodern in their pronouncements or methodologies, they do (a) try to put people before machines as they design machines—an unusual feat in U.S. society—and (b) recognize situational/environmental elements of design by exploring the particulars of interactions humans have with computers inside an organization. Taken together, these visions help us think about the political and ethical dimensions of the postmodern study of electronic communication. Our supplement to these two developments is rhetoric.

The paradigm we are advocating is less sanguine about the operation of power in the research setting and more actively attentive to the ethical and political implications of research activity. This paradigm resituates research methodology as praxis: as an ethical doing rather than as an observing of something, the "observing" metaphor being the problem with the traditional paradigm. What we are striving for is a resituating of methodology as a rhetorical, political, and ethical action that has as its goal the improvement of researchers and research participants.

Improving the lot of researchers and participants does not exclude the possibility that one way to improve their lot is to effect change within a given field. For instance, one way to improve students' writing is to work on behalf of better informed and more fully aware composition teachers. But we are also insisting that without direct benefit to participants during the research process, research risks being manipulative, oppressive, even matri/patriarchal. Also, please do not think that because we are challenging the assumptions of neutrality and objectivity, we do not advocate careful observation and thorough reflection. Actually, we think that the types of multiperspectival and heuristic observations, of double reflections and multiple mappings, we have been advocating in this book raise the standards for empirical study.

We find Feenberg's critique compelling, but we are also aware of the limitations of a strictly material notion of contextualization. Materialist Marxist and feminist theorists stress the importance of political situatedness and material conditions. Lisa Cahill (1990) articulates this as a key premise of Marxist/feminist ethical theory: "All human beings exist in spatial and material relationships which not only are constitutive of individual identity but are also the conditions of possibility of human communities and institutions" (p. 55). In other words, space and place matter (see Irigaray, 1993), a point with which we obviously agree. But sometimes such a materialist approach proceeds without sufficient regard for the rhetorical elements involved, or without regard for how rhetoric (situated language use) contributes to the perception of material conditions, and indeed at times to their very construction.

Thus, we want to move beyond materialist or essentialist notions of context to develop a rhetorical sense of modes of production. We agree with Young (1990) that the notion of institutional context should extend beyond the merely material (in the physical sense) to include what we consider the rhetorical, u.. include "any structures or practices, the rules and norms that guide them, and the language and symbols that mediate social interactions within them, in institutions of state, family, and civil society, as well as the workplace" (p. 22). Rhetoric is the third wheel that overlaps with both politics and ethics (see Porter, in press, Chapter 3)—and our contention is that we need to keep rhetoric, politics, and ethics together as a set of focuses informing research practices in significant ways. We are arguing that the dangerous and misleading thing to do in research is to pretend that research inquiry is (1) prior to rhetoric, (2) a-political, or (3) ethically neutral. Instead we argue for valuing the role of rhetoric/ethics/politics as an intertwined set of concerns influencing research activity.

Thus, our position bridges the concerns of rhetoric/composition, ethics, and computers and composition. It attempts to construct a "rhetorical ethics" (Porter, in press) to guide methodological decisions in the study of computers and composition. This rhetorical ethics borrows from diverse theoretical positions, including critical Marxism (Feenberg, 1991, 1995), feminist communicative action (Benhabib, 1992; Young, 1990), and rhetorical casuistry (Jonsen & Toulmin, 1988). This ethic focuses particularly on ethics as situated praxis, as central to human relations, and as particularly sensitive to the role of rhetoric (and language) in determining ethical action. It is an ethic of situated relations, that is, of situated rhetorical relations and of composing processes. It draws on both feminist and neopragmatic discussions in focusing on ethics as a rhetorical process and on rhetoric as an ethical process of constituting relations given the spatial and material conditions that define power (Porter, 1995).

THE AIMS OF CRITICAL RESEARCH

Research ought to situate itself ethically and politically, especially vis-à-vis participants and aims—that is the central point of this chapter. It ought to understand its ethical and political positionings, and, further, it ought to aim to "do good" and "avoid harm." At this level of Thomistic abstraction, we are likely to face little disagreement, except on the grounds of sentimental do good-ism, hopeless ambiguity, and political naïveté. An even harsher response—at times our own—might be "sanctimonious crap."

However, we intend to take the additional step of developing heuristics that will help us realize what doing good and avoiding harm might mean in particular settings and for particular studies. These heuristics provide criteria for judging political practices and effecting positive political change. For these criteria, we turn to several theorists, such as Foucault, Young, Benhabib, and Feenberg, who, we feel, understand the need for such criteria and have been relatively effective in articulating them—though none understands the framework they are developing as a heuristic.

Our Ethical/Political Goals for Critical Research are not laws, but rather are overlapping goals for critical researchers. At the very least, researchers should "respect difference" in their relations with research participants; but we also urge working proactively to improve the conditions of research participants. Some ethical systems, such as the feminist care ethic as expressed by Nel Noddings (1984), focus almost exclusively on ethics as relations between individuals. Other systems focus more on ethics as concerned with social and group issues. Because we think it important for an ethical system to install both individual and social viewpoints, on our continuum of ethical goals the first two principles focus more on participants as individuals, and the latter two think more about the group nature of research participants.

All four principles are important, but as you will see from our discussion below, we do not think that any one of them is sufficient. In a sense, each one needs the others to counterbalance its weaknesses. For instance, though we support the aims of the democratic ideal, we do not see democracy in itself as a sufficient political/ethical position. We have too often seen situations in which invoking a democratic ideal of equality in situations involving unequal participants led to the further oppression of less powerful participants. We are similarly wary of social theories of ethics or politics that do not assign sufficient value to distinct individuals.

Ethical/Political Goals for Critical Research (Overlapping)
- Respect difference
- Care for others
- Promote access to rhetorical procedures enabling justice
- Liberate the oppressed through empowerment of participants

Respect Difference

Show respect; this is a primary principle of numerous ethical systems. But postmodern ethics pushes this principle to a more specific form: Respect difference. Acknowledge Other. Postmodern ethics critiques traditional ethical systems because they have usually obscured difference and disagreement in an effort to establish community truths or to develop foundational principles of justice. Postmodern ethics critiques modernism because the dominant scientific principles of modernism—rationality, impartiality, and objectivity (in ethical theory as well as in research practice)—obscure difference and, in so doing, lead ultimately to domination and oppression of the Other, the one who is different. As applied to rhetoric, postmodern ethics insists that differences among audiences must not be obliterated. Distinct identities must be recognized. In a moral discourse readers should not be treated as an homogenous whole or as if they were all members of a universal collective (see Porter, 1992a; Porter, in press).

In her critique of the abstract impartiality of Jürgen Habermas's discourse ethic, Benhabib (1992) stresses this point in particular. Benhabib critiques Habermas for not stressing the importance of "the concrete moral self" (p. 146). One must avoid "generalizing the other" by engaging the concrete and particular features of one's audience: "The standpoint of the concrete other ... requires us to view each and every rational being as an individual with a concrete history, identity and affective-emotional constitution" (p. 159). Stereotyping of participant differences—for example, referring to women as a political or social collective—is what Benhabib means by treating the other as a generalized type. (Similarly, Feenberg sees the kind of formal abstraction represented by Habermas's ethic as too remote, from specific material technological settings as well as from the experiences and identities of real people.)

However, what is particularly dangerous about the principle "Respect difference" is the tendency of some abstract postmodern thought to essentialize Difference as the Other—that is, to recognize it but in so doing to marginalize it by reducing all groups' interests into the simple category of Other. An example of this would be linking all underrepresented groups into the category of Other—for example, equalizing Latino/Latina issues, black issues, gay/lesbian issues, feminist issues into the same soup of Difference. bell hooks (1981, 1989) is one critic who speaks to the particular histories, problems, and concerns of black women as a group whose interests were not being sufficiently addressed either by feminists or by black scholars. In computers and composition, Romano's work (1993) is especially noteworthy for her working through and beyond the too-facile category of "Mexican American" to notice sharper, more subtle complexities in her students' subjectivities.

We see a theological take on the principle of respect difference expressed in liberation theology. The ultimate sin, according to Enrique Dussel (1988), is instrumentalizing people as things. "Sin is domination over the other" (p. 61); it is failing to take into account distinct person-ness (needs, identity, character, gender, background, experience). From this theological perspective, formal abstraction does not simply result in bad theory or bad rhetoric; it is unjust and sinful. A balancing act is required, however: To achieve the critical mass needed for political change, one has to identify groupness in some way or other; and yet one must be respectful to differences between groups, to the particular histories and issues that accompany each group's subjectivity.

Feminist ethics in particular stresses difference, particularly gender difference, as a significant factor in ethical deliberations. Feminist ethicists (see Cahill, 1990; Cole & Coultrap-McQuin, 1992; Jaggar, 1992) have articulated the important ways in which feminist ethics differs from traditional forms of ethics: (a) It exposes the masculinity of traditional moral systems (which are not the gender neutral systems they claim to be); (b) it argues that gender difference is a (if not the) significant variable influencing ethical subjectivities (Irigaray, 1993, for instance, argues for physical sexual difference as the foundational ground for ethics); (c) it affirms the importance of concrete experience (vs. abstract principles), especially the concrete, lifeworld experiences of women; and (d) it reconceptualizes ethics as having to do with relations (vs. truths, vs. justice, vs. property). Feminist ethics sharply challenges universalist philosophies that attempt to develop a common set of principles for all persons (Rorty, 1991, p. 231).

Both Luce Irigaray (1993) and Young (1990) point to difference as a foundational principle. For Irigaray, sexual difference is the foundation of a relational ethics. For Young, acceptance of the validity of differences among social groups is the basis for political justice. Irigaray and Young both point to how traditional philosophy, or what Young calls "normative social philosophy and political theory" (p. 149), has worked to obscure difference. The result of such an obfuscation is domination by a privileged group that hides its "groupness" (e.g., whiteness or masculinity) under the coordinated claims of objectivity, impartiality, neutrality, and universality. The critical turn that Young makes is to view difference not as undesirable, or alien, or the Other (p. 170), not as the subordinate second term of a deconstructed binary, but as a value in its own right—that is, as "specificity, variation, heterogeneity" (p. 171). The turn Irigaray makes is a theological one: Embracing and celebrating difference brings us to a transcendent spirituality.

The first step, then, in achieving political or ethical justice through research practice is the process of acknowledging difference, including exposing the hidden or obscured difference that often ends up dominating. This is easy to say—yes, by all means respect difference—but sometimes hard to actualize. What if we can't see difference? Aha! That is where the critical research orientation provides us with some assistance. Respecting difference requires first of all an openness on the part of the researcher(s) to the possibility of difference, a willingness to concede to reciprocity as a critical principle in research relations, and ultimately a willingness to see who the participants are. The process of critical research engagement should encourage this to happen; it does not, however, guarantee it. The tactic of using competing narratives (discussed in Chapter 7) is one way to allow alternative voices to emerge during the research process.

In general, postmodern ethicists remind us of the importance of being "alert to exclusions and to forgotten aspects in a people's history" (Scott, 1990, p. 7). Our uses of discourse and our research practices must work to insure that the values we invoke, or the goals we establish, or the procedures we develop don't drown out alternative voices. In addition, a postmodern critical research ethic must do more than merely "respect" participants in a passive or detached way. It must work to liberate the Other by naming and making space for that which is taken for granted or "routinely excluded and silenced" (Scott, 1990, p. 8).

Difference must be respected, but we should move beyond merely "respect" for difference, which could be seen to promote a kind of distant, begrudging tolerance. Because difference is always foreign to us (and difficult to understand), because in the first place it may even be hard for us to see, it takes extra work to engage it. Irigaray argues that we have to move actively to embrace difference and to celebrate it, and that we should certainly be in awe of the mystery of difference.

Care for Others

One important source of the principle "Care for others" is the feminist ethical articulations of Nel Noddings (1984) and Carol Gilligan (1993), who view the ethical stance of the "caring one" as a distinctly feminist position that has been historically subordinated to masculine ethics. Challenging the deontological approach toward ethics (which values abstractness and impartiality in particular), the caring ethic views personal and emotional concern for the distinct person as a superior ethical posture.

Noddings, for instance, views the caring relation "as ethically basic" (p. 3). She defines caring as an act of commitment requiring "displacement of interest from my own reality to the reality of the other" (p. 14). Caring is not general or universal, but rather is focused on particular contexts, and, as Noddings frames it, pertains to individual, one-to-one relations. In fact, the model for Noddings's notion of caring is the mother-child relationship.

Gesa Kirsch and Joy Ritchie (1995) argue that the caring ethic should guide research activity in composition (see also Newkirk, in press). They urge the use of a critical "politics of location" that requires that researchers "recognize their own subjectivity" and examine their interactions with research participants through the course of a study (p. 16). Kirsch and Ritchie ask questions that, we agree, are critical to an understanding of the ethics and politics of research praxis, for example: "Who benefits from the research/theories? What are the possible outcomes of the research and the possible consequences for research participants? Whose interests are at stake? How and to what extent will the research change social realities for research participants?" (p. 20).

The ethical framework that Kirsch and Ritchie use to address these questions is that of caring. Caring for participants as individuals, and out of a spirit of concern and commitment, is how we should construct our ethos as researchers. The researcher should not proceed primarily out of a motivation to discover new knowledge, but rather should be motivated by a commitment to the participants, a concern for their welfare. The caring ethic, then, legitimates pathos, feeling for participants, as an appropriate ethic for the researcher, and does not treat such feelings as an emotionalism or bias to be eliminated from research activity. We are quite sympathetic to the case that the caring ethic makes for sensitivity to individuals within contextual circumstances (see Phelps, 1992, p. 14).

Kirsch and Ritchie are well aware of the limitations of the caring ethic, however. For example, the ethic of care tends to take a sanguine view of power, assigning the caregiver a position of more or less absolute determining power over the "one cared for" (that is, the assumption is that it is the caregiver who determines what is "right" and what is to be done in any given situation). In Noddings's (1984) version of the ethics of care, the "caring one" adopts a maternal position, and such a conception of the caring one can too easily essentialize women into the traditional labor role of "caregiver." Noddings's version of the caring one essentializes the ethical self as a "caring woman," an individual who does (or should) operate outside the constraints of institutions and communities (which in Noddings's system are always viewed as the source of oppressions). There are many ways in which the ethics of care can "reinforce oppressive institutions" (Kirsch & Ritchie, 1995, p. 21) and stereotyped roles. In addition, the caring ethic as framed by Noddings (in particular) does not create a space for the reciprocity or mutuality that we feel should characterize coparticipation in a critical research enterprise (Cushman, 1996a). Kirsch and Ritchie also recognize that the ethic of care limits their research agenda:

> A problematized politics of location leads us to research centered in the local and the individual while at the same time acknowledging that research has social consequences in the world. If we work from an ethic of care, we cannot ignore the political and cultural conditions that place us in unequal power relationships with the participants of our research. (p. 25)

Agreed: We cannot ignore "the political and cultural conditions" of our research location. But we are afraid that the ethic of care, by itself, leads to precisely that result: It assigns too much autonomy to the individual caring woman as the source of ethical judgment, and its effects focus too exclusively on the individual cared for. It lacks social/political punch, in other words. It leads us back to the liberal-individualist model of ethics (Porter, in press), which assigns ethical authority to the unself-determined individual, though it reconceives that individual as a "caring woman" instead of a "rational man." For a social and postmodern rhetoric, this is no less problematic.

We think that the ethic of care expresses an important value and establishes a role that researchers should embrace. But by itself, the ethic of care is not sufficient for the critical research agenda we are espousing, and which we think that Kirsch and Ritchie intend to espouse. Why? First, the ethic of care does not presume a dialogic relationship between researcher and research participants; it assumes a maternalistic/paternalistic one, and we object to that configuration of power. Second, the ethic of care assumes that the ethical determination lies with the lone, individual researcher, now conceived as a caring ethical female researcher, but still a lone individual. We question the individualist assumptions inherent in that ethic, because they do not sufficiently recognize the dynamic of institutional, communal, and historical forces that shape individual's options. Such a configuration does not allow a space for reciprocity, does not acknowledge the possibility of the participants' contributing to the reshaping of the project. Third, the caring ethic does not actively enough address the problem of social inequity, nor is it reflective enough about the possibility of domination by the caring one. Nonetheless, we agree with Kirsch and Ritchie in seeing caring as a necessary condition of critical research activity and an important principle of action balancing, and at times usefully counteropposing, more social principles.

Promote Access to Rhetorical Procedures Enabling Justice

It's easy to say "Promote justice," much harder to articulate what *justice* means in any particular context. You will not be surprised to hear that our notion of justice is tied to space and material conditions, and that our view on how to determine justice in any particular case relies on the heuristic operation of rhetoric. A helpful starting point for our thinking is Young's (1990) definition of justice as:

> The institutionalized conditions that make it possible for all to learn and use satisfying skills in socially recognized settings, to participate in decisionmaking, and to express their feelings, experience, and perspective on social life in contexts where others can listen. ... Justice ... requires, however, participation in public discussion and processes of democratic decisionmaking. (p. 91)

Young's definition helps us tie justice to a social and institutional rhetoric. First, Young does not define *justice* in the conventional way as an abstract notion of equality that is based on an abstract conception of individual identity/autonomy. Instead, her definition is tied to "socially recognized settings" and to human activities. You do not achieve social justice merely by assigning people citizenship, or by formally announcing constitutional rights, or by exclaiming "Democracy!" Rather, there are concrete and material criteria for determining justice; certain social conditions must be realized before justice can be said to exist. Second, Young's definition focuses on the "processes of decision making," that is, on the rhetorical nature of social life—raising particularly, for us, the issue of access. Justice is realizable only when people have access to the mechanisms of policy and decisionmaking. Access means accessibility of technologies in the technical sense, but it also means accessibility of the social frameworks for group decision making (that is, one must be socially accepted within the political processes of public policy making and must have the literacy competencies necessary for such participation (see Porter on "access," in press). In articulating justice in these terms, Young participates in the postmodern critique of "the liberal model of public space," upon which traditional Enlightenment theories of justice rely (e.g., Rawls, 1971).

The critique of this liberal model of public space—as articulated by Benhabib (1992), Martha Cooper (1991), Michel Foucault (1991), and others—attacks that model's assumption of neutrality and its instrumental view of technology and communication media. The liberal model of public space mythologizes, in a move of decontextualization, the idea that all citizens have equal rights, and that technology exists neutrally to assist citizens in their pursuit of life, liberty, and happiness. It's a model that fails to acknowledge power as a fundamental feature of discursive relations and access as a fundamental problem associated with technology.

Foucault's discussion of the knowledge-power nexus aims, in part, to explode the coordinated myths of equality, neutrality, and equal access. In general, his work critiques the Enlightenment model of scientific inquiry, which has as its aim the neutral (supposedly so) discovery of knowledge. But in particular, Foucault (1987) points out that there is no ideal speech situation free from institutional hierarchies, traditional alignments, and power relations—that all discourse occurs already in a situated practice of power relations. Though the liberal Enlightenment view assumes an assembly of people speaking their minds freely (as John Rawls says: "it seems reasonable to suppose that the parties in the original position are equal" [1971, p. 19]), no such assembly does or can exist.

> The thought that there could be a state of communication which would be such that the games of truth could circulate freely, without obstacles, without constraint and without coercive effects, seems to me to be Utopia. It is being blind to the fact that relations of power are not something bad in themselves, from which one must free one's self. I don't believe there can be a society without relations of power, if you understand them as means by which individuals try to conduct, to determine the behavior of others. The problem is not of trying to dissolve them in the utopia of a perfectly transparent communication, but to give one's self the rules of law, the techniques of management, and also the ethics, the *ethos*, the practice of self, which would allow these games of power to be played with a minimum of domination. (Foucault, 1987, p. 18)

Foucault's entire research project—the study of institutions like the prison and the hospital—investigates how the principles of liberty, justice, freedom, and equality espoused by Enlightenment philosophers were seldom realized in practice (that is, in the institutions and bureaucracies that their advocates constructed). In a way, he suggests, the utopian ideal makes things worse, because it can have the effect of blinding one to the exercise of power and thus of making power more invincible in its invisibility. Foucault's discursive theory insists that we cannot ignore the fact that all discourse occurs already in a situated practice of power relations, institutional hierarchies, technological systems, and spatial alignments.

Benhabib (1992) also considers the limitations of the liberal model of public space. She points out another problem with the principle of neutrality as it functions in this model: It is not helpful in getting new issues introduced into the public discussion, because it is neutral only in regard to stances that have already been assigned a place in the discussion (p. 100). If you're not in the discussion already, the liberal model won't help you get in, is the point that Benhabib makes, especially in reference to women's concerns (which historically have not been assigned a place in the public discussion).

Invoking Habermas's discourse ethic, Benhabib asserts two principles that can serve as rhetorical critieria for judging whether any particular discursive setting is indeed "doing harm": the principles of universal moral respect and egalitarian reciprocity (see Porter, in press):

> The 'universal and necessary communicative presuppositions of argumentative speech' entail strong ethical assumptions. They require of us: (1) that we recognize the right of all beings capable of speech and action to be participants in the moral conversation—I will call this *the principle of universal moral respect*; (2) these conditions further stipulate that within such conversations each has the same symmetrical rights to various speech acts, to initiate new topics, to ask for reflection about the presuppositions of the conversation, etc. Let me call this *the principle of egalitarian reciprocity*. The very presuppositions of the argumentation situation then have a normative content that precedes the moral argument itself. (Benhabib, 1992, p. 29)

These principles insist that all people have an equal right to participate in the public discussion and that all share the same special rights regarding the rules or conventions of public discussion (e.g., the right to initiate new topics, etc.). According to Habermas and Benhabib, these rules do not derive from some autonomous notion of self or contractarian philosophy; rather, the rules are implicit in the rhetorical nature of public communication media. In a sense, then, the principles derive from rhetorical theory rather than from a theory of self or government.

These principles extend from Habermas's (1990) distinction between strategic action and communicative action. Strategic action is manipulative persuasion, or public speech acts that attempt to coerce or manipulate audiences. Communicative action is Habermas's ideal ethical discourse action, the criteria for which are expressed in the two principles above. In ethical discourse, communicative action, the audience is treated not as a passive decoder or receiver but as an equal interlocutor with reciprocal rights.

There are problems with these criteria. As Habermas (1990) and Benhabib express them, they are formally abstract (and this is the basis of Foucault's and Feenberg's critiques of Habermas). The principles per se do not provide us with pragmatic criteria, and are perhaps hopelessly utopian (as almost no real public discourses are capable of meeting these criteria). Do they apply to all sorts of public fora in the same way? And how does one distinguish between public and private fora (in the latter, presumably, the same moral rights do not apply). Nor, according to Foucault, are these principles sensitive enough to the inequities of discursive arrangements, or to the presence of power and oppression in discursive settings. In her articulation of the Habermasian discourse ethic, Benhabib recognizes these limitations and works to address them, particularly in her effort to define public space in a more critical way and in her efforts to focus the ethic on the concrete self rather than on the generalized other.

Young's theory of justice and Benhabib's principles for discourse ethics provide us with additional criteria for our emerging ethic of critical research. We can these principles to critical research practices (a) in examining the status of participants as related to their community and institutional settings; and (b) in examining the status of participants as related to the researcher(s) and the research project itself. (See Table 5.3, for example.) We must look at the status of participants as decision makers. What position do they have in the communities and institutions to which they belong? How do they wield power? In what ways do they have access to the means of policy-making? Also, of course, we can see how this principles applies to a key topic in computer ethics: access to computing power. Who has it (and how do they use it)? Who doesn't have it?

A key condition to Young's theory of justice, and to our own, is the issue of access. Justice for a people means that they have access to the structures and processes of decision-making in communities and institutions—and it is at this point that her theory invokes Habermas's criteria for communicative ethics. There then can be a concrete test of whether a policy or decision or social activity is just: "if it involves the open participation of all those affected by the decisions" (p. 93). These criteria also require that we examine the status of participants within our studies to determine their moral discourse rights. Do our designs allow for "reversibility of movement" (Foucault, 1987, p. 3)—that is, do they allow participants a say in determining their status within research projects? These principles call special attention to the question of the rhetorical ethics of relations that exist in any research project.

Liberate the Oppressed Through Empowerment of Participants

We see "Liberation of the oppressed" as a fundamental ethical goal for human activity, including ethical research praxis. But what is "oppression"? Who is oppressed, and how do we adjudicate competing claims about who is more oppressed?

Let's start by talking about power, which must be distinguished from oppression. It's important to remember that in our Foucaultian construction "power is a relation rather than a thing" (Young, 1990, p. 31). It is not a possession, not something you have or don't have, but rather "consists in a relationship between the exerciser and others through which she or he communicates intentions and meets with their acquiescence" (p. 31). If power is a relation, then this implies that power relations can vary from setting to setting: A writing teacher may have relative power in the composition classroom, but when that teacher comes up for tenure or tries to secure additional campus computing facilities, his degree of power changes (wanes, probably) vis-à-vis dominant institutional forces. When a male student harasses a female part-time instructor, then we can see that the easy assumptions about power in a composition classroom—that is, the teacher has it, the students don't—no longer hold true. Relations of power, and thus of domination and oppression, are changeable from context to context, and that is one reason that we find context such a vital principle in our critical methodology.

Foucault makes a crucial distinction between "relationships of power" and "states of domination." Though all acts of rhetoric or research might be said to be acts of power, they are not all acts of domination; power is more general. Foucault says that relationships of power "have an extremely wide extension in human relations. There is a whole network of relationships of power, which can operate between individuals, in the bosom of the family, in an educational relationship, in the political body, etc." (1987, p. 3). Domination, on the other hand, refers to invariable relations of power—that is, to "firmly set and congealed" settings which "block a field of relations of power" and "render them impassive and invariable" by preventing "all reversibility of movement" (1987, p. 3). Elsewhere, Foucault (1983) says that domination is "a general structure of power ... a massive and universalizing form, at the level of the whole social body, [which entails] the locking together of power relations with relations of strategy" (p. 226). In short, for Foucault, domination refers to a social state in which the reversal and reciprocity that characterize freedom or liberation are missing.

This distinction between power and domination is important to our understanding of ethical research practice. Ethics is the practical art not of avoiding the exercise of power (which is unavoidable), but of making careful decisions about how power relations are to be exercised in order to avoid domination of the other. Even in a pluralist ethic, both Foucault and Lyotard suggest, and in the midst of deep ethical complexities, one must be able to make a judgment about what constitutes domination.

This distinction between the exercise of power and domination is important for critical research, as it provides a criterion for critiquing research activity. When we conduct research inquiries, we are engaging in acts of power, in Foucault's sense; our work with participants, our design and construction of a study, our data collection and analysis, our write-up of findings all constitute acts of power vis-à-vis the participants, other members of the field, the readers of our research, and so on. Rather than wring our hands in dismay over the arrogance of wielding this power—what Porter calls a "spasm of postmodern liberal guilt" (in press)—we should view the exercise of research power as common, as frequent, as unavoidable, and as potentially ethical. The important distinction pertains to acts of domination and oppression. For Foucault, domination refers to those acts of visible or invisible power that block "reversibility of movement" (or what Benhabib refers to as "reversibility of perspectives" [p. 145]); that is, they prevent a group or individual—or research participants—from expressing alternatives or exercising alternate choices. Though we cannot avoid the obligation of power when we do research, we can try to avoid doing it in a way that dominates or oppresses our participants, readers, and members of our research field.

Ethically and politically, it is also important to recognize a further distinction that Young (1990) makes between domination and oppression. Domination refers to "institutional conditions which inhibit or prevent people from participating in determining their actions or the conditions of their actions" (p. 38). We are subject to various forms of domination, but that does not mean that domination affects us all in the same way. "Not everyone subject to domination is also oppressed" (p. 38). Domination, in fact, may work to the advantage of some social groups (e.g., apprentices). A social group is oppressed, however, when the domination works to systematically inhibit people's abilities, freedoms, choices (p. 38). Thus, domination means that people are excluded from participating in the systems and institutions that guide or determine their actions. But oppression means that, because of this exclusion, a people's freedoms are inhibited. This distinction provides a criterion for distinguishing competing social groups' claims that they are oppressed.

Young distinguishes five forms of oppression of social groups, and her ethical/political orientation is indeed very much social, not individual: exploitation, marginalization, powerlessness, cultural imperialism, and violence (see Table 5.2 for descriptions of each). Exploitation, marginalization, and powerlessness "all refer to relations of power and oppression that occur by virtue of the social division of labor—who works for whom, who does not work, and how the content of work defines one institutional position relative to others" (p. 58). Cultural imperialism and violence refer to forms of oppression existing in culture generally, not specifically tied to labor conditions.

Young's criteria are helpful because they are contextually defined, located in particular types of circumstances and actions. Too often we have seen the arguments to "liberate the poor" and "oppose oppression" left on an abstracted level that achieves little political change. Without criteria, we are left in a position of uncommitted irony (Lyotard & Thébaud, 1985), or we are reduced to mere name-calling. If we have no criteria for determining what is truly oppressive, then it's too easy to slide into the fallacy of calling all institutional actions oppressive, or all uses of the computer. We end up equating the Macintosh interface with institutional apartheid in South Africa—after all, both are oppressive, right?

Young identifies particular groups, and particular sorts of oppressive divisions that occur in U.S. society, including divisions between men and women, between Native Americans or Africans and Europeans, between Jews and Christians, between homosexuals and heterosexuals, and so on (p. 58). Young's criteria "serve as means of evaluating claims that a group is oppressed, or adjudicating disputes about whether or how a group is oppressed" (p. 64). For instance, Young points out that "working-class people are exploited and powerless ... but if employed and white [they] do not experience marginalization and violence" (p. 64). In short, some groups are more oppressed than others, and the claims of various groups to be "oppressed" need to be critically examined.

Thus, oppression is a situation that has to be determined relative to other groups. White working-class people who claim that they are oppressed and who, therefore, oppose affirmative action (for instance) on the grounds that it advantages others (e.g., Blacks, Hispanics) at their expense may be using the fact of their own oppressed status to advocate a more serious form of oppression against

TABLE 5.2. Young's Forms of Oppression of Social Groups, as Applied to Cyberspace

Form of Oppression	Definition in Young (1990)	How Exemplified in Cyberspace
Exploitation	"a steady process of the transfer of the results of the labor of one social group to benefit another" (p. 49). Exploitive relations are "produced and reproduced through a systematic process in which the energies of the have-nots are continuously expended to maintain and augment the power, status, and wealth of the haves" (p. 50).	Use of a disproportionate percentage of underpaid graduate student and part-time labor (disproportionately female) to handle a significant amount of the teaching obligations of the university—for example, TAs who teach in computer classrooms, but whose own access to computer resources is limited or prevented.
Marginalization	"a whole category of people is expelled from useful participation in social life and thus potentially subjected to severe material deprivation and even extermination" (p. 53). Those who are dependent on others for at least part of their lives: "children, sick people, women recovering from childbirth, old people who have become frail, depressed or otherwise emotionally needy" (pp. 54–55).	School systems serving the inner city and rural poor not provided with sufficient funds for computers or for network access; thus, students are denied network access and participation (and the means to literacy, success, and political presence) (Piller, 1992).
Powerlessness	"Those over whom power is exercised without their exercising it; [those] situated so that they must take orders and rarely have the right to give them. ... a position in the division of labor and the concomitant social position that allows persons little opportunity to develop and exercise skills. The powerless have little or no work autonomy, exercise little creativity or judgment in their work, have no technical expertise or authority, express themselves awkwardly, expecially in public or bureaucratic settings, and do not command respect" (pp. 56–57).	Noninteractive hypertexts which provide users no means for response, or control, or rebuttal. (Johnson-Eilola, 1995) Changes made in interface design or operation by institutions (university, corporation) without input from students, faculty, or workers.
Cultural Imperialism	"the universalization of a dominant group's experience and culture, and its establishment as the norm" (p. 59). "The dominant meanings of a society render the particular perspective of one's own group invisible at the same time as they stereotype one's group and mark it out as the Other" (pp. 58–59).	Interface designs that establish white as racial norm or office setting as environmental norm (Selfe & Selfe, 1994).
Violence	"random, unprovoked attacks" on one's person or property, or harassment and intimidation because of one's group affiliation (p. 61).	Harassment of women in cyberspace (Takayoshi, 1994a).

an even more marginalized group. Hence the oppressed become oppressors in a misguided effort to improve their own status.

We think it very dangerous to proceed without guiding criteria, because not to carefully distinguish forms of oppression is to equalize all forms of oppression, and that tends to make the truly harmful forms of oppression more, not less, innocuous. As Lyotard (1984) says (even as a committed ironist), we must be able to stand up against the Holocaust—to say with conviction: This is wrong. Young's distinction between domination and oppression, and her distinction between forms of oppression, allows for these sorts of judgments. The Macintosh interface may represent a form of oppression (cultural imperialism), but it's certainly better than the old DOS command-line interface. In any case, neither should be equated with other forms of surveillance and harassment that constitute more extreme, and violent, forms of oppression.

These criteria can function as a heuristic that balances between proceeding without criteria (what we argue against above) and proceeding with too-rigid criteria which function as rules, and thus fail to give us the contextual flexibility we seek. Young's criteria also work to distinguish a wider range of forms of oppression than typically are addressed in conventional "ethics of research" discussions. Most such discussions focus on egregious violations of research ethics—direct violence, or physical or emotional harm to participants—but does not address the subtler forms of oppression (e.g., exploitation, marginalization, cultural imperialism), which to some degree we feel are a prerequisite of the traditional mode of research and its insistence on the neutrality of the researcher.

Once oppression is identified, there can be only one ethical stance toward it: Oppose it. Hence we arrive at a fundamental communitarian philosophy articulated by liberation theologians such as Boff and Boff (1986), Dussel (1988), Freire (1993), Gutièrrez (1973), and others: Liberate the oppressed.

"Liberate the oppressed" is an ethical position that fits both our advocacy of situated theorizing and also our effort to heal the theory-practice binary as it operates within theory and empirical methodology. Similarly, liberation theology as a movement aims to heal the binary between formally abstract theological speculation and situated pastoral care as it intersects with the material conditions of people; it is an effort to transform a decontextualized form of inquiry (traditional theology) into praxis. Liberation theology formally emerged in the Medellín document (written by 130 Latin American bishops in 1968), which denounced political and institutional systems that subjugated the poor. It argued that theology must reconceptualize itself not as abstract formulations but as a form of action directed at both critiquing economic and social systems which oppress and at improving the material conditions of the poor (see Berryman, 1987; Smith, 1991). Liberation theology has a Marxist component to its articulation—in the respect that it combines a Christian/Catholic theological emphasis with a Marxist praxis. Liberation theologians insist that theology and ethics must be situated in the material conditions of people, and they focus particularly on how ethics intersects with economics, labor, production, and the ownership/distribution of property in a society. In this respect, liberation theology is very much a situated ethic.

"Liberate the poor" is the foundational principle (Dussel, 1988, p. 73) of this ethic, because it provides a linkage between both real persons in a community (and their material status) and the notion of a transcendent/utopian existence. It provides the linkage between current actual conditions and a hoped-for ideal state. It is an ethic that does not satisfy itself with merely expressing the ideal state (e.g., "equality for all") or articulating generalized action (e.g., Aquinas's "Do good"), but situates the expression of an ideal in a demand for action that takes into account present circumstances. The implication is that since we do not have this ideal we hope for, the only ethical thing to do is to work to achieve it.

The ethical standpoint of liberation theology addresses relations between humans, both on an individual and a communal level: How should I be for/to others? How should we be for/to others? In what manner should I/we relate to them? In this respect at least, liberation theology and feminist ethics overlap: both focus primarily on the representation of ethics as relations, or in postmodern terms, subjectivities. Dussel (1988) defines praxis as "both act and relationship ... praxis is the actual, here-and-now manner of our being in our world before another person" (p. 8). Dussel's definition seems to posit a one-to-one praxis, but he posits this relationship as necessarily occurring within a community framework.

Given conditions of fundamental inequity, or faced with a situation of oppression, this is the only ethical stance possible for a community or individual to take. It's the chief operative principle in such situations, and it's a principle not present per se in democratic ideals, not inscribed in the U.S. Constitution: Liberate the oppressed. The principle is not a static claim, but a pronouncement of an intention and an action. It indicates the fundamental posture one must take toward oppression. Liberation theology expresses this action as a "preferential option for the poor and marginalized." In the view of this theology, the principle is necessary to moralize the communitarian framework. Communitarianism without this principle runs the risk of further oppression of the marginalized; it runs the risk of the majority determing the rules for the minority. Situating this principle within the communitarian framework allows communitarianism to work without oppression. Hence, the argument implies that having a "preferential option for the poor and marginalized" is how a community maintains justice for its members.

We are always left with the issue of defining the oppressed. Who are they exactly? Paulo Freire (1993) draws a sharp distinction between "oppressors" and "oppressed," between practices (especially educational practices) that humanize and those that dehumanize, and between right and left. The appropriate ethical position vis-à-vis these concepts is of course to avoid being an oppressor and to assist the oppressed in improving their status. Freire's binaries arise out his lifeworld experiences in Latin American cultures with a dramatic difference between the poor and the privileged classes, and Freire's understanding of these binaries is quite materialistic: The distinction is based on socioeconomic factors—who has wealth, who doesn't; who has access to the mechanisms of political influence, who doesn't; who has food and clothing, who doesn't. It is easier to "see" oppression in countries where the socioeconomic gap between rich and poor is immense, and where the disadvantaged condition of the poor is observable in every city and village. It is harder to see in relatively affluent countries or communities, or in towns where everyone is in a similar condition. It is often masked in the arena of technology access. You never see who's not on the Internet.

We now want to complicate Freire's binary by asking, How do we determine who is oppressed in any given situation? Does all research involve oppression of research participants? Are all researchers oppressors, more or less? We are uncomfortable with what we see as a tendency in composition scholarship (for instance) to bemoan all classroom-based writing instruction as "hegemonic" or to decry all uses of the computer to teach writing as "capitalistic" (Ohmann, 1985). Similarly, we are not willing to view all research or all uses of computer technology as necessarily dehumanizing, and we think it important to develop criteria for distinguishing what we would regard as perfectly ethical forms of research from research that involves the exploitation of participants.

When Dussel and Freire talk about the poor, they mean poor in the material sense, and this is the the first and most important sense of oppressed we can imagine. Food and clothing, housing, access to health care, basic safety and security for self and property—these are fundamental material needs, the first order of business for all. But we think that the principle can be extended to cover those who are "oppressed and marginalized" in other ways; for instance, because of race and gender. There are those who may have the basic human needs, but whose rights and opportunities are limited in other ways.

Now, there is some danger in articulating the goal of "Liberate the oppressed," because the articulation can too easily fall into presuming that the researcher is the primary agent effecting this liberation. As we develop our position, as we look toward the goal of liberating participants, we have to be wary—critically wary—about the assumed superiority of such a stance. We do not want to become missionary researchers whose attempts at liberating participants take the form of colonizing them. We are suspicious of the matri/patriarchal implications of such a view of research liberation (what we feel Brian Fay, 1987, strays toward).

Rather, the research paradigm we envision aims to position researchers and participants in a reciprocal relationship. As we enter into this research community that is created through the research activity, we get and we give. Our participants provide us with stories and experiences ("data," in the old vocabulary) that enrich our understanding of human experience, and of course also always of ourselves, and probably give us more than a few of our own stories to tell. We take this knowledge/experience to our research communities, and obviously we benefit from sharing this knowledge within the academic economy. We publish, we get raises, we get promoted—we claim academic capital.

But what do we do for our participants? The traditional paradigm, which values the objective neutrality of the detached observing scientist, values leaving them as little as possible. The goal, in fact, is as little change (known as "intrusion") as possible. The critical research paradigm attempts to change, to liberate, but we are also extemely wary of entering a research community with a preconceived notion of what the participants' liberation ought to look like. Equally problematic to us is the assumption of liberal superiority: the "good" missionary who brings truth and salvation to the ignorant natives.

Along with Ellen Cushman (1996a), we are distrustful of those forms of critical theory that presume to know, in advance of practice, what liberation looks like. When we enter into research arrangements, we do not know. We only know that liberation or progress is bound to take different forms for different groups at different times; thus, our notion of liberation is a micropolitical one that is tied to particular practices. We also know that the role relations between researcher and participants in any given study are bound to shift over time, as well may our goals.

Thus, we have to attach two caveats to our understanding of "Liberate the oppressed." The ethics of the critical research arrangement requires (a) that we do not presume, in patronizing fashion, to know in advance what is good for our participants—that "good" needs to be co-constructed with the participants; and (b) that we leave something behind, that we negotiate through the research activity to contribute something to the betterment of the group or community we are studying. That is, we enter into the research activity with our participants in an effort at mutual liberation—ours as well as theirs—and in a spirit of reciprocity.

In many literacy studies, the something that the researcher leaves behind is a set of literacy skills that will help the oppressed negotiate their daily lives. An example is the inner-city poor that Cushman (1996b) describes in her dissertation, who must learn institutional literacy practices in order to maintain their health, their homes, their safety. Cushman's ethnography focuses on several black women (Lucy, Mirena, Raejone) who must learn how to use language to negotiate the government social service agencies and other institutions that offer the support they need for their families and the means by which they can improve their economic status. Quite literally in this study (an instance of critical research, though the project does not focus on technology issues), if the women do not learn how to negotiate the bureaucratic maze, they will end up homeless. Cushman charts how these women used their rhetorical skills and also struggled to learn new discourse conventions that would enable them at least to engage in the power struggle—though they did not in every case succeed. In this study, language education is presented as a means by which a disadvantaged group can engage in the struggle, and Cushman positions herself explicitly as an agent of change in the study; she tutors the participants to help them acquire the literacy skills they need to apply for government housing, to write letters to their landlords, and to apply for admission to universities; she also counsels them in negotiating the bureaucracies of power (e.g., government in the form of social agencies and law enforcement) that have an impact on their lives. And, in turn, she learns from them, and becomes one of their community. One of the ethical problems that Cushman addresses, as a critical researcher, is the matter of when to get involved and when not; she establishes as her guiding principle that she can only get involved when the participants explicitly ask her. This principle respects the status of the participants and allots them some relative power in the research relationship, yet it provides some space for the researcher to assist.

Not all research projects focus on studying the oppressed. Sometimes we are studying the oppressors—or, to be less essentialist about it, some research projects focus on understanding those who are relatively powerful (say, writing teachers, for instance, or professional managers in the workplace). It may be that as we study such groups or writers, we question our advocacy role a bit: Perhaps we should not work to liberate our participants so much as work to liberate those who our participants oppress? Perhaps our efforts should be aimed at helping our participants understand the ways in which their writing practices are themselves oppressive. As teachers and researchers in professional writing, we are keenly conscious of this positioning in our own work: In our respective programs at Purdue University (technical and business writing), we teach students who will comprise the managerial middle class of powerful organizations. Though our efforts are aimed at helping them succeed in their professional lives, we are also very alert to the importance of teaching them how to recognize and not to abuse the power they are likely to hold over others.

The articulation "Liberate the oppressed" has to be considered in terms of three conventional stages of change as articulated in critical theory: first, enlightenment, second, empowerment, and third, emancipation (see, e.g., Fay, 1987, p. 29). Enlightenment is a necessary precondition of change. Freire stresses the importance of "critical consciousness" (*conscientizaçao*), the awareness that one develops about one's place in the world. Developing such an awareness is the first step toward liberation of the poor. It is based on the understanding of whether one is oppressed or an oppressor.

Critical theory is obviously not satisfied with the first stage only; enlightenment of participants is not sufficient (because knowledge of one's condition alone does not guarantee that one will have access to the means of changing it). Enlightenment is too passive a stance for the critical researcher. There must be some effort to empower participants, which is a necessary precondition of their emancipation.

What do we mean by *empowerment*? According to Foucault (1983), empowerment refers to the process by which a class, a group, or an individual who is primarily acted upon comes to exercise change on her/his own behalf to "act upon" and to effect change in status. Empowerment does not entail the dominated becoming the dominator; but rather, empowerment means that there is a shift in the power relations to a state where there is a "reciprocal appeal" (Foucault, 1983, p. 226), and the formerly dominated are able to engage in a power struggle over the possibility of attaining some kind of change in the system or reversal of their

TABLE 5.3. Points of View Toward Oppression in the Critical Research Process

Point of View	Criteria for Action	Example of Advocacy
participants vis-à-vis their environment	Researchers examine status of participants in their own environment. Researchers do not stand back and neutrally observe participants who are in a condition of oppression. Rather, they work to reduce participants' oppression—not at some future date, but in the here-and-now of the inquiry process.	Researcher not only interviews participant to collect data, but helps participant negotiate literacy challenges in her life. (Cushman, 1996a, helps her participant write a letter to a government agency requesting assistance for housing.)
researcher vis-à-vis environment researcher vis-à-vis participants	Researchers examine their own relations with participants and work to avoid oppression. Is the project exploiting participants, marginalizing them—or is it empowering them? Is the research process blocking or enabling "reversibility of movement"? (Foucault)	In a usability test session, the tester breaks through the one-way mirror syndrome to help participants who are struggling with the technology. Researchers show findings to participants and interrogate the differences in opinions in ways that give voice to participants in the interpretation of the project.
researcher vis-à-vis research events and research design	Researchers examine their own understanding of oppression vis-à-vis the events of the research in order to improve themselves and in order to develop research designs that better assist participants.	

status. Similarly, Jennifer Gore (1992) calls upon Ellsworth's definition of *empowerment* as the process of:

> Expanding 'the range of possible social identities people may become' and 'making one's self present as part of a moral and political project that links production of meaning to the possibility for human agency, democratic community, and transformative social action.' (p. 59)

Thus, what we are advocating here is a position whereby the critical researcher works to liberate the oppressed by empowering research participants. The empowering goal in this case aims to avoid the problem of the researchers positing an a priori emancipation for the participants by creating a space for the participants to construct their own form of liberation. Table 5.3 provides some prompts for critical researchers to help determine their status vis-à-vis participants. It expresses some positive action that critical researchers can take to instantiate the principle of "Liberate the oppressed" in their research activities, but it also provides prompts aimed at checking the researcher's ongoing role relationship with participants.

HOW POLITICS AND ETHICS SURFACE IN THE STUDY OF COMPUTERS AND WRITING

It would be nice if we could now turn to examine empirical studies in computers and composition that meet the criteria for political and ethical action that we have articulated in the previous section. Unfortunately, we can't. As we mentioned in Chapter 3, there are no published studies that implement the kind of critical research practices we are advocating—because, fundamentally, empirical research in computers and composition (or rhetoric/composition or professional writing, for that matter) has not operated by the rules we are constructing. However, as in Chapter 3, we can find traces of critical research in various studies. Though many of the studies we examine here are not empirical and do not claim to be, some of them do exemplify the kinds of critical tactics we are advocating.

How did we select these studies for discussion? First, we looked for studies that foregrounded political and ethical issues in talking about or studying computer use. This criterion eliminated from consideration most of the research explicitly identified as empirical studies, as such studies often said little about political or ethical factors; this paucity of critical discussion bothers us. But numerous studies in computers and composition published in the 1990s do focus on what we would consider political issues: for example, how computer networking affects relations between participants (empowering the marginalized or not?); or on how it constructs gender, racial, and ethnic identity; or on how the discursive identities of writers and audiences are modified in cyberspace. We have seen less direct discussion of ethics, though ethical issues are often surfaced through the political discussions (e.g., Janangelo, 1991).

Second, we looked for well-known and often-cited studies that serve as benchmarks for both topical interest and scholarly excellence in the field. Despite our criticisms of these pieces, we want to make it clear that we think these represent excellent work. In two cases (e.g., Faigley, 1992; Romano, 1993) the pieces won awards—and we think those awards are well deserved. Our criticisms are then, in a sense, unfair; we are using others' studies to make our own case about critical research practices, and thus we are not judging these works on their own merits. For this, we apologize, and we hope that the authors will sympathize with the aims of our criticism. Third, we selected studies that had some empirical component, or the possibility of it. Our discussion moves from those that we find least situated—that is, that are least "contextualized" in the sense we have developed from Feenberg—to those we find most situated and most representative of the critical viewpoint we are espousing.

What questions and principles guide our discussion of the stu⌐ need to point out that in this chapter we are not looking at process is⌐ did in Chapter 3); nor are we examining framing issues (as we did in Ch⌐ The overriding questions in our analysis here are: To what degree does the ⌐ front political and ethical issues? How does the study situate itself politically a⌐ ethically? Subquestions extending from this include questions deriving from our discussion in the first part of this chapter, such as: To what degree does the study contextualize (participants and technologies)? To what degree is each study respectful of technological situatedness? to differences among participants? to the political and ethical status of participants? To what degree does the study work to liberate or empower or care for participants? to assist them in attaining some degree of improved freedom? to improve access to computing tools? We look at how these researchers represent technology and participants/users in their write-ups. We look at how they situate themselves in the study (the degree to which they articulate their involvement vs. the degree to which they stand apart/above/behind the study). We look at how they describe their research process (to the degree that they do—most don't). We look at how they frame the goals of their study, and we look at the expressed telos of the study: What changes do the researchers hope to effect through the study?

One strand of research in the field of computers and composition is keenly aware of the political implications of writing with computers (see Part 4, "The Politics of Computers: Changing Hierarchies" in Hawisher & Selfe, 1991; Kaplan, 1991; Moulthrop, 1991; Poster, 1990, 1995; Selfe & Selfe, 1994). Their work has been important in alerting writing teachers to the ideological implications of teaching with computers, to possible dangers of computerizing the writing curriculum (Janangelo, 1991), and to new models for thinking about design (for example, Moulthrop's [1991] discussion of the rhizomatic model of Deleuze & Guattari, p. 254). One popular strategy for developing this discussion has been to apply a metaphor of oppression—say, Foucault's concept of the panopticon— to the workings of networked writing and its environments (Janangelo, 1991; Provenzo, 1992). We find this work promising, and it is helpful in laying out an agenda for empirical research to pursue. But we worry when such treatments drift off into the Big T sort of Theory (and they occasionally do), the formally abstract kind of theory that does not situate itself in particular technologies or sites or users (except for the use of confirming examples).

One form of theoretical abstraction that we see in the field is a remnant from literary modes of analysis: the assumption that the form of the technology—or the form of Ideal Text that a particular technology encourages or "allows" (Landow, 1992)—will determine writing or reading patterns within that environment (see Porter, 1993). This is a type of formalist fallacy; that is, it assumes that the nature of the process can be determined by examining the formal structure of the text or technology. Michael Heim (1987), for instance, argues from an idea of an Ideal Text (for him, "the book") to make the claim that "the formulation of electronic writing is less contemplative" (p. 210) than that of the book and that the electronic text "may lead to the disappearance of the authentic and determinate human voice or personal presence behind symbolized words" (p. 212). Heim's claim has political and institutional implications, of course, as it is the sort of claim that can easily be used to oppose using computer technology to assist writing instruction.

Jay Bolter uses the same sort of strategy as does Heim, but he arrives at an opposite conclusion. Bolter's ideal text is a hypertext, and in *Writing Space* (1991), he grants "text" considerable power over readers. He claims: "To read is to choose and follow one path from among those suggested by the layout of the text. In confronting an ancient papyrus roll, the reader had few choices. The earliest ancient writing was strictly linear" (p. 108). Thus, for Bolter reading is limited to those paths explicit in the layout of a given text, whose form is determined by the technology that produced it. Similarly, George Landow (1992) warrants his entire optimistic discussion of hypertext with a notion of an Ideal Good Hypertext, which he pits over and against the Ideal Bad Print Text. The assumption that textual layout or technological form determines reading and writing practices is what we consider a formalist fallacy—one form of an overreliance on Big T Theory—and one that does not take into account situated practices.

We see similar statements coming from Poster (1990), who claims that:

> Computer conferences upset the power relations, both economic and gendered, that govern synchronous speech. Factors such as institutional status, personal charisma, rhetorical skills, gender, and race—all of which may deeply influence the way an utterance is received—have little effect in computer conferences. Equality of participation is thereby encouraged. (pp. 122–123)

Based on an abstracted characterization of the technology that is coupled with some anecdotal material (e.g., about Minitel in France), Poster's claim shows the political danger of formally abstract theorizing. In this case, he looks at the general form of computer conferences and concludes that the technology encourages equality. Of course, some studies in computers and composition suggest that gender difference (for instance) is by no means erased in virtual space (Hawisher & Sullivan, in press; Selfe & Meyer, 1991). There is some evidence to suggest, in fact, that electronic space is as sexist a physical place as conventional print forums (Takayoshi, 1994a).

We are not against theorizing as an intellectual mode of inquiry—that's obvious—but we are urging more situated, empirically tested theorizing, and we are cautioning researchers to be wary of decontextualized theory, especially the kind that proceeds untested by situated uses of technology by various types of users and especially the kind that derives from formalist (and perhaps, literary) assumptions about Ideal Text. This particular brand of inquiry, we feel, too much obscures practice, variability among users, and variability in technologies. But theorizing, when informed by practice, has a far greater chance of effecting constructive political change.

So we have mixed views of this research. On the one hand, we admire it for engaging new issues, for making us aware of the political and ethical implications of our uses of computers, and, conversely, for the valuable critiques of the dominant systems-based approach to the design of computer systems. We are awed by its global scope. These theorists are the ones raising substantive (in Feenberg's sense) questions about the design and use of computer systems for teaching writing, and trying to counterbalance the culture's dominant instrumentalist tendencies. On the other hand, we wish that these theorists would critically engage situated uses of the technology by particular kinds of users. Why? Because by doing so they could, perhaps, more effectively underscore the inequities for that group and be more likely to achieve the political change they advocate.

We regret, for instance, that the insights of these theorists have had almost no impact on usability studies in the computer industry. On the surface the lack of impact can be traced to writing and reading practices: The theorists who write these pieces do not address issues in usability, and those doing usability studies do not read theory. But usability is an important site of change, because usability research, at least to the degree that it is truly sensitive to the needs of users, has the potential to effect product change in the computer industry. (An example: A former professional writing students of ours, who graduated from Purdue in 1989, was the principal usability researcher working on Microsoft's Windows '95. We hope that we taught him well about user awareness and situated research. We think we did. But we also know that while he reads, he doesn't read critical theory. Hardly anyone does.) We feel that the theory that fronts political and ethical uses of computers has important insights to contribute to product development, but to the degree that such theory decontextualizes, its influence on the design of computer systems wanes. As Feenberg points out, the philosophical privileging of formal abstraction, especially the kind that pontificates about politics from on high, does little to effect the design of technology. We know that computers and composition researchers think about how they can change their students' writing (and thinking) practices for the better—but do they think about how their students, soon to become working professionals, could change society for the better? Do they develop situated ethical and political scenarios that engage students in thinking about the aims of their work lives? It is time, we feel, to bridge the gap between classroom studies (in composition, in computers and composition) and workplace research/practice (in professional writing). Solving this problem requires the development of a transdisciplinary viewpoint that the typical academic alignments resist.

Some researchers doing work on online instructional text (e.g., Johnson-Eilola, 1996; Mirel, 1996a) aim for political action by effecting fundamental changes in institutional and technical learning conditions. They are not fighting systems rationalism from afar, but rather are going into the heart of systems rationalism, especially in the computer industry and in the engineering design curriculum, in order to change the ways that users learn and are treated by the dominant technologies. These researchers are fighting decontextualization—the abstractions and atomizations that predominate in system design—by urging a contextual approach to the design of computer systems. They are fighting the bias of systems neutrality; as Johnson-Eilola (1996) says, "being neutral is biased." Their agenda challenges the presumed neutrality and advocates approaches to the design of computer systems (e.g., for online help) that will help nontraditional users whose views/problems/needs are not addressed by the dominant system: women, minorities, high school–educated laborers.

This is the kind of practical/situated work that we advocate. Postmodern theorists and researchers working in computers and writing are by and large ignoring this significant political work being done in professional writing on the design of computer systems—or else they do not recognize its political efficacy.

Stuart Moulthrop's discussion in "The Politics of Hypertext" (1991) provides a classic case of a theory-driven, decontextualized approach to the discussion of computers (see also Kaplan, 1991; Provenzo, 1992). Moulthrop's procedure, which is modeled after literary theorizing, is to apply the analyses of various postmodern theorists—such as Foucault, Deleuze and Guattari, and Fish—to issues in electronic writing. Moulthrop's characterizations of technology remain on an abstract level: he talks about "technology" and "electronic writing" in broad terms, only occasionally focusing on situated use of particular applications.

We do not wish to overlook the important contribution of Moulthrop's piece; nor do we wish to diminish the value of theorizing as an important form of scholarly inquiry. As Louise Phelps (1991) says, theory serves an important purpose insofar as it "galvanizes and disrupts the system, changing its very questions, undermining long-held beliefs, introducing ambiguities, revealing complexities, setting new tasks, forcing risks" (p. 883). Moulthrop's theorizing helps us to rethink our models and conceptions of electronic space. It does intend to effect a political change in the way that teachers conceive of the design of digital writing space. He is urging teachers and theorists to look beyond "the printed page and the bound volume" (p. 255) for their models of writing space. He is urging his readers, most importantly, to recognize the presence of the political in electronic space. At the time of publication of his work, this was an important message for a field steeped in instrumentalist assumptions.

His treatment is a good example of a theoretical discussion calling upon postmodern theory in the service of more enlightened understanding of the ways computers can assist in the teaching of writing. However, its abstractness leaves some important questions unanswered: Do the new writing technologies by themselves determine the dramatic changes that Moulthrop predicts—or can teachers and students resist these changes? Is hypertext per se liberating—or do some forms of hypertext, which place users in a passive audience role, actually achieve a higher degree of oppression than some print? How do his hypotheses pertain to particular users using different forms of writing technology? Moulthrop says that he wants to break through the "confining ... hothouse of literary theory" by applying such theory to "technological development" (p. 254). This he does, but his theory and methodology are still very firmly planted in another hothouse, that of literary theory of technology (whose chief caretakers are Landow and Lanham and, on the postmodern side, Poster). The filter Moulthrop uses is enabling in one way, disabling in another.

Joseph Janangelo's article on "Technopower and Technoppression" (1991) uses Foucault's discussion of the panopticon to consider how electronic discourse can be misused, by students as well as teachers, as a tool for surveillance and oppression. He relates stories about students and teachers misusing computer technology in various ways, including spying on one another through unethical trespass into others' computer accounts (or files) and using electronic conferences as a forum for ridiculing and humiliating others. Janangelo's treatment provides discussion of cases; his treatment is, you could say, thoroughly situated in the activities of the composition classroom. But the cases are paradigmatic in the sense that though they are detailed, they are perfect examples supporting the theory that Janangelo offers. None of the cases challenges or complicates the theory offered. Thus, though Janangelo's treatment is situated and "empirical" in one respect—he provides detailed case scenarios of teachers and students, even providing transcripts of personal conversations—the scenarios are suspect in another respect. Did Janangelo (a) construct the examples to support the theory, or rather (b) did he listen to his experience to see how it might or might not confirm the theory? or maybe even (c) did he come to the theory after his experiences with teachers and students? While all of these are possibilities, we think it is important for Janangelo to position his theorizing vis-à-vis his data.

Cynthia Selfe and Richard Selfe's study of "The Politics of the Interface" (1994) is another example of research that applies postmodern theory to particular forms of technology, but their study articulates a clearer agenda for technological change in the direction of liberating users. Selfe and Selfe describe "some of the political and ideological boundary lands associated with computer interfaces" (p. 481), and begin the process of critiquing interfaces with an eye toward their deployment of power, particularly in the composition classroom. They are particularly interested in identifying "some of the effects of domination and colonialism associated with computer use" (p. 482), so that writing teachers can become more alert to the ways that they use technology in the writing classroom and, eventually, effect change in the direction of more egalitarian computer designs.

They notice, for instance, that the Macintosh interface, which represents the virtual world in terms of a desktop metaphor, presents "reality as framed in the perspective of modern capitalism, thus, orienting technology along an existing axis of class privilege" (p. 486). Further, they note how this metaphor aligns with "the axes of class, race, and gender" (p. 487). Entry in this interface signals to users that they are entering a certain world, and that to attain the power that this world represents requires adopting the "values of white, male, middle- and upper-class professionals" (p. 487).

The hypothesis that Selfe and Selfe develop is that computer interfaces are not neutral, that they assert cultural value and, in so doing, practice a power. But what is the effect of that deployment of power? Their examination of the politics of interface features proceeds without reference to the ways in which users interact with those interfaces. What they provide, instead, is demographic data that show the diversity of the student population in U.S. universities (p. 483). Their analysis, then, juxtaposes the values and norms established by the interface against the demographic realities of U.S. students.

Once we have critiqued interfaces, where do we go from there? Selfe and Selfe say that we should:

> Work with students and computer specialists to re-design/re-imagine/re-create inter-faces that attempt to avoid disabling and devaluing non-white, non-English lan-guage background students, and women. Our goal in creating these new interfaces should be to help rewrite the relationships between the center and the margins of our culture. (pp. 495–96)

Their answer, then, is for teachers to move in the direction of influencing the design of computer spaces, certainly the design of the screen, but also the design of computer classrooms and other technological arrangements. In this respect, their political agenda instantiates the proactive (but generalized) goals espoused by Feenberg and by Paul LeBlanc (1990). Selfe and Selfe's article is strong in its program of action for the redesign of computer space to promote the aims of democratization. (Johndan Johnson-Eilola's study, 1995, of hypertextual inter-face features in terms of postmodern theorizing uses a comparable methodology, though Johnson-Eilola's treatment is even more technologically situated.) Selfe and Selfe's study is not an empirical project, and it makes no claims to be one. But we do consider it a situated project that advances a political and ethical agenda.

Where their work is less critically situated, we feel, is in its articulation of the specific program for democratization. By what criteria do we distinguish between good and bad interfaces? ones that promote democracy vs. ones that dominate? Here is where Foucault's discussion of power or Young's criteria for forms of oppression would help their analysis by providing some framework for theorizing ethically. An examination of the effect of the interface on particular users would also complicate their findings. It is perhaps misleading to represent users only in terms of demographic data. As Susan Romano's research (1993) tells us, users identify themselves in ways very different from those suggested by the demo-graphic information about race, gender, and ethnicity. How do we know that the computer systems we use necessarily "support racist, sexist, and colonial atti-tudes" (Selfe & Selfe, 1994, p. 484)? Are users always passively constructed by the culturally hegemonic interfaces they encounter? Or do they themselves con-

tribute to the redesign of the interface in the way they choose to use it? To wha.
extent do they employ tactics that enable them to resist the hegemony of the interface?

We also want to raise questions about the definition of the interface as the
visual and physical features of the computer—as "those primary representations
of computer systems or programs that show up on the screens used by both teachers and students" (p. 485). We would posit, instead, that a study of the interface
has to take into account the situated uses of the interface by practicing writers, the
interaction between users and physical/visual components of the computer. Elizabeth Lopez's study (1995) of computer use in several professional writing
classes suggests: (a) Different forms of technology allow/promote different
degrees of student freedom, and (b) teachers' use of the technology helps determine its degree of freedom/domination.

In other words, it's hard to make judgments about the hegemony of the technology itself (as formalized, abstracted system) without examining the situated
interactions between technology and users, the "framework of strategies of domination and democratization" (Feenberg, 1991, p. 91). A situated study would
complicate their critique in useful ways. (Note: The manuscript version of Selfe
and Selfe's article, which included numerous screen shots, is more technologically situated than the published version of the article that appeared in *College
Composition and Communication*—which, interestingly, contains no visuals. Did
publication in *College Composition and Communication* require a more abstract,
less situated and detailed treatment of the issue? Or did Apple Computer refuse
permission to reproduce images of its interface in a less-than-congratulatory analysis?)

The study that perhaps comes closest to thoroughly situated treatment of participants is Romano's *Computers and Composition* article "The Egalitarianism
Narrative" (1993), which won the award for Best Article in Computers and Composition for the year of its publication. Romano examines the "egalitarian myth"
that she sees as prevalent among computers and composition professionals: that
the use of computer technology in composition classrooms, especially the use of
synchronous conferencing, "facilitates the restructuring of power relationships"
(p. 7) in the direction of greater equality for the participants involved.

Romano's study specifically questions whether "quantitative" (p. 8) methodologies are really appropriate methods for addressing the question of whether computer technology can be, or is, egalitarian. Romano places "a higher value on
readings of transcript excerpts" and argues that "careful, interpretive readings are
valid legs of the triangulation or quadrangulation that constitutes responsible
research" (p. 8). At one point, she calls her methodology "anecdotal" (p. 8), but
what is interesting about her treatment is that she specifically articulates her
hermeneutic methodology *as* a methodology, and argues for its contribution to
empirical discussions of computer conferencing. Unlike much interpretive,
hermeneutic, text-based analysis, Romano's approach overtly reflects on its meth-

odological status and configures itself relative to more conventional empirical studies. This is being up front and reflective about one's methodology.

Romano provides some background about the classroom context for her study, but she provides relatively little information about the technological setting (Daedalus INTERCHANGE) for her study. Because the Daedalus program is well known in the computers and composition community, a lengthy description of it might seem unnecessary in the journal *Computers and Composition*, but we are also not told anything about its contextualized use in Romano's particular class.

Where her study is strongest, we feel, is in the way that it identifies research participants, giving voice to participants and focusing in detail on the Mexican-American students in her class, through presentation and careful analysis of INTERCHANGE sessions. What Romano notices in her observations of her students is how they resisted, negotiated, and realigned themselves in terms of the dominant marking categories used (for instance, by computers and composition theorists) to denote race and ethnicity. As the course and electronic conferencing unfolded over a semester, Romano noticed how the nominal Mexican-American-ism of nine of her students (out of 21 total) became more complex.

Romano's study is not an empirical study by conventional norms; nor does she claim the mantle of empiricism (she explicitly identifies her study as an alternative to quantitative studies, though that does not mean her work cannot claim to be empirical). But we think that her study is probably the closest of any published work to bridging the gap between empirical and theoretical modes of inquiry in computers and composition. The theoretical discussion is not segregated, as it often is, in some distinct literature review section of the article. Rather, her discussion mixes presentation of data, with analysis of data, with theorizing about data. Romano provides a section offering an alternative viewpoint to her own reading of the data. In a section entitled "Undermining My Reading" (p. 24), Romano considers other ways her data might be read, which suits our own instincts about critical research practice.

Romano is highly sensitive to her data, the transcripts of her students' electronic conferences, but her methodology is still a form of interpretive reading of text. Did she involve her students in the design of her research? There is no evidence that she did so. Did she check her readings of the students' texts against other forms of data collection, such as interviewing? Apparently not (the only data used in the study was transcripts from the INTERCHANGE sessions). Was the good of participants a primary goal of the study? Indirectly, yes, as Romano hopes to complicate the ways that composition teachers think about the relationship between technology and difference (gender, race, ethnicity) in their classrooms; she wants teachers not to assume the egalitarian myth, but to be alert to the ways in which our uses of technology might be creating other sorts of institutional oppressions, or even reinforcing the same old "institutional hegemonies" (p. 21). However, we do not see evidence of a follow-up with these participants. Were the nine Mexican-American students who were the primary subjects of this project involved in the writeup? Did Romano share her results with them? seek their reactions? We don't know—this sort of material was not part of the final write-up.

We see much of promise in Romano's study. Per se, it may not be an empirical study, but we don't think the exact labeling matters much here. Her study is a thoughtful, careful, analysis of a well-defined set of data. It is certainly a critical study; it is certainly postmodern and rhetorical in its theorizing. It's also a study that would be quite compatible with the kinds of feminist approaches we describe in Chapter 3. (Similar in many ways to the Romano study is Faigley's description and analysis of two INTERCHANGE sessions in "The Achieved Utopia of the Networked Classroom," Chapter 6 of *Fragments of Rationality* [1992, pp. 163–199], which also meets many of our criteria for politically and ethically alert research practices.)

Gail Hawisher and Pat Sullivan's (in press) study ("Women on the Networks: Searching for E-Spaces of Their Own") provides an example of a feminist approach to empirical analysis, one that is alert to the situations of users and to the constraints of particular technologies, and one that also expressly articulates its aim as the betterment of research participants.

Hawisher and Sullivan studied thirty women in composition, trying to learn more about their views about and habits for using online communication. Begun in 1994, the study collected online interviews, ran an intensive LISTSERV discussion, held a face-to-face meeting at the 1995 Conference on College Composition and Communication, and then moved into a phase of discussion online. The researchers first conceived of the study as a way to gather a more interactive view of what these women thought about online communication, and wrote an account of the interviews and LISTSERV discussion in early 1995. But they also broadened and extended their work as they realized that though they had gathered over 500 pages of data in the interviews and LISTSERV transcript, they were not satisfied with certain dimensions of the study—some related to feminist principles (e.g., involving participants in analysis), some related to technology (e.g., rapidly shifting participation in technology, and by extension notions of online communication). Hawisher in particular came to see the LISTSERV function (originally conceived as a means of collecting data) as a potential safehouse for women who experience mistreatment online.

It is interesting to think of traditional methods in relationship to this study, and then to turn to examine the ethical implications of those methods. The authors write in "Women on the Networks" that they could find little methodological guidance for conducting online interviews in previous studies (feminist studies in composition and studies of online communication) because studies of online communication "typically deal with 'found' texts, those which are transcribed or printed, rather than with online interviews or texts in the making" (p. 6). Most of the research they found that dealt with gender online was concerned with these found texts and included little (or more usually, no) direct contact with those who produced the e-texts. They noted that Cynthia Selfe and Paul Meyer (1991), in one of the earlier studies (and certainly an influential one), took the transcripts of a LISTSERV discussion and analyzed them to discover gender elements of participation. Selfe and Meyer, however, did not interact with participants to get their take on what was happening or on what the researchers found; instead they treated the discussion as a playscript, using discourse analysis to unlock its crafted meanings.

> While such an approach is a useful one for describing the marking of gendered interaction in electronic texts (and given the prominence of the reduced social cues model such work is an important corrective), this approach cannot be used to get at how people (women and men) responded to or felt about a particular discussion. ... Transcripts [are not] able to capture the emotion or dynamism; they flatten and freeze the experience. (methodological notes, Sullivan, 12-27-94; see also Sullivan, 1993b)

Again, we have here an example of how the research process itself—in this case, a deliberation about a data collection strategy—intersects with politics and ethics. The data collection procedures are the "academic mode of production" (Stanley, 1990b) that establishes ethical and political relations between researchers and participants. The procedures themselves influence (determine?) how participants will be represented (that is, how their subjectivity will be constructed) in the eventual write-up of the study.

The researchers wanted to have a more complete understanding of participants' responses to public discussion than was possible with just transcripts. This concern prompted them to ask participants to debrief with them about the discussion (another interview, this one short), to ask for feedback at a thank-you breakfast at the Conference on College Composition and Communication (a few months later), and to ask several participants to read a draft of their first paper. This concern about the thinness of the data was accompanied by another ethical concern— about misrepresenting the views of participants. The concern had two sources: (a) The researchers were grateful to the participants and did not want any of them to feel slighted in the write-ups, and (b) the researchers agreed with Michelle Fine (1992) that including only selected quotations from the participants too easily allows researchers to "mystify the ways in which we select, use, and exploit voices" (p. 219).

In some sense, the Hawisher and Sullivan study involved handing over the collection strategy to the participants by creating an online list where the participants could voice their concerns in a community of discourse (and thereby assist the development of the community). This move could be judged negatively as a loss of control of the process. But in this move, the study instantiates at least one of Feenberg's proactive goals: The study works to establish a collegiality among the participants. The data collection process in effect was based on the construction of a community: a kind of online focus group, but one in which the researchers' own questions did not necessarily guide the discussion. In fact, the authors note, "the participants directed this phase of the research" (p. 9). What happened during the LISTSERV exchange was that the women on the group (called woman@waytoofast) attempted to construct the group as a utopian group; for instance, they attempted to treat one another with a respect that they did not always find in other groups (p. 16): they were "welcoming, disclosing, polite, inclusive, and often personal" (p. 17). In a sense, then, the research process itself facilitated the redesign of at least one computer writing space.

But another feature of this research project is that the online community established through the LISTSERV group did not end when data collection ended. The list woman@waytoofast continued sporadically after the project, serving as a support group, an "emergency space" (p. 30); women who experienced harassment or marginalization online could get assistance, in the form (for instance) of strong responsive action against such behavior. In short, the research process itself very clearly demonstrates commitment to those in an oppressed (marginalized) situation. It does not leave the participants stranded.

The purpose of this research went beyond simply reporting results to a field of researchers who do not belong to the group being studied. Rather, the participants in this study were also members of the field of the researchers (computers and composition), and would likely be readers of the study. The research process itself has a liberating effect, insofar as it provides a safe place for participants to express their views, but it goes beyond being merely a counseling forum in its proactive involvement in the online lives of participants beyond the parameters of the list. While the study does not aim directly at effecting large-scale change in computer systems, it does have as its clear aims (a) establishing women's online lives as important and valuable in themselves (and not just as related to men's), and (b) creating a community of support among researchers and participants.

Any methodology offers researchers a set of filters—which of course are also blinds—that the methodological theory hopes will be useful in structuring a systematic study of a phenomenon. Those filters often focus on ways to observe (and measure) the behavior(s) of interest and on determining what counts as knowledge in the content area under investigation, but they also include political and ethical stances, even when such stances are backgrounded. Our position is that backgrounding of politics and ethics usually is dangerous, though we admit that at times it is attractive.

Why would any group want to construct a method that is politically and ethically neutral—that is, one that allowed researchers to claim that a phenomenon of interest was a foundational concept, to claim that a behavior is universally measured thus, to claim that they had no stake in the outcome of a study (i.e., that both positive and negative results would equally advance the course of science), to claim that their data analyses held no interest in the outcome, to claim that following certain procedures de facto resulted in validity, to claim that the results could be generalized to all people with certain characteristics, and so on? In research in the human sciences, individual differences (race, gender, class, ability, religion, personality) typically have been "controlled" (e.g., allowed to vary randomly or matched by certain attributes) in order to unravel how certain truths shine through us all (i.e., the move toward a formal abstraction that effaces the problematics of situated difference). Received wisdom in traditional methodology has attempted to set up such a system for Method. It portrays the researcher as a man in a white lab coat who is the instrument of scientific truth, that is, he is industriously uncovering the natural laws. This lab-coated man is working from the basis of previous research, using methods established and accepted by other researchers, and adding to our understanding of the world around us. This researcher theoretically allows all answers to emerge (he is unbiased and neutral, almost powerless in the face of observed truth) and focuses on extending the explanatory power of theories through observation. Researcher power is never discussed; power is only used in the presence of explanation or prediction, and then observed behavior is the source of that power (the subject's behavior, not the researcher's). Ethics is only voiced in the realm of egregious researcher misconduct—someone who falsified data or its analysis or someone who mistreated or harmed subjects (e.g., exposed them to harmful chemicals without their knowledge). Put this way, a better question than "Why would we want a neutral method?" is "How could we force ourselves to give up such researcher power that is cloaked by this set of methodological filters?" or "Do we really want to surrender this power?"

Of course we do not have a choice. Methodologists of the past 20 years have dismantled the position that asserts the neutrality of methods (and methodology) and the presumed authority of the scientific observation. They have shown, among other things, how neither the claim to impartiality and objectivity nor the hiding of research procedures is innocent politically or ethically. Such claims, Young (1990) says, "feed cultural imperialism by allowing the particular experience and perspective of privileged groups to parade as universal ... and legitimate authoritarian hierarchy" (p. 10). Assuming an ethos of neutrality when one is actually in a superior position of power (e.g., the researcher position) is to risk manipulation or paternalism. In order to counter the imbalance of the research situation, we suggest, the researcher is required to take ethical action to empower the researched—which is one reason that we so much stress contextualizing one's project, and which is one reason we view "Liberate the oppressed" as such an important ethical/political stance for critical researchers.

Postmodernists are of course alert to the dangers of the neutrality thesis, and some dismantle this thesis as a way to reject bodies of research findings or approaches to research—in other words, the popular pastime of bashing empirical research. We do not agree that previous research is devoid of value; we look, instead, to historicize and qualify it in many of the same ways that we historicize and qualify other approaches to method and knowledge making. As we stated in previous chapters, we see research as local, contingent, malleable, heuristic, and generative of situated knowledge. Consideration of ethical and political dimensions is critical to such a stance. These dimensions can no longer be marginalized, ignored, or considered to be calcified in the rules of procedure. As we hope we have made clear, especially in our discussion of the Hawisher and Sullivan study—the procedures of research are by no means neutral. The procedures themselves always involve relations with participants, and it is those relations, as developed (and perhaps changed) through the research process, that researchers have to interrogate and articulate. It is through those relations that power—and perhaps, at times and unfortunately, oppression—is manifested. That is why the activity of research has to stop overlooking and start articulating its political and ethical situatedness.

6

The Emergence of Research:
A Convergence of Personal,
Political, Professional

In this chapter we discuss critical research practices within the context of our own projects as a way to explore critical stance-making during the emergence of research (i.e., the front end of our critical practices depiction of the research process, shown in Chapter 3). Thus, we focus on our emerging study of electronic pages. Actually, we talk about several interrelated projects (that we were working on between 1992 and early 1996) that share a common interest in electronic pages: In one we are developing a case study of our department's struggle to develop an online identity (or, more simply, a home page) on the World Wide Web (WWW); in another we are investigating our attempts to include the Internet and the World Wide Web in the advanced writing courses we direct (which includes pedagogy and teacher training); in the third we are exploring gender and online communities as they are portrayed in web pages.

With projects such as these in mind, we proceed. They lend the weight of particulars to our discussion of how to enact critical research practices. In our lingo, they rhetorically situate our discussion. It is much harder (and actually much easier) to talk about the constellation of critical concerns within the framework of a particular study.

Instead of presenting an example that illustrates the smooth operation of the kind of critical practices approach we have been advocating, we turn now to the messy process of beginning research as a way of demonstrating our lack of easy answers for research methodology. We are writing about a process that we are just beginning, as we are beginning it (in early 1996). Thus, it's a mess, and you may find this chapter somewhat frustrating, if not exceedingly tedious. Bear with us, because we are trying to describe a process that is not often acknowledged in published literature. We have no precedent for writing it.

While sometimes covered by research manuals (see the characterizations of research processes in Chapter 3), "How we begin/began" is not recognized in the write-ups of research, in part because research hopes to be systematic and certainly represents itself that way. Relegated, then, to retrospective reflections that researchers sometimes speak or write after a line of research has been published (see, for example, Lisa Ede's 1992 discussion of how Lunsford and Ede, 1990, was shaped throughout its process as well as her postproduction thoughts on the project), "How we begin/began" becomes a story, a reminiscence, a war tale. Yet the critical tale of the emergence of a research project is key to our notion that research is a rhetorically situated activity. Thus, our goal for this chapter is to describe the social and political work environment—the primal ooze, if you will—out of which some of our own research is emerging. Confession time: Since a key component of critical research practices is coming clean, but in a critical as opposed to a confessional way, we will work to minimize any urges to confessional excess. Forgive us, please, if we stray.

Knowledge-making is not innocent or neutral, despite the attempts of many to make it appear so. This has been a central tenet of our discussion. But what does embracing the charged nature of knowledge-making mean for researchers as they are beginning their research? First, it means that we articulate our positions while that process is still under way. Second, it means that we examine how our positions may lead us to seek certain themes or to embrace certain explanations and to be tempted to do so with or without supporting evidence. Third, it means that discussions of our research include, as one of the foregrounded issues, how we tried to be reasonable despite our own predispositions.

Thus, this chapter concretizes the "how" of critical research practices by discussing how we are struggling to instigate these practices in several closely linked projects that can be clustered around the topic "producing electronic pages." The research topic, stated thusly, highlights the ambiguities inside our general community—that is, researchers in computers and composition. "Producing" calls up process but does not specify whether this process involves computers (we suppose some people might think of producing a page by handwriting it or by sending typed pages to a printer for design and publishing), or classes (this could be an assignment, a task for an intern, or a classroom demonstration), or software (this could range from a straightforward task requiring simple word-processing software to a complex page layout task requiring scanning, manipulating, importing, coloring, animating, and so on), or conditions (the process could be related to learning or to work, it could be a time-pressured activity, it may lack the materials it needs, it may focus on the task, it may be routine, it may be considered critically important or decried, and so on), or culture (who controls the process, who reviews it, what standards are held by the group, how important is group acceptance, and so on).

"Electronic pages" mute the distinction between print and digital objects and also inhibit our ability to concentrate only on the content of the text at the expense of the other elements of meaning on those "pages." The term also unsettles us: It plays with the fact that we think of pages as paper we can hold, even though digital pages cannot be so tactilely encountered; it conjures a medium that is technical (electronic) and not as understandable as paper is; and it hooks a medium we are more comfortable with (paper) to the mystery of the technical. Thus, we can worry that electronic pages are more technically sophisticated and remote, that they act differently from real pages, and that we need to learn more technology in order to produce them.

"Producing electronic pages" is also ambiguous about who is producing the pages, what relationship producing electronic pages has to our more traditional consideration of writing processes (conceivably we could be talking about print shop activity—say, producing color prints from a computer file—that does not involve creative control of content in the sense that writing teachers mean content), what community surrounds this production process, how technology transverses and interfaces with this production process, and how readership and evaluation might be factored into the equation. We intend this ambiguity, urging an uneasy framing of issues by the ambiguous phrasing, and we intend it as a constant reminder of the complexity we seek to study. But we also think it important to honor ambiguity and to suspect research ideas that are seemingly devoid of it.

In our discussion of the fabric grounding these studies and grounding any study we might cut out of that fabric, we concentrate first on setting the scene, then on complicating it. Such moves help us discern relationships that are key to our research as we question them. In essence, then, to understand how these projects are emerging for us, we need to describe how the complex search for key relationships helps us to forge research projects that link our local needs with our research interests.

DESCRIPTION OF THE FABRIC

As you read this fabric, please keep in mind that we have not forged these components into a nicely formed narrative, and we have kept ourselves from tidying it up because we want to allow those rough edges to show. If we could describe this fabric concisely and insightfully, it would not have such a powerful hold on our thinking. Instead we might believe our memorably crafted story to be the one, true, and immutable interpretion—and that would be dangerous for researchers aiming to deal in critical research practices. Keeping the rough edges gives our stories a heuristically generative quality. Thus we meander through the site, discussing those topics that we find in some vague way potentially important to our research.

Let's begin with the pressures to inhabit the Internet as the starting point for our discussion of the environment we live and work within. In the past few years those pressures have intensified. Before 1990, the field's participation in the Internet was modest: email, electronic discussions, and telneting to library catalogs were the focus of group consciousness in computers and composition, and this was also mainly the case in our experience at Purdue. (Hawisher & Sullivan, in press, report that their participants, all of whom were using the Internet when interviewed in Fall 1994, were using a computer by 1990, but only 68% were using email by that time.) There was not widespread experience with netsurfing; many in composition and in computers and composition were just getting connected and learning about electronic communication. In the early 1990s, as people surfed enough to realize what Gopher sites (and more recently World Wide Web sites) could offer composition—for example, places to store materials that can be accessed worldwide (as Blythe, 1997, argues for Writing Centers)—attention has turned to this new conception of networking as a world to navigate and colonize through the production of e-text. After Mosaic was released in 1993, "everyone" began setting up their sites and/or their web pages. Matthew Gray's (1995) study of the growth of web sites estimated that in June 1993 there were 130 sites, and by December 1994 that number had burgeoned to 11,576 sites; further, Michael Neubarth (1995) predicted that this number would skyrocket to 40,000 by the end of 1995. Though numbers vary, most discussions of WWW growth are similarly impressive about its rapid rise to prominence. By 1996, Mary Meeker and Chris DePuy (1996) reported that 35 million people used email and that 9 million were using the World Wide Web. They further predicted that "email users could number 200 million worldwide by the year 2000, and that about 150 million of these could access the Internet/Web, with slightly less than half representing U.S. users" (p. 3–1). Clearly the Internet in general is a huge presence in our nation's consciousness (this has been true since we began trying to understand the Information Superhighway after the 1992 presidential election), and WWW excites almost all who use it. Networks also dominate our thinking about new technologies for the teaching of writing via the computer, in part because they show us a direction for distributed computing that involves more than email.

The importance of the web becomes more pointed as we bring to mind the local pressures on the rhetoric and composition graduate faculty and on the professional/technical writing graduate faculty at Purdue to keep current with developments in computing as they have an impact on theory and pedagogy of writing. The sources of this pressure are the status of Purdue's Ph.D. program in rhetoric and composition (and its desire both to improve and to maintain that status) as a serious site for the study of writing (with both "study" and "writing" constructed broadly); our program's need to compete for the best graduate students; our graduate students' need for a range of teaching and learning experiences; and our own research needs. We do not think we can aim to educate future contributors to the professional writing field without providing up-to-date computing experiences; nor do we think the best students will attend institutions that neglect this aspect of their education; nor will the best students want to study with us if we are not publishing interesting computing-related research. But the Department of English does not have the resources to hire computer support. Thus, faculty and other teachers must expend considerable effort convincing the Department and University to provide the technology we need for instruction. We also must deal with general undergraduate computing support that is not customized to assist us with the special needs of our various writing classes. Given the current institutional support, these goals require a constant struggle.

Another set of complicating factors is found in our institutional roles as administrators, curriculum developers, and teacher trainers for business writing and technical writing courses at Purdue. Our jobs, as we see them, include developing curricula that help our undergraduates function more effectively as communicators in the workplace. For this, too, we have a critical vision; that is, we hope that our students exercise a thoughtful concern for others in their work as professionals. Our view of rhetoric insists that an active concern for audiences (users, clients, customers, fellow workers, the public) be at the center of writing work. As we project the changes in workplaces, we expect that networked communication will be increasingly important to the work that college graduates perform (see Dautermann & Sullivan, 1996). Thus, we need to project the changing shapes of communication technologies so that we may help students deal with the rhetorical challenges that await them. Because this technological imperative has been layered on top of already full syllabi, we spend considerable effort folding technology into these classes and then remaking the classes in new ways. It is an ongoing process that is situated within the realities of the facilities we have, the changes in university software and procedures (i.e., if you need to change documentation, you cannot spend that time revising curriculum), the teaching backgrounds of new teachers, and so on. In a sense our workplace mirrors the types of changes we project for our graduates. We cannot reach the seamless integration of technology and classroom activity because each year we have new technology and new teachers.

Let's also consider our interest in and experience with teaching page design to writing majors. Both of us have taught and published on page design, fascinated by (a) the ways in which technological change in the 1980s made page design an important consideration for (and ultimately duty of) professional writers, most of whom were not educated in visual design or page layout, and (b) the fact that few people thought to consider the page from a rhetorical position. We saw some repetition of that move in the design of online documentation. We now see more in the design of home pages for WWW, though we should add that the various style sheets developed to promote good principles of design often strike us as poorly designed or as advocating principles we don't follow (see Yahoo, 1995).

Further, there is our involvement in the making of institutional policy. Jim has been a member of a university subcommittee charged with making recommendations regarding long-term planning for instructional computing on campus. Much of the work takes place on the World Wide Web—but since Jim did not have an office hookup to the campus backbone until March 1996, he was hampered in doing committee work and could not participate at the same level of involvement as others on the committee (e.g., file sharing). Jim was the representative for Liberal Arts, yet Jim did not have equal access to network resources (because Liberal Arts receives fewer resources for campus computing than do others schools, and because English receives less within Liberal Arts), and he could not leverage the kind of influence that Liberal Arts needed to leverage in order to change its second- (or third-) class status. In such ways does an inequality of access perpetuate itself.

We also are influenced by our own publishing. Both of us have focused considerable energy on computers and composition in the last five years, with Jim recently completing a book on ethics in electronic writing situations, this collaborative effort, and Pat working on gender online. Both of us came to our considerations of electronic communication from backgrounds in rhetorical theory and in professional and technical writing, as well as with experience teaching writing with machines. These backgrounds and issues shaped our early views of this evolving space.

The fabric can be further described by discussing the projects we see emerging out of our work in this place (does place, as we mean it here, reflect the larger field of education? the field of Rhetoric/Composition? the field of Computers and Composition? the Big Ten? Purdue? the Professional Writing Program? the graduate Rhetoric program? or perhaps this set of facilities? this curriculum? and so on?).

THE HOME PAGE PROJECT

An ongoing publishing project that interests us is the development of the English Department's home page. This online page project has been convoluted in its development because of the territorial disputes that swirl around the development of home pages representing Purdue University. In Fall 1994, the central administration dictated that all schools must develop home pages for the University's World Wide Web site; Liberal Arts, in turn, decided that each of its departments would develop a web page to support the college's web page. Liberal Arts purchased a server and allocated a consultant's time to coordinating the school's effort; each department sent a representative to the committee that was to develop the school's page. At the same time, each department was supposed to form a committee to build a departmental page that would be nested in the school page. English was hampered in its efforts because it was one of the very few departments not connected fiberoptically to the campus network; some faculty had a 2400 baud modem, but only a few administrators could run Netscape from their offices.

The campus had been led in World Wide Web activity by the University Libraries. In Fall 1993 the Libraries had started a Gopher site that included the University libraries' online catalog, a number of databases, assorted online journals, links to other University information servers, resource information, and pointers to other information. They had used the advent of the Z39.5 protocol to gather a variety of information sources together under a common interface. This Gopher site was the Libraries' initial vision of a CWIS (Campus-Wide Information Server) for Purdue, and it was marked by a fluid conception of joining many types of information (that would be owned and maintained by groups across the university). The Libraries initially focused on the concepts of Purdue and clearinghouse, thinking that Purdue-related information could all be found in this electronic clearinghouse.

Two efforts in English also preceded the Liberal Arts initiative:

1. The Professional Writing Program (inside English) had been talking with the libraries about a Professional Writing page that would gather appropriate research and research pointers as a way to build an electronic library for professional writing.
2. The Writing Lab, with funding from the dean, started a Gopher site and then a World Wide Web site. Their OWL (Online Writing Lab) already was operational when the College directives took force and thus was exempted from the current style guidelines and administrative oversight.

These various groups overlapped in mission and approach, yet they aimed to coexist harmoniously. The teaching units began to see their territory as dispensing academic information and demonstrating academic prowess, while the Libraries began to view their project more as an Electronic Library (and less as the shaper of the CWIS). Of course the groups affected ranged wider than these two, as computing services had to provide technical support for both efforts and the Office of Publications was recruited to develop guidelines for home pages that were linked to the University home page. Lest you think the coordination flawless, we offer the following example: We know about the Office of Publications document only coincidentally because Pat's husband saw it in an Athletic Public Relations meeting in August of 1995 (Athletics is not part of the project); as far as we know those specifications never reached the departments that are involved.

Perhaps the Libraries' idea of a CWIS was muddled or lost through this process; perhaps it was saved by a wider interest in presenting and maintaining information. We do know that the 1994–1995 school year at Purdue was a time of demarcating and defending cyberspace territories. The Professional Writing Program (the group we obviously identify with), because it lacked monetary support to start its site before the cyberturf disputes began, was buffeted among these forces. The English Department's page was delayed because its technological resources lagged behind the college's and because it did not want the professional writing faculty to dominate efforts to represent the whole department (at least that is what we suspect, somewhat paranoically). The Libraries ultimately refused to house a site that might be viewed as renegade. But Professional Writing was not the only resource-poor group. English was not connected to the fiberoptic backbone until 1996 (two and one half years after the project started—the last department on campus to be connected); there was (and is) little money to upgrade faculty systems enough to use cable in the offices; and there are no computers in teaching assistants' offices. While development swirls around very quickly, English had remained almost in neutral—a point we feel nervous admitting because of our programmatic need to be current in technology (will admitting a weakness upset our program's reputation?).

The institutional politics of writing, then, became more clearly foregrounded in this project as groups sorted through that age-old disciplinary and administrative problem: Who owns what knowledge? This emerging focus allows us to articulate the power issues related to web site/web page development in ways that make the rhetoric of web pages more radically contextual and more politically situated. Yes, they become much more situated than theoretical or research issues that are shaped through accounts of the processes of students who are contructing their own home pages, but are doing so seemingly in isolation from their environment.

TEACHING PROJECTS/TEACHER PROJECTS

Developing teaching uses of the Internet in general, and web page projects specifically, is a related set of activities that has occupied the same time period as the home page project and has suggested several teaching projects. Perhaps we have focused effort here because our goals for the professional writing web page were blocked. Perhaps we have focused effort here because we are tenured, which allows us more flexibility to devote time to building a learning community. Whatever the reasons, we have urged/helped/nudged/ordered the various professional writing curricula (business writing, technical writing, the professional writing major, and the graduate program) to integrate Internet projects into various classes. As of Fall 1992 all of the technical writing classes were taught in computer classrooms, with business writing (the largest upper-division writing course at Purdue) adding as many sections per term as it could. Further, in Fall 1996 we received a curriculum grant to develop the web materials needed to run all advanced writing courses in computer classrooms by Spring 1998.

Why have we spent so much effort on developing the online curriculum in our respective professional writing programs? What goals motivate our keen interest in this development? First, we see electronic writing (including word processing, email, Internet file transfer, World Wide Web) as the key site for future writing. Very shortly, if not already, *writing* will mean "electronic writing." Thus, if we are to be responsible to our professional obligations as writing instructors, we have to recognize this development and deal with it. We have to learn how writing works online, and we have to learn how to teach writing online.

Second, because electronic writing is an emergent phenomenon, we see an incredible opportunity to affect changes in the way that this type of writing instantiates itself. We don't see the same opportunity for change in the print realm, only because the habits and practices of print are so firmly established. Working against a long-dominant grain, it is harder to effect change in rhetorical procedures. We see more potential to influence the pattern of the grain in electronic writing. For instance, Pat's research on women's uses of electronic networks attempts to fashion the Internet in a way that will make it hospitable to women; that research can influence the design of systems (both the software design, the interface, as well as policy and practice). Jim's research into copyright issues on the Internet has led him to become an advocate for copyleft laws and policies that favor more open access to and distribution of electronic information. As Co-Chair for the Intellectual Property Caucus of College Composition and Communication in 1996, Jim has worked to oppose electronic copyright legislation that favored large commercial publishing interests at the expense of smaller publishers and educational uses of the technology. In short, the teaching and professional goals intersect with political interests that are also tied to ethical concerns about how online subjectivities will be formed.

Third, in order to empower our students as agents of change—in the public realm, in their professional lives, in their personal lives—we need to learn how to teach them electronic writing. If they are to participate as citizens in the transformation of society, in the making of a better society, then they need to understand the rhetorical procedures and technologies that enable writing to happen. It is our fundamental duty as writing teachers to assist them in this as best we can.

And fundamental to this duty is our obligation as faculty within a graduate program in rhetoric and composition to help train new teachers. In fact, as our professional identities have developed at Purdue, we are now much more thoroughly focused on teacher development: the fact is that our workloads are more thoroughly focused within the graduate program, and thus directed to teacher/faculty development. This focus probably explains our keen interest (in this book and elsewhere) in matters related to mentoring and curriculum design; it probably also explains why we tend not to see the isolated writing classroom as a primary unit of analysis. We view this perspective of ours as a strength, because it is relatively atypical within the field. However, we know that it is also a bias that perhaps makes us a little impatient—well, to be honest, extremely impatient; let's even admit it, frustrated—with the field's continued nearly exclusive obsession with the first-year composition classroom.

Our curricular interests in computing and professional writing have led us to develop many approaches to computers and pedagogy. The technical writing course (directed by Pat), for example, from 1992 to 1995, turned more directly toward the Internet. In 1992–1993 the staff focused its instruction on the use of email, online libraries, and bulletin boards; in 1993–1994 it dealt with locating material relevant to students' majors via Gopher; in 1994–1995 it located online resources via the World Wide Web, with more experienced teachers requiring students to develop web pages which instructed others in how to use the Internet to do something relevant to their field; in 1995–1996 new teachers built their own web pages for instructional materials as a way to prepare them to teach producing online writing.

The rapid turnover in the technologies used to teach technical writing, though, has posed problems for curriculum development, staff development, and for teacher training. Materials were placed on the lab server under a common account, as a way to divide the work and keep current, but teachers both wanted to contribute their assignments and for there to be an "authorized" version: the question of authority became a complex one. Some staff members enjoyed constantly integrating new technology into their classes, and felt that it added to their development, while others found the course too time-consuming (because there were always new assignments and technologies) and uncomfortable (because it was hard to feel like you had mastered teaching it). The staff's hard work to deal with these shifting technologies clearly has been successful: they have given conference presentations related to their teaching at the Midwest Conference of the Association for Business Communication, the Conference on College Composition and Communication, Writing Center Conference, and Computers and Writing; all who are no longer graduate students have jobs. But several staff members who are still graduate students have quit teaching technical writing, and we suspect that they were disappointed by their experiences.

We know, from research done about the technical writing staff by graduate students in another class, that those studying the staff meetings found the level of discussion very technical and did not understand many issues we discussed—a perception that underscored the general graduate student perception that you teach technical writing if you are a computer nerd. Thus, we think that the course processes have not evolved sufficiently well to handle the technology in ways that make it quickly understandable to new teachers (i.e., it still takes a big commitment on the part of new and experienced teachers). The problem of developing curriculum that integrates technology into the course's texture during times of profound technological change is a very important one for us. We are particularly concerned about the difficulties new teachers have, the gaps that grow between the classes of new and experienced teachers, and the problems encountered when we not only try to teach writing with/through technology but also try to instill a critical stance toward technology.

Purdue's business writing program (directed by Jim) teaches approximately half of its sections each semester in computer classrooms; in the 1995–1996 academic year, for instance, 24 sections serving 480 students were taught in a networked computer classroom. For some time, the program has wanted to move its instructional materials online, both because it would be easier to update them online and because putting them online would be a way to help some students avoid the expensive copying charges associated with purchasing a printed coursepack. In 1995, the program moved much of its materials to the central campus server. While this location made it possible for the director of the program to distribute materials among the teaching staff, access to students was still stifled because of the design of the Purdue central server (which stresses security and restrictions, not information access). The staff agreed that it would be ideal to make course materials available through a web site that all business writing students could access.

As we previously mentioned, institutional politics and lack of resources have hampered this vision. For one thing, in 1995 the business writing program was told that it could not develop its own home page until the College of Liberal Arts, and then the Department, decided on protocols for program web material. (This reason for this restriction was that the Department and College wanted to assure that material affiliated with Purdue conformed to certain standards of appropriateness and design, but, inexplicably, some departmental programs were allowed to place their materials on the web before any such standards were issued.) This restriction apparently did not apply to individual instructors, though, so some instructors developed their own materials, which of course were accessible to program teachers and to students. Tim Krause, for instance, developed a comprehensive site linking students to online job ads and research sources; he produced print documentation helping students use an HTML editor to create online resumes (see http://omni.cc.purdue.edu/~tkrause). So, although there was no official business writing program web site until 1996, there were business writing materials available on business writing teachers' web sites.

Lack of resources also hurt the plans to develop a comprehensive set of online materials in support of both business writing and technical writing. Not having a web hookup in their offices hampered both Jim's and Pat's efforts to contribute to the development of a web site. The business writing program used to have an assistant director, as did technical writing, and the professional writing program had a "computer liaison" person; all three of these positions focused on developing instructional computing resources for professional writing. During the campus budget crunch of the early 1990s these positions were eliminated—and they have never been restored, despite the improved budgetary conditions since early 1995. In 1995, Jim applied for a university-wide development grant ($12,000) to support the purchase of a server and development of a web site. The application made it to the final round of consideration, but was not funded. Three other grant applications that featured upgrading equipment were also unsuccessful. (Note: In late 1996, the professional writing program did receive two grants, totaling $22,898, to promote technological and curricular development.)

University copyright policies also impede the development of web materials for the business writing program. Because the university insists on laying copyright claim to instructional materials developed on University equipment, teachers in the business writing program are reluctant not only to develop new materials using campus equipment, but even to place materials they have developed elsewhere on the campus server. In general, there is a national trend developing in which universities are beginning to exercise the work-for-hire doctrine of copyright law to an extent that they have not in the past, especially as pertains to faculty development of multimedia products. This strategy is intended, reasonably enough, as a way for a university to recoup its considerable economic investment in computer resources. But ironically, such a policy can also have the effect of stifling the development of innovative instructional materials.

The irony—in the nonfunny sense—of the situation is that Purdue is a campus that is incredibly rich in technological resources, and yet even within this environment there are significant differences between haves and have-nots. Campus attitudes toward English and the humanities generally, and attitudes within English about the status of professional writing and the use of computer resources to teach writing, all conspire politically to influence the emerging situation. Of course you would not find anyone at the University who would not say that these resources are important (well, maybe you would find one or two in English)—but in the current climate it has been difficult to find anyone willing to pay for them.

In the professional writing major and the graduate curriculum we have been helped by Johndan Johnson-Eilola, a new faculty member in 1994, who was hired to contribute courses and course components in hypermedia and multimedia. His knowledge of and enthusiasm for home page development—in his words, "becoming producers"—has kept us moving up the learning curve. Johndan has worked to get tools to people, added home page construction to our undergraduate documentation course, and held workshops on constructing home pages. Currently he is requiring graduate students to build their own home pages in the computers and composition seminar, which we think will help develop a critical mass of knowledge.

Actually, the use of technology in graduate classes has been key to our efforts to raise the base of technical knowledge in the department and to build a community of technical knowledge. We have built technical knowledge for the writing program through course assignments consistently in this decade. Jim has taught email tutorials as preface to assigning an online forum analysis in his audience (and now postmodernism) seminar. With the purpose of socializing students into online environments as teaching and research resources, the online forum assignment has two key components: (a) an online community journal, and (b) an electronic forum analysis (descriptive). Teachers of professional writing theory have included units on using computers to produce program materials as a way to increase knowledge of the computer as a document production resource. Pat also includes a group project that gathers data about some computers and writing topics in her composition research seminars. In these projects graduate students have compared the teaching issues of new and experienced teachers in computer classrooms, have investigated English graduate students' online lives, and have interviewed other graduate students who have home pages. This use of the technology in the postmodernism and in composition research courses (both required courses for Ph.D. students in Rhetoric and Composition) is particularly important because it raises the general level of knowledge about technology among all members of the community.

Within the climate of the classroom, our graduate students and staff are developing curriculum and presenting it at conferences. We are particularly interested in their growth as teachers and professionals as it is shaped by and as it shapes the curricular moves made to teach electronic pages. From our roles as teachers of teachers, we worry about how to develop technologically rich curricula that new teachers can teach. This project seems to dovetail with the interests of teacher researchers (see Cochran-Smith & Lytle, 1993), and it could profit from paying careful attention to their approaches to research and to identifying and empowering teacher knowledge.

However, the fit is made uneasy by three facts. First, which classroom is the focus is not clear. Are we studying the undergraduate classrooms where our graduate students are teaching writing to juniors and seniors in various majors, or the graduate rhetoric classes where we are trying to establish the knowledge with and interest in technology, or the teacher training classes where we also are trying to establish knowledge with technology (though in this case the knowledge is used in the service of teaching)? Second, who the researchers are and who the participants are is not clear. While students would be participants, which students: the undergraduates? the graduate students in rhetoric classes? the graduate students in teacher training classes? And would we be informants, or participants, or bystanders? Third, what community of knowledge is prized is not clear either. Is the goal of this work to promote the general technical knowledge needed for web page construction? or to help teachers feel comfortable with technology? or to teach producing electronic pages? The instability of the concepts of classroom and teacher unsettle teacher research, which seems much more able to identify teachers, students, and classrooms than this project is.

An aside: If this example were to accomplish nothing more than to push researchers to question some of these natural categories, we would be satisfied. If the discussion were to push readers of research to look askance at classroom research that seemingly is unaware (a) of the complex relationships and power exchanges among the players in a class, and (b) of the instability of classic terms of teacher, student, classroom, and instructional technology, and (c) of the local politics that surround and impact on the uses of technology in particular classes and programs, we think our field would see progress.

GENDER AND THE WEB

A third project that intersects with these (and is also independent of them by virtue of Pat's collaboration with a colleague at another school, Gail Hawisher), is our interest in gender on the web.

Gender attracts attention in discussions of online participation. Although Leslie Miller reported in *USA Today* (1995) that participation by women in cyberspace has grown dramatically to 43% (the source was the Yankelovich survey of pay services such as America Online), we still contend that women have considerable barriers to full online participation (see Damarin, 1992; Herring, 1993; Spender, 1995; Taylor, Kramarae, & Ebben, 1993). And this conviction spurs an interest in the Web because it is touted as easy to build and easy to use. Do women experiencing the web agree with the ease-of-use claims? Do they find it invigorating? How do they experience the e-spaces that WWW have cultivated? Do they build their own sites? We are interested in better understanding the gendered experience of this new technology, in the gendering of web writing.

Of course that means that we do not believe that gender is abandoned in e-space. What positions does that belief entail, and in what ways are our assumptions likely to filter what we see? We know, for instance, that we see gender as a perspective that can illuminate inequities for women in society. Yet, is it reasonable for us to extend that perspective into cyberspace; that is, are cybersocieties busy reproducing the organization of and lines of power that identify current societies? Or are these cyberspaces forging, in Michel Foucault's (1986) terms, utopian or heterotopian societal units that will stand in contrast to daily life? To what extent e-spaces are reproducing regular space and to what extent they are challenging it are important concerns for feminists (though feminists already contend that much of e-space is reproducing the dominant power structures in force in "regular" society).

DISCIPLINARY POLITICS AND COMMUNITY BUILDING

The task of writing this fabric has already been useful to us in focusing our work on the electronic pages. As we have thought about our own interests in light of field issues we have realized that producing electronic pages has been the general topic driving our recent work, but it is not the driving force behind this work. We are far more invested in building a community of scholars of writing who are thoughtful about electronic page development. Now how has that emerged, you might ask. We see it as an amalgam of the projects and roles. We had as a goal in these projects to explore, and to promote the exploration of, electronic pages. When some of those experiences started to blend with our normal discourse about teaching, about theorizing electronic writing, and about negotiating life within a university setting, we found the nurturing of community far more important to us than were the other dimensions of the projects. Perhaps it was our teacherly selves asserting themselves; perhaps it was our research selves saying, "Hey! There are participants for research in every direction you turn."

Of course we should note a potential disciplinary problem. While the gendering of e-spaces is a suitable focus for the study of computers and composition, neither of the other projects, which revolve around developing published pages (in the case of the home page) and studying teachers (in the case of the teaching project), is the "normal" focus of study for those who study computers and composition. Computers and composition is much more likely to study the writing of students and/or the happenings in a first-year writing classroom. Although it does include professional discourse in its study of networked communication, and there are some studies of first-year composition *teachers*, classrooms and students are its primary focus. Thus, our study will have to be justified (and tied to issues in computers and composition) as we speak or write about them. Ironically, though these projects could be cast as a study of writing in the workplace (home page project) and a study of worker enculturation (teacher/ing project), they would not automatically be seen as central to professional writing research either because (a) they are focused on technology as much as communication, (b) they are set in universities (usually thought to be in contrast with workplaces), or (c) at least one addresses teaching and teachers (and those who can, do, while those who can't, teach). Does this disciplinary road block mean that we will study the gendering of e-spaces because that topic is more acceptable (or even more central) to the field? We hope not. But we have to admit that the temptation to work with issues that are easier to explain to the discipline is a real one.

The act of narrating the contexts, origins, and relationships we see in these projects has not resulted in traditional research questions, but they do urge us to see the perimeters of our curiosity about electronic pages and help us establish focuses for the more general project. We are particularly interested in the fact that the departmental home page project is not as central to computers and composition as is the study of the ways our teachers learn to teach electronic pages (both their production and their use in research), and that neither is as acceptable as the gendering of web writing. The reduced field relevance of projects that involve us as professionals strikes us as odd, but it also shows our dual involvement in computers and writing and professional writing (because in professional writing the work of professionals is always relevant). If we tried to publish the research about the home page in computers and composition venues, we would not get published unless and until we convincingly explained why we did not focus on students' writing and how this work is relevant to the study of students' writing and learning to write with computers. Thus, a project that is helping us define the political

...es that can shape electronic pages is not, in our opinion, immediately connected to the published discussions of home pages—even though we think it key.

We are also becoming more keenly aware of what it means when we say "It is our job to build learning environments as well as to study them." That dual role, once recognized, lends a focus that is far more involved and aware, but the learning focus does not always meet tenure/promotion expectations for research. Hence, our emerging focus for this group of projects grows beyond that topical statement "producing electronic pages" to one that examines the continuities and contrasts between the community-building that is happening in our program and the specific electronic page projects we study.

Although we are involved in critiquing web pages and other online documents from other sources, we do not expect that we could be interested in a study of web pages that only performed a content analysis using text-based hermeneutic analysis (though we admit that the new media available through web pages lend verve to textual studies). This type of study—one that gathers web pages meeting certain criteria (e.g., all the opening pages for online writing centers), and then compares and contrasts their approaches to placement of prominent services, inclusion/exclusion of surfers, page design, and so on—could not yield the contextual information we think is needed to understand each site (the local jokes and hidden criteria that shape a page, the local space limits or other considerations that dictate media use, the local style requirements that constrain the page design, and so on). This data could contribute to a study, but could not yield a critical study in and of itself that would be interesting to us as we try to understand the interplay of physical and electronic community in the construction of electronic pages.

Neither would an isolated study of the development of one person's page necessarily yield contextual information about the motivations of the communication. The reason that the person was developing the electronic page is important to the process that made it and the attitudes and choices displayed. For example, the composition research class studying graduate students' home pages has proposed a number of general purposes displayed in those web pages: institutional (i.e., keeping up a page for a writing center or a student group), instructional (providing help for students who must develop home pages in their classes), class assignment (one given to them), personal (for fun and serious hobbies), blatant job hunting, though they recognize that there can be mixtures of purposes too. They have interviewed page owners, with one of their purposes to find out how the owners see their own pages, what motivated the pages, and to what extent they identify their work with the purposive typology that the class has advanced. We expect that their work will yield information about context and about the web identities sought by graduate students. But a study that watched a particular person's web page construction and focused on the decisions at a move-by-move level might not contextualize the process in ways that yield any information about the clash between local and electronic cultures.

The approaches we are taking, then, as a means to illuminating the local and electronic cultures, mix ethnographic, case study, and even teacher research approaches as we try to develop a sense of the cultures involved and the clashes they spark. We are assembling, through the use of informants, a multi-perspectival view of the community—with the perspectives of faculty, graduate students, undergraduate students, computing center staff, departmental administration, and college administration important to assembling that view. We are also assembling snapshots of the online personas of various participants and maps of physical and electronic space at different times. We are also developing some case studies of the development of electronic pages, with the development of the English Department's web page a key case in that it helps us to identify political issues from an institutional perspective that we think vitally important to an understanding of computers and composition. After all, the linkage to composition is a linkage to a group that has traditionally performed yeoman service to universities without gaining power or even status.

The ways that graduate students negotiate the tightrope of roles as teachers, students, new teachers, and colleagues—both off and online—is another case that interests us, though we are reluctant to ask them to participate, except as researchers. The institutional disputes are played out in a different way through the bodies of these people, and we hope that they are not too exploited by the extra time and learning that teaching with technology requires of them. There is always (we feel) a keen tension between what grduate students need to learn/know and what they are expected to do. Their normal teaching duties place considerable burden on them, and yet those normal duties don't always provide them with the experiences they need to be successful professionals. The difficulty they all face is in carving out the time necessary to do that "extra" stuff which is really not extra, because it is ultimately vital to their development. We try, insofar as possible, to position the extra stuff (e.g., technology development) within the realm of the normal (i.e., their normal teaching loads and coursework), but the bottom line is that graduate students have to work very hard to get it all done. The effort stresses their bodies, and ours.

In addition to these local cases of building a web community, we are also interested in electronic communities that are facilitated through these web pages. It is less clear how a web page participates in online community than it is how an electronic discussion participates in one (particularly a LISTSERV list for which the members can be identified). We can examine internal and external links as one way to think about community-building, and we can also look to sites that include interaction as another. But, our basic approach is through interviews as we talk with users of web pages and with owners of web pages. Our goal is to assemble a number of cases that participate in this general physical site (Purdue University between 1993 and 1997) and also link to electronic page construction and to online communities.

We have surfaced several critical issues in our narrative: First, our work does not immediately (or even easily) fit the categories for research in computers and composition or in professional writing, a fact that gives us a disciplinary wedge with which to examine our assumptions, our research questions, and our actions (i.e., in what ways are the two disciplinary interests shaping and disrupting our thinking about the project?). It also allows us to offer the work several names (Is it a study of producing home pages, or of teaching—and learning to teach and learning to teach new teachers—networked technology, or of building web communities?) as a way to highlight differing categorizations. Second, our work contains several voices that have differing goals, political interests, and institutional positionings. We certainly do not occupy the same institutional positions as our graduate or undergraduate students, nor do we have the same problems and goals. By including their views in the theorizing of issues related to community building in web space, we can highlight a multivocality that may lead to ways in which the voices in the process provide a diverse view of the project as well as critiquing each other. Third, our work values community building and learning to the extent that clashes between what we need to do as teachers and what we need to do as researchers could be sources of ethical dispute. Because we intend to put the good of our learning environment ahead of our research, we suspect that we will have trouble finding a standpoint that allows us to decide how to balance these differing goals. Yet we also see that it is in issues such as these that collaboration has its merits; that is, we hope that one of us will have a cooler head about problematic issues.

Since we haven't completed these projects, we have no easy conclusion to this chapter. We cannot point to the answer—the correct study is the one behind curtain number 2—or even satisfy our own curiosity about how this research will be told in conferences and written in journals. Perhaps that lack of closure reinforces the focus on emerging research that this chapter has sustained. As we promised, it's messy.

If we gain a "clearer" focus for our project through our investigation of the relationship of the fabric to the focus, why do we then need to invoke critical tactics such as those described in Chapter 7? Won't they destabilize our project just as we begin it—at a time when we must investigate the situations thoroughly, generating an immense amount of material, and needing to keep it in some kind of order? Won't they shake whatever confidence we have that we know what we are doing in these projects? Yes, there is danger in invoking critical tactics at the same time that you are trying to build a scaffolding for a study. There is always a danger of losing purpose, identity, or even your way. We cannot minimize that possibility, though we think that it is in this area that a community of researchers sustains the researchers who are questioning their way.

The difficult and, we think, rewarding activity of research is built around "rigorous" thinking—around painstakingly careful framing of projects, assembling and analyzing of data, and arguing interpretations. A critical research practices approach does not abandon the idea of "rigorous" or its instantiating criteria. Instead, it makes preordained criteria more difficult to accept without justification. Why? Because it blurs the rules and blunts the stability of criteria by exposing them as historical/discipline-based/political/gender-based/racial-based artifacts rather than as rules of nature aspiring to be timeless.

7

Enacting Critical Research Practices

Q: What did the subject say to the postmodern ethnographer?
A: "Can we talk about me for awhile?"

—David Shumway, as told to Patricia Harkin

As researchers, we act, always mindful of the multiple tensions impacting on and impacted by the actions we take. Thus, in this final chapter we focus on the kinds of tensions we want to expose by the actions taken during the research process as a way to discuss some of the key tactics of critical research practices. We offer this discussion of tensions and tactics as exemplary of the kind of doubling action needed in postmodern critical practices research.

Chapters 3, 4, and 5 have already examined three aspects of critical research practices that we contend are key to enacting this type of approach to research—making the practice of method critically aware (Chapter 3), mapping multiple frames that comprise a study in its distinct historical moments (Chapter 4), and articulating the political relationships and establishing the good of participants as an ethical goal (Chapter 5). Chapter 6 probed the impact of these approaches on research we are instigating. Because we want readers to end this book with some specific ideas of how to enact critical practices in the study of technology and writing, this chapter takes up several analytic tactics that we see as key to research of this type. We do not mean to suggest by this chapter's discussion that you need pay attention only to the tensions and tactics found herein, because methodological awareness, critical framing, and political/ethical goal setting are certainly overarching concerns that direct critical practices during research. But we do want to direct our discussion to specific critical moves that can occur at various points during a research project—hence the interplay of tensions and tactics.

EXPOSING TENSIONS IN OUR RESEARCH PRACTICES

Normally, the focuses of a study are culled from concepts, people, events, machines, or environments that for one reason or another capture our attention as researchers. When we are operating in scholarly mode, we don't just wander, we wander with a purpose—that is, noticing, observing, examining and theorizing some object we have in (or bring into) focus. In Chapter 6 particularly we have argued that the foci of our studies emerge over time and as a result of critical engagement with participants and events, rather than as responses to preset questions we have derived from theory and then must test empirically. These foci are constructed heuristically out of the interplay of tensions that drive and obstruct the processes of investigation. Some of the key tensions that researchers struggle with and must expose include:

- potential disciplinary tensions
- tensions in the environment
- tensions between ideal methods and realizable possibilities
- tensions between researchers and participants

Postmodern research already considers some of these tensions. Feminist methodology, for instance, insists on constructing narratives that give voice to participants as well as to researchers and on positioning researchers in the fabric of the research as their answers to exposing the tensions between researchers and participants. Postmodern geography examines the historical situatedness and ahistorical instability of its objects of study by mapping them in multiple ways (including across time periods). However, it is extremely difficult to find research that displays (and promotes) an awareness of all the components of critical research practices necessary for composition or computers and composition research in part because disciplinary tensions are rarely exposed. Perhaps not all of these tensions are equally important to every phase of a project; indeed, we have found, for instance, that we articulate global disciplinary frames at the start of a project and again during analysis and during our write-ups, but that we do not challenge those framings as we collect specific data (say, postings from a LISTSERV) or as we apply a coding scheme, unless we have problems (perhaps an uneasiness about the categories being used). But, we would argue, all of these tensions speak to important critical research practices, and we hope that more detailed discussions of these key tensions and tactics used to explore them will demonstrate their importance to critical research practice.

We link up tensions and tactics in this discussion because we have found that we conduct research often on the tactical level and because we see that the doubling of our attention on the tensions and the tactics allows an interplay that offers a critical space for negotiating both of them.

Disciplinary Tensions

The disciplinary framing of an interdisciplinary enterprise—such as the study of writing and technology—is not straightforward, nor is it stable. Composition itself acknowledges that it naturally crosses disciplines (see Gere, 1993; Lauer, 1984), with computers and composition seeming—by its very name—to acknowledge computers to be at least alongside and perhaps outside this multidiscipline. Further, when studying writing that transpires in workplace settings, computers and composition intersects with workplace writing research in professional writing, which itself is connected in complex ways to composition and to English (see Sullivan & Porter, 1993b). When studying how well people can use interfaces, computers and composition intersects with technical communication, computer science, sociology, information science, and human factors (itself an interdisciplinary field). But these intersections presuppose original disciplinary framings that differ; they suggest that someone in computers and composition who is studying an interface does so for a different reason than someone in human factors who is studying that same interface. And, indeed, there is evidence that such a difference exists. Sullivan (1989b), for example, articulated the different approaches taken toward the study of word processing by computers and composition and by human factors. The two groups, while studying ostensibly the same phenomenon (learning to write using word-processing software), had such different framings of that phenomenon that their findings were not very transportable to the other group's issues. Nor did either group have much interest in the other (as is evident by the lack of cross-quoting and a minimum of shared conference presentations).

Methodological Framework Mapping

As we pointed out in Chapter 4 (Figure 4.5 depicts the concentration of research along the axes of classroom to workplace and technology-poor to technology-rich environments), there are distinctly differing foci among the ways that these groups approach the study of technology and writing. Neither composition studies nor professional writing singles out technology as an object of study very often. When Sullivan and Jennie Dautermann (1996), for example, contacted workplace writing researchers about contributing to a collection on computers and writing in the workplace, many prominent researchers said that they do not study the use of computers for writing in the workplaces they enter (even though so admitted that most of their nonexecutive participants use computers when they write). Even though the computer is used by almost all of the professionals studied, it is invisible to many professional writing researchers. We think this is true because professional writing for the most part views the computer either as office equipment (e.g., calculator, filing cabinet, or phone) or as an innocent tool that operates as pen and paper or typewriters do (this is the case despite Joanne Yates's, 1989, historical work connecting the typewriter and other office technologies to changes in U.S. management philosophy). It's almost as if the computer's impact is muted or even eliminated for workplace researchers because everyone uses computers—as if it is a variable that can be ignored because it is distributed equally across the population.

By contrast with research in professional writing, the computers and composition literature has two overarching foci for studies of writing technology that are derived from its title: The use and development of technology for communication/ writing, and the ways writers and their societies employ (and learn to employ) technology in the service of that writing. This literature, by and large, is also focused on studies of writing technology in the first-year (computer) classroom.

A further contrast comes from the fact that neither composition studies nor professional writing claims technology as a main focus of its literature. Composition focuses on first-year composition instruction in college—theorizing and pedagogizing writers and their societies and the teaching and learning of writing. Professional writing focuses on writers at work and on writing classes (usually junior- and senior-level classes) that aim to prepare college students to write in various professional settings. Its theory/research takes place in workplaces and is adapted/evaluated in classrooms.

Thus, as we think about the study of technology and writing as it is conducted in composition, computers and composition, and professional writing, we find that unless we include computers and composition and professional writing as subgroups within composition—which actually makes the discussion hopelessly murky—the question of disciplinary focus vis-à-vis technology is indeed complex and in flux.

Murky or not, the disciplinary framing of the relationships for a study is/can be/ought to be addressed by each study. We have found that it is easier to conceptualize through a map such as the one shown by Figure 4.5, but we also think that multiple binaries could be used to tease out disciplinary framing, as could the analysis of assumptions. We also find considerable evidence that such framing is at least attempted by researchers as they write the introductions and accounts of previous research. Janice Lauer and Sullivan (1993) offer one example of how this framing works as they examine how three professional writing studies try to establish the validity and reliability of their efforts. In these studies, a major way that the authors seek to establish validity is by constructing the issues and researchers with whom they agree and disagree. By choosing a particular constellation of issues and formulating the issues as they do, authors declare theoretical loyalties—for example, "I want my research to be thought of as cognitive research on planning," or as "social processes research on planning," or as "cultural constructions that block planning." By allying themselves with some researchers (or positions) and arguing with or omitting other researchers (or positions), authors also disclose the disciplinary framing they aim to invoke as they write. Although these framings are the ones the researchers settle on when they publish the work and do not necessarily reflect initial or intermediate framings that accompanied the research process (careful tracings of the frames across the history of a project are usually found only in dissertations), these framings do announce a disciplinary framing for the work.

Multiple Binaries

Another tactic useful to the articulation of disciplinary tensions is multiple binaries. Binaries certainly unite and divide the study of writing technologies at various times and in multiple ways. A central feature of discourse in computers and composition is its movement on a pendulum between technological optimism and technological critique. We divide, for example, theoretical approaches to technology into instrumentalist and substantive perspectives as we aim to move toward critical perspectives (Feenberg, 1991). We approach innovation in technology and education as innovation-focused (positive) and social system–focused (negative) (Bruce, 1993). We see systems as stand-alone or networked, as command-based (CLI) or graphic-based (GUI). We see machines as geared for real work (technically-oriented) or for play (end-user-oriented). Documentation, too, is system-oriented or user-oriented, expert-oriented or end-user-oriented, technical or nontechnical.

The urge to divide an issue into two positions—pro and con, the classic "us vs. them"—is difficult to fight as it is lodged in Western cultural traditions of analysis. Kenneth Burke (1969) views division—along with its counterpart, identification—as an inevitable feature of rhetorical action (Porter, 1990); dividing is implicit in the rhetorical situation. One exorcism may be found through the move of constructing as many binaries as you can in an effort to give a more complex contour to your position. At least that activity works for us. Though we usually would prefer to claim that we do not fall prey to the problem of creating binaries (be they true or false), actually we do. What, for example, is this discussion of evoking tensions but an exercising of multiple binaries? Indeed, we have found binaries addictive, as they are sewn into the fabric of most discourse theory (e.g., syntagmatic/paradigmatic, competence/performance, nature/nurture, skill/talent, private/public). Our institutional and theoretical problems with a prominent binary—theory-practice—actually began the collaborative work that this book partakes in (see Sullivan & Porter, 1993a). Thus, it seems a more reasonable approach to admit to one's sins: Acknowledge binaries as a theorizing tactic, and take a position that uses multiple binaries in order to frame a more complex view.

Of course, the use of multiple binaries is not without its dangers. Feminists often point out the dangers of binary thinking (Evelyn Fox Keller, 1985, 1992, is eminent in this discussion). Gillian Rose (1993), for example, attacks disciplinary thinking in geography for its use of binary oppositions, whereby geographic knowledge is:

> Organized through a stable term against which other terms are contrasted. This structure is homologous with the masculine subject's identification of himself as the centre against all non-masculine Others....Both the repression of and a fascination with its Other constitute the masculinism of geography. (pp. 65–66)

Rose goes on to argue that feminists cannot simply invert the binary oppositions created by a masculinist geography as a corrective to that view, because such a move accepts the masculinist target terms as "normal" even while they reinscribe an inversion of them. Instead, Rose argues that binary oppositions have to be seen as "warnings about a potential complicity with the structures of domination that feminists seek to overcome" (p. 66). She takes aim at those binary poles (of masculine same and non-masculine other) by oscillating between them, offering challenges wherever one lands, and thus breaking down the authority of those binary poles.

In *Feminism and Geography,* Rose enacts this tactic as she offers a list of multiple binaries used in several masculinist portrayals she is critiquing.

time-geography	-	humanistic geography
public	-	private
transparent	-	opaque
social	-	body
knowledge	-	maternity
rational	-	emotional
space	-	place (p. 75)

She argues that listing binaries of this type is reinforcing (and perhaps reinscribing) the masculinist view of disciplinary knowledge as moving between self and other, and we do see the problem. Instead, Rose wants to use a complex oscillation between the dual poles in ways that displace the dualism. She offers multiply constructed others that do not allow the debate to be framed as between two, using the work of Teresa de Lauretis (1987) and others who challenge dualism, and then offering a paradoxical approach that establishes a position that oscillates in such a way to place women at margins and more centrally.

Victor Vitanza (1991, 1994), too, challenges simplistic binary thinking (which insists on the One truth and ignores the Other) at the same time as he stands against deconstructive binary thinking that merely flips the terms of the binary, pointing to the one truth and saying "two." Vitanza argues for the ethical importance of a third place, which he counts as "some more." The third place is constructed out of a move of affirmative deconstruction which entails a playful and farcical resisting and disrupting of attempts to solidify, stabilize, homogenize, and systematize rhetorics (or, we would guess, methodologies generally): "It attempts, instead, infinite 'radical heterogeneities and parataxes'" (1991, p. 133). We doubt that Vitanza would approve of this systematized operation.

Yet, despite the criticisms of the use of binaries mounted by Rose, Vitanza, and others, we also see in the example Rose provides (and the critiques she mounts in her work) that by positioning the binaries found in geographic texts in the way she does above, she exposes problematic assumptions of geographic knowledge. She uses this listing of multiple binaries to align the sides as they are "normally" drawn, then points out the problematic views of geography that flow from such an alignment, as her way of fashioning a critique of the same-other constellation in geographic writing. Thus, Rose participates in using the tactic of multiple binaries; indeed she teaches us one way to exploit that tactic.

Applied to the study of technology and writing, we might use multiple binaries to explore potential disciplinary tensions by aligning assumptions about the usefulness of technology argued by those optimistic about technology's usefulness in counterpoint to those engaging in technological critique. To destabilize the dualism of those binaries we might also chart how those binaries are configured differently by different researchers or research communities. We might also construct and explore the binaries that uphold scientific/technical vs. traditional humanities positions, theory vs. practice positions, leading edge (technology) vs. backwater (technology) views, or even masculine vs. feminine conceptions of technology. By offering multiple constructions we would be less likely to be unreflective about the disciplinary assumptions underlying our study. The strength in articulating research foci using multiple binaries, as David Sibley (1995) has suggested in his study of boundaries, lies with articulating and investigating the ambiguities suggested through these multiple views. Careful considerations of how a problem has been/could be placed onto the binary poles that turn our intellectual disputes may help us to unmask the hidden assumptions that underlie our deeper intellectual desires. Once unmasked, these hidden assumptions are more open to critical examination.

Tensions in the Environment

Computer environments, most particularly the online ones, we think, invite several types of tensions. The first is for researchers who began their research into the ways of the classroom or the workplace in less computerized times. Those researchers who have studied traditional classroom environments—to focus our discussion on one type of environment we research—need to make as radical a set of adjustments when they study computer classrooms as do teachers comfortable in traditional classrooms when their writing classes move to computerized classrooms. Instead of being able to listen to (and note or tape) a verbal classroom discourse taking place between teacher and student or, occasionally, among several students (and place it in a frame of discourse—say, Courtney Cazden's, 1988, initiation-response-evaluation framework), these researchers have to include in their possible dialogs an electronic discourse that is silent and is also not the same for each student in the room (e.g., in a session dealing with email all students will not be reading the same texts at their screens) and a classroom that is not always attentive to the instructor's every word. No longer is the teacher automatically the center of classroom talk. Instead of being able to videotape the classroom from a stationary camera, these researchers have to choose a group to videotape, try to include their screens (notoriously hard to do because of the flicker in old or cheap monitors), and hope not to miss critical information; the focus for the camera's eye is not so clearly directed as it is in traditional classrooms. And those are only a few of the considerations.

Computer environments also participate in tensions highlighted by the contrast between ideal technological conditions and the here and now of computer equipment. Often technology in a particular research situation is at odds with our more idealized notions of technology and its operation—in part because of the ways in which a particular site mixes its equipment, physical space, cultures, and curriculum; in part because of the people who encounter and inhabit that site. A sumptuous computing facility with fabulous machines and ample computer classrooms does not necessarily yield cutting-edge use of that facility. Perhaps those who run the facility are invested in keeping it clean and protected at the cost of access, playfulness, or even open hours outside of class time.

We could go on, as we see tensions between the technologies and the particular research situation as quite openly important and including such considerations as:

- The remade place: How is a classroom, a workplace, a scholarly group made more complex by its computer technology?
- The remade events: How does observation of the events shift when a computer is a component of the environment for at least some of the events? (e.g., how do you watch group behavior when part of that behavior includes using the computer for drafting or for contacting others outside the room for comments about a problem?)
- the remade teacher-student (or boss-worker) positioning: How does authority flow in a computer classroom when there is no dominant teacher position and students are as likely to face their monitors (TV screens?) as to find and face the teacher? How does authority flow in an electronic discussion about a work problem when messages tread over other messages, ideas get misattributed, and mention of one's hierarchical position within the institution (or organization) may not be sufficient to ensure obedience of those at a lower position in the hierarchy?
- The remade data collection/storage capabilities: How do you deal with the possibilities of increased data collection through history programs (that cap-

ture keystrokes), text analysis programs (that are easy to use because your students submit electronic copies of their work), archives (that save the postings from electronic discussions), sign-on surveys for web sites (that ask questions of all visitors), and so on? Does the increase in easy-to-collect data result in better analysis, or more confusion?

Technology and writing research focuses at various times on the various relationships among places, writers, readers, texts, and institutions. Often it proceeds from the assumption that all of these relationships occur inside a framework that accepts technology as an inevitable part of writing (for good or ill).

If we historically examine the literature surrounding emerging technologies, we find optimism, followed by criticism, followed by a dénouement of direct discussion (unless the technology continues to be evolving and in some way remaining new). Take the first wave of research in computers and composition as an example: In the early 1980s, when line editors were the norm and word-processing software was being introduced, considerable enthusiasm accompanied the discussions of its use by writers and in classes. Often this research tried to show the ways in which teaching/learning/writing with word processing software was superior to pen- and paper-composition. The questions the research posed seem obvious to those of us who remember the political struggle to get computers accepted for writing classes (and not to be regarded a waste of class time): In what ways does writing on a word processor facilitate the teaching of writing? As has been argued elsewhere (Kaplan, 1991; Sullivan, 1991), the political climate was such that proponents of computers for the teaching of writing did not want to claim that computers changed the writing process; rather they claimed that these machines provided programs that remediated problems through drill and practice and word-processing software, a tool that facilitated writing. Thus, institutional and political relationships were backgrounded in this early research. While it was clear that the research intended to justify buying computer labs and using computers to teach writing, the focal questions did not address the politics of access in relationship to class (or other such concerns). Instead the focal questions were those about student writers, word-processing software, written texts, and (sometimes) composing processes (Hawisher, 1989).

Obviously, those early research issues have changed, as has the disciplinary focus of research. Articles such as Joel Nydahl's (1991) expose the ways in which the field's thinking has shifted to bring about the dénouement of research into word processing and the learning of writing, even though word-processing tasks continue to be important in computerized composition classrooms. New technology, in part, urges us to research new issues, or at least new technology. Computers and composition's fascination with the new certainly reshuffles the relationships among the objects of study; the study of how one student interacts with an interface may quickly be replaced with studies of how groups of students interact in an environment, just to name one example. What is just as important to critical practices in a particular study, and to this discussion, however, is keeping track of (and being critical about) changes in the relationships between these typical objects *inside* a particular study. We are interested, here, in the tensions in the relationships of the objects of study in specific research.

Research Scene Mapping

The environment is constructed as much as it is accepted, even in a particular study. A key to that construction is the relationships established/sought among these components of place, writers, readers, texts, and institutions. We can use research scene mapping (see Chapter 4 for a detailed example of this tactic) to demonstrate what we mean. Take the study of teachers in computers and composition: There is none. While many in composition are busy researching writing, classroom activities, and students, few are engaged in the study of teachers of writing (though there is a strong anecdotal literature about training teachers for first-year composition). In a sense this is understandable; after all, we are teachers and also researchers—our problems and approaches are inextricably linked with our experiences with teaching. Yet we seldom study ourselves. Why not? There are various alternatives: We may not study teachers because they are ourselves and we have been socialized feminine (our work in teaching writing is skill work, foundational, personal/not public, and therefore not worthy of public funds or discussion), or because we have focused on students (they are more interesting to us), or because we just run out of time (there is so much to know about the students that we cannot indulge ourselves)—and not many of the alternatives are pleasant. Most of the reasons we can spin are related to diminished status, self-confidence, or self-awareness. Yet our lack of focus on teachers might result in a dangerous situation: What if we cannot understand some aspects of our students' actions because our published depictions of them are drawn (unconsciously or unreflectively) using a teacher's eye?

The blind spot about teachers is not total within computers and composition. But if you view the discussion of teachers, you find a number of articles on teacher preparation (Holdstein, 1989; Kiefer, 1991; Selfe, 1992) but little direct study of teachers in computer classes (Sullivan, 1995). Indeed, in *Literacy and Computers: The Complications of Teaching and Learning with Technology,* which Cynthia Selfe and Susan Hilligoss edited in 1994, there is talk of teaching, but there is no direct examination of teachers. Teachers are present, but they are not often foregrounded. Although we have several recent studies of teachers at Amherst—one of new teachers' responses to teaching in a networked class (Klem & Moran, 1992), another investigating online voice in a group of teachers (Carbone, et al., 1993), and a third of teachers' responses to technological change (Klem & Moran, 1995)—this research is most startling for the fact that it is the only group of articles that studies teachers in computer classrooms. We hardly have a prolonged consideration of teachers; indeed, we have just begun.

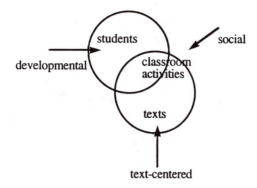

FIGURE 7.1.   Typical filters for composition classroom research.

But, returning to our example about the construction of scene maps, if we begin to position a study of teachers in computer classes using lenses typically invoked by classroom-oriented studies of writing, we are likely to start with the study of writing classes in composition (see Figure 7.1). Most studies focus on particular issues related to students, classrooms, and/or texts, using a theoretical approach to the observation (which we label *filters* in this discussion because the research and theory establishing this concept also give the approach a focus that directs the researcher's gaze). For example, researchers who are interested in how students learn to write often will study the developmental dimensions of what is happening in a classroom, and they may even take students out of a class setting. Researchers interested in the quality of texts normally focus more on the texts produced than on the classroom activities or even the students themselves. Researchers interested in classroom activities often are trying to chart the social impact of a curriculum, and thus they pay attention to what happens in the classroom and sometimes to texts as measures of success, or to students' opinions as measures of success.

When an awareness of teachers is added to the depiction of classroom relationships, the possibilities for study expand. Certainly those who are teachers doing research (teachers as researchers) filter their studies of classroom activities through their roles as teachers and foreground that connection, even if they are not particularly critical about their positioning as teachers within an institutional setting or about the status of the knowledge they produce within a disciplinary setting. (Note: Marilyn Cochran-Smith and Susan Lytle, 1993, sidestep the disciplinary debate as they argue that teacher research produces a different kind of knowledge than does academic research about teachers.) But any of the filters, regardless of their focus, will draw a more complex portrait of a class when the consideration of teachers is added to the mix, as Figure 7.2 shows.

If you think Figure 7.2 is complex enough to account for all of the popular filterings found in the study of writing classes, think again. The filters shown do not

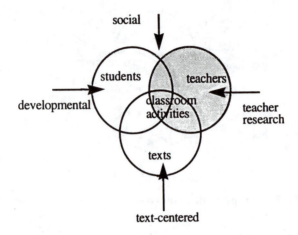

FIGURE 7.2.   Complexity added by considering teachers.

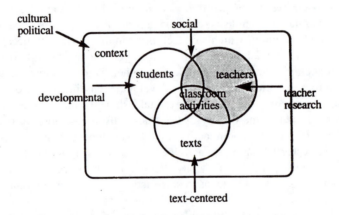

FIGURE 7.3.   Complexity added by considering context.

yet address contextual framings of the class that are focal to the study; that is, Figure 7.2 lacks a framing filter. Typically in composition, those who are interested in context focus their view on or through culture and/or politics and/or history and foreground the fabric surrounding the class, as is shown in Figure 7.3.

Though certainly complex enough to show the variety of focuses available for study in a composition classroom, and to give us yet another reason why teachers are not often the focus of those studies, Figure 7.3 has not yet managed to include another key element (at least key for our interests): Where are the computers?

To make focal that this classroom is a networked one, we add even more potential complexity to our mapping of potential filters to the study of a writing

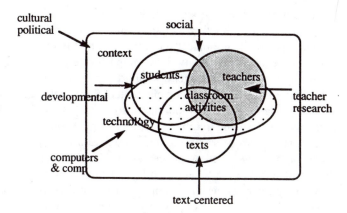

FIGURE 7.4. **Complexity added by considering technology and foregrounding teachers.**

classroom, as Figure 7.4 does. In fact, this diagram shows the reasons that studies holding complex views of the networked class are so difficult to enact and so important to our thinking. The technology can be depicted as intersecting with these other relationships, because for the most part it does. Further, if we view activities in that classroom through the filters of both technology and teachers (because we are researching teachers in computer classrooms), we find that important questions surface, such as those about contested authority (students may wonder "Whom do I believe—the teacher or the television?"; teachers may wonder "How do I cover all the skills required by the composition director and also teach my understanding of the nature of writing?"; and so on) or about ethical curricular disputes (composition directors who believe in teaching writing online may not have the equipment they are convinced the students need and may be unable to obtain it; teachers may be convinced that a standard curriculum for teaching email does damage to students' understanding of how email will work at work; and so on).

Also foregrounded are potential clashes between teachers' abilities and experiences with particular technologies, or between teacher and student knowledges of technologies, or between changes to curriculum that are made to match the technology and the impact the new pedagogy has on classroom activities—just to name a few possibilities.

This final mapping shows why foregrounding teachers in networked computer classrooms can become a messy business. Context, students, classroom activities, texts, and technology all have the ability to complicate or obscure our understanding of the teachers, their issues, their needs, and their contributions. But the notion of "final mapping" bothers us. We do not see Figure 7.4 as the answer to this question: How do you configure the relationships in a study of computerized writing classes that features teachers? It still is talking generally and directing us to consider context rather than interacting with the cultures and conventions of a particular site. In other words, the notion of "environment" is still too general. It also puts the placement of teachers in that environment in perspective. Other mappings of these relationships might add teachers' support systems (which certainly is important to the Amherst studies) as a main element, or they might see classrooms as a main element (particularly if it is important to contrast classrooms using computer technology with those using traditional settings), or they might deemphasize some of the key channels from traditional classroom research shown in Figure 7.1. The teacher might be depicted as the center, her/his own panopticon of the electronic writing experience that oversees all other (and smaller) entities. The possibilities are many for reseeing this mapping; it is not final or in some way immutable. It is merely a tactic used in this case to clarify environmental components and to establish your view of their relationships in the study under way.

Metaphor Analysis

Metaphor analysis is another tactic we might use to expose tensions in the environment we construct for a study (see Table 7.1 for a heuristic to use). A favorite tactic in cultural studies analysis of popular cultural icons, metaphor analysis as we consider it is a critical activity rather than a descriptive or imaginative one. Cynthia Selfe and Richard Selfe provide an example of metaphoric critique in their assessment of the Macintosh interface (1994), and Cynthia Selfe's (1996) discussion of gender in advertisements for technology adds another—if somewhat different—example. Selfe and Selfe, as we discussed in Chapter 5, examined the ways in which the desktop metaphor guides the look and feel of the GUI interface for Macintosh OS, from a perspective that interrogates the deployment of power. They focused on unmasking metaphors that at first glance may appear innocent but that actually require the successful user to adopt the "values of white, male, middle- and upper-class professionals" (p. 487). And to the extent that they could raise consciousness about the metaphoric nature of that interface, Selfe and Selfe were able to open up an aspect of the computing environment to critical appraisal.

Selfe, in her 1996 discussion of advertisements, looked to popular metaphors, asking, "What kinds of metaphoric messages do technology companies think will sell computers?" and finding out that the 1950s-style *Leave It to Beaver* family huddled around their new television was a popular metaphoric connection, as was the standard image of a beautiful woman, and the futuristic cyber warrior. Women, according to Selfe, were objectified and/or marginalized in these attempts to project the kinds of technological self-images that might urge a customer to buy. In both discussions the authors aim to show how the ordinary, and seemingly innocent, can use metaphor to shape the scene.

Certainly, there are many technology metaphors at large. Even in this book we can recall connecting television screens with computer screens, hypertext with books, email with conversation, and people with users and inhabitants. But this

TABLE 7.1. Metaphor Analysis

System Metaphor	Participants' Metaphor	Researcher's Metaphor	Tensions Across Metaphors & Breakdowns

metaphorizing can be invoked in differing ways by different groups. The Internet, for example, is often called the information highway, and we have also heard it referred to as a town hall. But feminists also see it as a dark alley populated by lurking (and potentially violent) males, and we can imagine people of color characterizing it as a whites-only country club. Such metaphoric clashes, particularly when they are abutted against one another, show how perspective can adjust the metaphor used as well as the attitude taken toward that metaphor, and this clash is what makes metaphor analysis helpful to critical practices research.

The tactical task of metaphor analysis, then, is to probe the uses of metaphor—both those comments that characterize the metaphor for a particular person or group and the clashes of metaphor that might occur across the various perspectives vis-à-vis the environment under scrutiny.

Tensions Between Ideal Methods and Realizable Possibilities

What about the tensions surrounding methods that unfold as the study develops? (a) You may need racial diversity in your study of online discussion, and you may secure African-American participants but then find that several must quit the discussion because of other commitments, equipment problems, and other reasons. What do you do? Is the study not viable anymore? Or (b) You may plan to study a group's use of networked discussion over the course of a year. During the first semester no major problems arise, but in the second semester a new teacher for this group is not as computer-interested as the first-semester teacher and does not make networked discussion central to the class. What are your alternatives? Or (c) You may be studying online communication in a company and two of your best participants are downsized out of their jobs while several less productive participants are kept. You have lost participants and also have critical comments to make to/about the company that approved your research. How do you handle it? All working writing researchers know this problem. The "realizable possibilities" of a study do not match your planned methods. But in what ways do they chafe against the "ideal" methods you outlined at the start, in what ways do they open up new possible insights, and in what ways do your possibilities move you too far from the information you needed to conduct the study you intended to conduct?

Further, how do the "realities" occurring during the process challenge your research ethics?

Experienced researchers realize that problems such as these typically happen in studies and that researchers need to be prepared to argue for the continued viability of the methods after adjustments have been made to smooth out the design problems. Such maneuvering is to be expected and can be approached pragmatically. But what if these occasions are also seen as sites of critical as well as pragmatic deliberation? What if you saw the mismatch of planned methods and realizable possibilities as related more to serendipity or kairos or timely opportunity than to the inevitable data-gathering dilemmas discussed in methods classes? What if the mismatch is seen as inevitable, as related to the emergence of the focus of your research? Such are the tensions we seek to articulate and examine.

Assumption Analysis

Assumption analysis can be used to help clarify these emerging tensions between planned methods and lived experience. As you realize there are problems with how the study's methods are unfolding, you can chart the differences between what you expected to be able to do and what you are actually able to accomplish in order to articulate the gaps between planned and lived research (see Table 7.2 for a heuristic to use). These mismatches may be minor glitches that you decide to ignore, but they may also challenge the integrity of the fabric of your study, and as such, are ignored at your peril. Regardless of the outcome, examining the mismatches between your planned methods and what you actually can (and do) do is key to enacting certain critical practices—most obviously the charge to involve participants in the making of a study.

Analyzing your working assumptions and procedures as they are challenged by the realizable possibilities of the study can lead to a number of plausible resolutions: abandon the study (if the problems are so extreme as to make it difficult to continue—though we rarely find researchers who abandon research for this reason); realize these assumptions should be changed (also rarely done because assumptions are tied to theory and belief); change the course of your actions; accept the mismatches as not problematic enough to cause serious rumination or change (obviously not our favorite choice, and reporting conventions' bare cover-

TABLE 7.2.   Assumption Analysis

Goals/assumptions/ procedures of the planned method	Goals/assumptions/ procedures that can be used in this study	Goals/assumptions/ procedures that I am using	Mismatches	How I resolve (or don't resolve) mismatches I find problematic

age of process makes it difficult to know how popular this option really is); or accept the mismatches and qualify some aspects of the study. Suppose that in your study of online discussion, to expand a bit on one example, you begin with the expectations that you can unravel the dynamics of race in online discussions. You secure participation from a number of racial and ethnic groups, and you interview all the participants online before staging an online discussion, only to find that your online discussion records little participation by anyone but Caucasians. What are your options? You can hardly focus on textual analysis of the interaction online; there is little interaction. You do have information from interviews, so you could say, "My interest was in the dynamics of problematic interaction because I assumed that there would be interaction and that interaction would have problems; perhaps there is only silence or silencing." Such a reframing would send you to gather more information about silencing and would push you to find out why those who are not white did not participate in the online discussion, and how many of those who are white did not participate, and so on. The data collection would take a turn toward a focus on understanding nonparticipation in online discussions. The ways in which this new approach was a mismatch with the previous approach would need to be explored and explained.

This process, and the resolutions you reach through it, strengthens your research process in at least two ways: First, it helps you defend the integrity of your method from critics who claim that you have not documented your research process. Not only have you described this process, as most genres of reporting require, but you have also documented the reasons why you made (or did not make) the changes you report. Second, it gives you a systematic way to evolve methods (and even new focuses) while the study is in progress. Mark Constas (1992) has argued that the origins of coding schemes for qualitative research in education need to be documented and rationalized in systematic fashion in order to support claims of rigor and to trace how insights evolved out of data. We think assumption analysis can function analogously to rationalize the evolution of methodological insights.

Tensions between Researchers and Participants

One of the more talked about tensions is between researchers and participants in that research. We are used to researchers (and their research write-ups) positioning their participants in multiple ways as a condition of analysis. This is a central marker of researchers' power over participants in a study; that is, researchers' freedom to "position" participants in a study allows researchers to in some ways own them (notice that we refer, in the previous sentence, to "their" participants). Routinely, researchers sort participants during analysis by professional roles (teacher, administrator, student, parent), by gender (biological or preference), by ability level (high/middle/low, expert/novice, advanced/basic), by race (majority/minority, ethnicity), by socioeconomic status (poor/working class/middle class/

upper middle class), by theological practice (church-goer/non-church-goer), by political affiliation (liberal/conservative, democrat/republican/third party), and so on.

These sortings that "discriminate" among the participants' data are culled to be factors or variables in explanations that are developed as findings or positions. In a sense, analysis seeks to search through the potential multiple positionings of participants and to select the proper positioning lens for the community to use as it tries to make sense out of the events presented. But as researchers, we seldom report the positionings of participants that were not chosen, nor do we usually explain why our approach to understanding the data is better than the approaches not chosen. (Note: This is less true of quantitative studies that report statistical analyses that were not significant.) When we construct our analysis as a story, we closet the other stories in the data that we decided not to tell—and we certainly do not allow the participants to choose how they are depicted in those stories. Even when we include participants' words in our written accounts, it is usually our decision to quote, what to quote, and how to discuss the quoted words of partici-pants. Our participants can only protect themselves by not agreeing to be quoted.

We are less used to researchers' positioning themselves in more than a per-functory manner vis-à-vis the study they are presenting. Although feminist meth-odologists require such positioning and, indeed, most qualitative methodology supports such disclosure, researchers are wary—justifiably, we think—of describing themselves or their motivations in less than flattering light. Will a jour-nal accept for publication an article on differences in male and female involve-ment in computing when the author admits that the source of that work is her religious beliefs that men have certain intelligences that make them computation-ally superior? or even, less volatilely, if the author generally credits her religious beliefs as a source of motivation? Further, how much disclosure equals overdis-closure? When do personal disclosures bore readers, constituting a form of exces-sive self-absorption? We think that every researcher suspects there are certain disclosures that cannot be made, and perhaps many think it is better not to exam-ine one's reasoning and motivation too closely. We cannot deny that self-exami-nation and disclosure is a potentially painful process, nor can we avoid the fact that such discussion, unskillfully done, threatens the dissemination of research. Nor can we gloss over the fact that the process is potentially exacerbated by meth-odological differences. Current critical and postmodern urges for researchers to bridge the gap between themselves and participants, to esteem participants, and to disclose themselves to participants and readers in order to situate their work are at odds with traditional urges for researchers to distance themselves from the research situation, the subjects, and the events to be observed (and analyzed) in order to achieve impartiality, critical distance, and/or rigorous analysis.

These points—namely, the power of researchers over participants and the need for critical researchers to take self-reflexive positions within their studies—are at the crux of the tensions between researchers and participants.

Competing Narratives

One technique for exposing the tensions between researchers and participants can be competing narratives, in part because narrative is used so frequently in computers and composition. Stories of technology experiences have been important in technology and writing as a way of describing a new technology and/or its uses in teaching writing. If a technology is new, then few have seen or used it as yet in the writing classroom. How do you evaluate an emerging technology's usefulness when few people have a clear sense of what it looks like, how it operates, and what impact it has on the pedagogy of writing instruction? You may be able to demonstrate the technology with an overhead or video, but the pedagogical impact is more subtle and difficult to discuss. A story of how X worked in the classroom helps listeners/readers to catch on to how X operates. It helps them envision how the technology may (or may not) work for them. Thus, the new technology narrative has played a particularly key role in discussions of technology and writing. A particularly memorable early story—say, the mid-1980s' story of Lucy, the disabled bulletin board participant who was found out to be a middle-aged male psychotherapist—can shape years of discussion and research on an emerging technology or on a particular issue attending it—just as Lucy's story has.

If the stories that dominate the public discourse about a technology or its use are unrelentingly positive, that may signal a wave of revisionism on the way. People who have had negative experiences may package their experiences in competing stories and may peddle the "rest of the story" to the public.

We think that this natural use of storytelling in computers and composition is good. By now, you can probably guess "how" we want to change the practice, though: Instead of advocating only one story as capturing a phenomenon, we suggest that multiple competing stories be collected and developed as a way of keeping the conflicts alive. These stories can be real or constructed. If, for example, we were collecting multiple narratives about teacher authority, we might include the bulletin board story above as a technological whammy or as a story about the trials of new women teachers. But instead of settling there, we would look for other stories about those issues, or, if none are forthcoming, consider what-ifs: What if the teacher were a man? What if the teacher responded differently to the post? What if the students were technologically sophisticated? and so on. Multiple narratives can help you put off reduction to a simple story and can help you sharpen the points that particular stories make.

Thus, those who are speaking or writing about an innovative technology or an innovative use of technology are apt to use stories as a way to relate that new technology to the broader practices of teaching. This is particularly helpful (a) if readers do not have the technology in question, and the stories model how those new technologies operate; or (b) if readers do not have much experience teaching in computer classrooms, and the stories give them expectations of what might happen. But these narratives are seldom used as a voice that competes with the narrator. Even in his famous triptych of oppression stories, Joseph Janangelo (1991) presents single-voiced narratives that generally work to make the points he intends, even though the narratives compete with each other and with the general points that they are challenging about the egalitarian effects of technology.

We think the competition needs to be more pointed. Take a local example to illustrate: A story we use frequently at Purdue is the one of a new teacher in a computer classroom who is teaching her students to post to a USENET group for a class assignment. She posts a message herself that recommends they comment on something they have in common, say, stories in the student newspaper. But before any of the students can learn to post, a flame comes online from someone else in the university who noticed the teacher's post. That flame derides and belittles the teacher for suggesting that the student newspaper contains anything worthy of comment, shocks the students, and results in the students' refusal to post to the bulletin board. Because the teacher had planned to use this technology rather than email, the loss minimizes the class's participation in electronically held discussion. We use this story in various ways: tell it to new teachers; use it to assert (a pedagogical) authority over the campus computing center (they had bullied the teacher into using bulletin boards rather than email out of a concern for economizing on disk space); relate it in conference papers (often to complain about poor teacher training or to show how female teachers get intimidated by the system); and mention it in dissertations (Takayoshi, 1994b).

The story is not just one narrative, as its morals and focuses change according to the situations of its use. Yet if we take all of its uses into account, we see that it functions to discuss authority and the ways in which it gets constructed differently in networked classrooms. Although most who use it intend it to make one point or another about the relationships among teachers and students in networked classes—indeed, they find that the story gives voice to the vulnerability of a teacher's authority, especially when that teacher is new to using technology—we think the story lends itself to the multiple voices of new teacher who is unsettled, students who are uncertain, outsiders who are terrorists, an institution that is at best insensitive and at worst malicious about setting up new teachers, and disciplinary overseers (of the new teachers' mentors or bosses) who are not paying attention to the risks of use. Those voices are connected with the event; others are added as the story gets retold across the staff. Each voice can give us a slightly different story, and to develop one narrative suppresses the richer story. At the same time, to tell the richer stories allows the dissonances between teacher and students, teacher and other teachers, teacher and bosses, teacher and administration to show. Such tensions drive research.

Advocacy Charting

Another tactic that can be useful in exploring the tensions between researchers and participants is advocacy charting (see Table 7.3). Advocacy charting assumes that at least two sides are in contest over resources, or other kinds of power, and that a depiction of the positions and actions taken by researchers over the course of the research project helps the researchers to assess the impact of actions taken during the study. (See Table 5.3 for discussion.) The work of advocacy charting, from the perspective of understanding researcher-researched relationships, is organizing and reflecting on:

- For the researcher: the process of articulating the positions you ultimately hold (both your own positions and those of the participants) and the recording of advocacy actions you take during the process of research.
- For the participants: the process of articulating the positions actively held by participants and the recording of advocacy actions participants take (as well as the evidence you, as researcher, have that participants actually hold those positions).

Table 7.3 folds into the tactic of advocacy charting a space for commentary on roles that various people (both researchers and participants) play (a) because role analysis is so prominent in communication research (see Berger, 1991) and (b) because roles in relation to technology are beginning to be interrogated in composition and communication research (see Mark Simpson's dissertation, 1989, for one of the first in-depth studies of roles in the computerized development of books for the computer industry; CMC research has also included organizational roles in its consideration of online communication). We also see the two as related because one's ability to advocate positions and actions successfully in most institutions and organizations is related to one's role(s) inside that institution/organization. It is of particular analytic interest when advocacy and roles clash in a situation, as when, we try to advocate an action while we are positioned in a role

TABLE 7.3. Advocacy Charting

Date	Positioning	Advocacy Description	Action Taken/ Evidence of Advocacy	Role Relationships Involved	Advocacy-Role Clashes
	participants vis-á-vis their environment				
	researchers vis-á-vis their environment				
	researchers vis-á-vis their participants researchers vis-á-vis research events and design				

es not have sufficient force to sustain our advocacy of that action. Thus, we are careful not to conflate advocacy and roles in this charting because we see advocacy charting as an activity that tries to point out places where action is taken to better the lot of the participants.

Advocacy charting has another positive effect. Because advocacy may be seen as "contamination" by some researchers (see the discussion of traditional researchers in Chapter 3), our tactic of charting it helps researchers to become more aware of when and how it operates in their research. Simultaneously the charting can be used to document how relationships have developed over the course of the study both for the purpose of showing yourself to be an advocate of participants and also for the purpose of being critically aware of what is happening in the research process. We see this as necessary analytic activity if you are going to engage in dialogue with researchers who oppose advocacy as an approach during research.

SUMMARY: USE VARIOUS CONTRASTIVE TACTICS TO CLARIFY THESE TENSIONS

As this chapter (and ultimately this book) no doubt has suggested, we use various tactics to articulate the tensions that drive critical research practices. At the risk of appearing mundane, or of asking you to suffer yet another chart, we offer Table 7.4 to summarize tactics we see as key to highlighting these tensions.

To our way of thinking, this chart concedes our need to stabilize our discussion, if only momentarily, so that researchers can act. We worry that it will be perceived as more a tablet of truth-seeking than it is—that researchers will flip through this text and copy Table 7.4 as representative of this approach. (The idea makes us cringe.) While such a response would represent either a profound mis-

TABLE 7.4. Summary of Tactics for Exploring Research Tensions

TENSIONS		TACTICS					
	Multiple mapping	Multiple binaries	Competing narratives	Metaphor analysis	Assumption analysis	Advocacy charting
Across disciplines	•	√			•	
In the environment	√	•	•	√		•
Across methods		•			√	
Participants-researcher(s)		•	√	•		√

√ = used in this discussion   • = useful tactic for exposing this tension

understanding of our intent or a willful corruption of that intent, on a certain level we would applaud such a misreading as well. To anyone who decides that doing critical practices research in computers and composition requires you to focus on the tensions across disciplines, inside the environment, across methods, and among researchers and participants, and to articulate those tensions via tactics such as multiple mapping, multiple binaries, competing narratives, metaphoric analysis, assumption analysis, and advocacy charting: You have a good start toward taking critical research action. Just remember: Using the chart alone does not guarantee sound research practice or critical integrity.

CONCLUSION: OPENING CRITICAL SPACES

Reluctantly, we stop our discussion of critical research practices for the study of writing technologies here. We hope our discussion has served to open up new spaces for research.

One space we have tried to open is one that invites the cooperation among three camps inside composition studies that have unique perspectives on the study of writing technologies but have not sufficiently appreciated one another: computers and composition, professional writing, and rhetoric theory/history (or composition). We have argued that these groups have several distinct blind spots in current work that we believe offer opportunities for needed work:

1. For general rhetoric/composition research, we want to encourage more study of writing technologies and of workplace literacies.
2. For professional writing research, we want to encourage more study of the role of writing technologies in defining workplace literacies.
3. For computers and composition research, we want to encourage more study of the use of writing technologies in the workplace.

Another space for research that we have sought to open combats the currently too limited view of literacy that we think underlies composition studies (see Grabill, 1997). We see the parameters of "literacy" as too limited in each of these three fields, and we would like to encourage a kind of cross-fertilization between the fields of both methods and sites in an effort to enrich notions of literacy. In particular, we think the separation of "workplace" and "classroom" studies—a binary we find ethically problematic as well as methodologically limiting—needs to be breached. The classroom is not the only potential site for education or social change.

Another space we seek to widen is the one supporting a critical postmodern approach to research methodology. We see the beginnings of such a methodology in the work of cultural anthropologists who take a reflective-situated view (Bourdieu, 1977; Geertz, 1983), in the work of computer theorists and human factors specialists who are developing a situated view (Bødker, 1991; Ehn, 1988; Green-baum & Kyng, 1991; Suchman, 1987), and in the work of feminist methodolo-gists (Bell, 1993; Lather, 1991; Roman, 1992; Rose, 1993; Stanley, 1990a). But, we think researchers in computers and composition have too easily accepted the divisions in composition studies among modes of inquiry. Stephen North (1987), for example, divides research into communities of knowledge he labels lore, his-tory, philosophy, and research, while Janice Lauer and William Asher (1988) argue for complementary modes of inquiry that are philosophical, rhetorical, his-torical, and empirical. While those modal distinctions can be useful, they also have made it easier for the larger community of compositionists to think of empir-ical work as traditional in its approach (or, worse, positivistic). This book has tried to show that empirical research does not have to equal positivist research, and it also has tried to link research in computers and composition with other critical efforts. We find the divisions between two of the main methodological camps in rhetoric and composition—between empirical research and critical/postmodern theory—unnecessary and counterproductive, and we hope others think so as well.

Thus, by involving a critical practices methodology for writing technologies we argue that empirical research can be postmodern in its methodology. What does a postmodern methodology look like? First, it promotes researcher situated reflexivity, addressing especially the issue of the researchers' standpoint relative to (as well as relationship with) research sites and participants. Second, it recog-nizes the distinct and situated nature of any observation; it is especially sensitive to "local conditions" (such as particular forms of computer technology in use). Third, it is conscious of the role of power, politics, and ideology in any setting, starting perhaps with the researchers' power over participants; institutional hier-archies that may perhaps impact researcher role or participant behavior; gender factors that may influence how a researcher participates in a study; and so on. Fourth, it is especially reflective of the shifting relationships through the course of a study: Researchers' perspectives probably never remain consistent through a study, and researcher roles may change from study to study. We think that the old categories for studies—case study, ethnography, experiment, meta-analysis—are probably not adequate for foregrounding relations within any particular study. (They have the tendency to favor commonalities across, rather than differences between, studies.)

Most of all, the research space we are advocating for the study of writing tech-nologies is one that involves praxis, a perspective that sees research as a kind of reflection-in-action (Schön, 1983). We think empirical research can generate use-ful local knowledge as long as it exercises a kind of postmodern critical-reflective praxis. We find James Sosnoski's distinction between modernist Theory and post-modernist theorizing helpful for an understanding of this position: *Theory* is the "modernist notion of an explanatory metacommentary ... [or] paradigmatic explanations of natural phenomena," and postmodern *theorizing* is reflection/action that is "not 'meta' to other discourses" (1991, p. 199). Obviously we are doing, and encouraging, a lot of theoretical reflecting in this book, but we hope the kind of theorizing we are advocating is postmodern in the sense that the research processes we enact do not map neatly into conventional rules for method but are heuristically forged out of a study's needs. Indeed, out of participants' needs.

As we approach the study of computers and writing, we are urging researchers not to look for the One, Holy, and Perfect Methodology, but to embrace working across methodological interfaces. We want researchers to expand critically and creatively the boundaries of writing technologies research. Why? Because to do less risks our larger aims as teachers of writing: that is, to help empower and liberate through the act and art of writing.

References

Allen, Thomas J., & Hauptman, Oscar. (1987). The influence of communication technologies on organizational structure: A conceptual model for future research. *Communication Research, 14*, 575–587.

Augé, Marc. (1995). *Non-places: Introduction to an anthropology of supermodernity* (John Howe, Trans.). London: Verso.

Barthes, Roland. (1977). The death of the author. In *Image—music—text* (Stephen Heath, Trans.) (pp. 142–148). New York: Hill and Wang.

Barton, Ben F., & Barton, Marthalee S. (1993). Ideology and the map: Toward a postmodern visual design practice. In Nancy Roundy Blyler & Charlotte Thralls (Eds.), *Professional communication: The social perspective* (pp. 49–78). Newbury Park, CA: Sage.

Beabes, Minette A., & Flanders, Alicia. (1995). Experiences with using contextual inquiry to design information. *Technical Communication, 42*, 409–420.

Bell, Diane. (1993). Yes, Virginia, there is a feminist ethnography. In Diane Bell, Pat Caplan, & Wazir Jahan Karim (Eds.), *Gendered fields: Women, men, and ethnography* (pp. 28–43). London: Routledge.

Benhabib, Seyla. (1992). *Situating the self: Gender, community and postmodernism in contemporary ethics*. New York: Routledge.

Berger, Arthur Asa. (1991). *Media research techniques*. Newbury Park, CA: Sage.

Berkenkotter, Carol. (1989). The legacy of positivism in empirical composition research. *Journal of Advanced Composition, 9*, 69–82.

Berkenkotter, Carol, & Huckin, Thomas N. (1993). Rethinking genre from a sociocognitive perspective. *Written Communication, 10*, 475–509.

Berkenkotter, Carol, & Huckin, Thomas N. (1995). *Genre knowledge in disciplinary communication: Cognition/culture/power*. Hillsdale, NJ: Erlbaum.

Bernard, H. Russell. (1988). *Research methods in cultural anthropology*. Beverly Hills, CA: Sage.

Berryman, Phillip. (1987). *Liberation theology: The essential facts about the revolutionary movement in Latin America and beyond*. New York: Pantheon.

Bitzer, Lloyd. (1968). The rhetorical situation. *Philosophy and Rhetoric, 1,* 1–14.

Blyler, Nancy Roundy. (1995). Research as ideology in professional communication. *Technical Communication Quarterly, 4,* 285–313.

Blyler, Nancy Roundy, & Thralls, Charlotte (Eds.). (1993). *Professional communication: The social perspective.* Newbury Park, CA: Sage.

Blythe, Stuart. (1997). *Conceptualizing the technologies of writing center practice.* Unpublished doctoral dissertation. Purdue University, West Lafayette, IN.

Bødker, Susanne. (1989). A human activity approach to user interfaces. *Human-Computer Interaction, 4,* 171–195.

Bødker, Susanne. (1991). *Through the interface: A human activity approach to user interface design.* Hillsdale, NJ: Erlbaum.

Boff, Leonardo, & Boff, Clodovis. (1986). *Liberation theology: From confrontation to dialogue.* San Francisco, CA: Harper and Row.

Bolter, Jay David. (1991). *Writing space: The computer, hypertext, and the history of writing.* Hillsdale, NJ: Erlbaum.

Bonington, Paul. (1995, April). The fourth media. *Internet World, 6,* 6.

Bourdieu, Pierre. (1977). *Outline of a theory of practice* (Richard Nice, Trans). Cambridge: Cambridge University Press.

Bourdieu, Pierre. (1988). *Homo academicus* (Peter Collier, Trans.). Stanford, CA: Stanford University Press.

Bourdieu, Pierre. (1990). *The logic of practice* (Richard Nice, Trans). Stanford, CA: Stanford University Press.

Bruce, Bertram. (1993). Innovation and social change. In Bertram Bruce, Joy Kreeft Peyton, & Trent Batson (Eds.), *Network-based writing classes: Promises and realities.* New York: Cambridge University Press.

Burke, Kenneth. (1969). *A rhetoric of motives.* Berkeley: University of California Press.

Cahill, Lisa Sowle. (1990). Feminist ethics. *Theological Studies, 51,* 49–64.

Campbell, Donald T. (1988). *Methodology and epistemology for social sciences.* Chicago: University of Chicago Press.

Campbell, Donald T., & Stanley, Julian C. (1966). *Experimental and quasi-experimental designs for research.* Chicago: Rand McNally.

Carbone, Nick, Daisley, Margaret, Federenko, Ed, McComas, Dix, Moran, Charles, Ostermiller, Dori, & Vanden Akker, Sherri. (1993). Writing ourselves online. *Computers and Composition, 10,* 29–48.

Cazden, Courtney B. (1988). *Classroom discourse: The language of teaching and learning.* Portsmouth, NH: Heinemann.

Clark, Gregory, & Doheny-Farina, Stephen. (1990). Public discourse and personal expression: A case study of theory-building. *Written Communication, 7,* 456–481.

Cochran-Smith, Marilyn, & Lytle, Susan L. (1993). *Inside/outside: Teacher research and knowledge.* New York: Teachers College Press.

Cole, Eve Browning, & Coultrap-McQuin, Susan. (1992). Toward a feminist conception of moral life. In Eve Browning Cole & Susan Coultrap-McQuin (Eds.), *Explorations in feminist ethics: Theory and practice* (pp. 1–11). Bloomington: Indiana University Press.

Consigny, Scott. (1974). Rhetoric and its situations. *Philosophy and Rhetoric, 7,* 175–186.

Constas, Mark A. (1992). Qualitative analysis as a public event: The documentation of category development procedures. *American Educational Research Journal, 29,* 253–266.

Conway, Glenda. (1995). "What are we doing today?" High school basic writers collaborating in a computer lab. *Computers and Composition, 12*, 79–95.

Cook, Thomas D., & Campbell, Donald T. (1979). *Quasi-experimentation: Design and analysis issues for field settings*. Chicago: Rand McNally.

Cooper, Marilyn M., & Selfe, Cynthia L. (1990). Computer conferences and learning: Authority, resistance, and internally persuasive discourse. *College English, 52*, 847–869.

Cooper, Martha. (1991). Ethical dimensions of political advocacy from a postmodern perspective. In Robert E. Denton, Jr. (Ed.), *Ethical dimensions of political communication* (pp. 23–47). New York: Praeger.

Curtis, Marcia, & Klem, Elizabeth. (1992). The virtual context: Ethnography in the computer-equipped classroom. In Gail E. Hawisher & Paul LeBlanc (Eds.), *Re-imagining computers and composition: Teaching and research in the virtual age* (pp. 155–172). Portsmouth, NH: Boynton/Cook.

Cushman, Ellen. (1996a). The rhetorician as an agent of social change. *College Composition and Communication, 47*, 7–28.

Cushman, Ellen. (1996b). *The struggle and the tools: Oral and literate strategies in an inner city community*. Unpublished doctoral dissertation, Rensselaer Polytechnic Institute, Troy, NY.

Damarin, Suzanne K. (1992). Where is women's knowledge in the age of information? In Cheris Kramarae & Dale Spender (Eds.), *The knowledge explosion: Generations of feminist scholarship* (pp. 362–370). New York: Teachers College Press.

Dautermann, Jennie, & Sullivan, Patricia. (1996). Issues of written literacy and electronic literacy in workplace settings. In Patricia Sullivan & Jennie Dautermann (Eds.), *Electronic literacies in the workplace: Technologies of writing* (pp. vii–xxxiii). Urbana, IL: NCTE & Computers and Composition.

de Certeau, Michel. (1984). *The practice of everyday life* (Steven Rendall, Trans.). Berkeley: University of California Press.

de Lauretis, Teresa. (1987). *Technologies of gender: Essays on theory, film, and fiction*. Bloomington: Indiana University Press.

Deleuze, Gilles, & Guattari, Félix. (1987). *A thousand plateaus: Capitalism and schizophrenia* (Brian Massumi, Trans.). Minneapolis: University of Minnesota Press.

Derrida, Jacques. (1977). Signature event context. *Glyph, 1*, 172–197.

Derrida, Jacques. (1977). Limited Inc ABC ...*Glyph, 2*, 162–254.

Dieli, Mary. (1988, October). *Integrating usability evaluation into the computer documentation development cycle*. Paper presented at the ACM SIGDOC Conference, Ann Arbor.

Dillon, George L. (1986). *Rhetoric as social imagination: Explorations in the interpersonal function of language*. Bloomington: Indiana University Press.

DiMatteo, Anthony. (1991). Communication, writing, learning: An anti-instrumentalist view of network writing. *Computers and Composition, 8*(3), 5–19.

Doheny-Farina, Stephen. (1989). A case study of one adult writing in academic and nonacademic discourse communities. In Carolyn Matalene (Ed.), *Worlds of writing: Teaching and learning in discourse communities of work* (pp. 17–42). New York: Random House.

Doheny-Farina, Stephen. (1992). *Rhetoric, innovation, technology: Case studies of technical communication in technology transfers*. Cambridge, MA: MIT Press.

Driskill, Linda. (1989). Understanding the writing context in organizations. In Myra Kogen (Ed.), *Writing in the business professions* (pp. 125–145). Urbana, IL: NCTE & ABC.

Duin, Ann Hill. (1993). Test drive—techniques for evaluating the usability of documents. In Carol M. Barnum & Saul Carliner (Eds.), *Techniques for technical communicators* (pp. 306–335). New York: Macmillan.

Dussel, Enrique. (1988). *Ethics and community* (Robert R. Barr, Trans.). Maryknoll, NY: Orbis Books.

Ebert, Teresa L. (1991). The "difference" of postmodern feminism. *College English, 53*, 886–904.

Ede, Lisa. (1992). Methods, methodologies, and the politics of knowledge. In Gesa Kirsch & Patricia A. Sullivan (Eds.), *Methods and methodology in composition research* (pp. 314–329). Carbondale: Southern Illinois University Press.

Ehn, Pelle. (1988). *Work-oriented design of computer artifacts*. Stockholm: Arbetslivscentrum.

Eisner, Eliot W., & Peshkin, Alan (1990). Introduction. In Eliot W. Eisner & Alan Peshkin (Eds.), *Qualitative inquiry in education: The continuing debate* (pp. 1–14). New York: Teachers College Press.

Eldred, Janet Carey, & Hawisher, Gail E. (1995). Researching electronic networks. *Written Communication, 12*, 330–359.

Enos, Theresa, & Brown, Stuart C. (Eds.). (1993). *Defining the new rhetorics*. Newbury Park, CA: Sage.

Faigley, Lester. (1992). *Fragments of rationality: Postmodernity and the subject of composition*. Pittsburgh: University of Pittsburgh Press.

Fay, Brian. (1987). *Critical social science: Liberation and its limits*. Ithaca, NY: Cornell University Press.

Feenberg, Andrew. (1991). *Critical theory of technology*. New York: Oxford University Press.

Feenberg, Andrew. (1995). *Alternative modernity: The technical turn in philosophy and social theory*. Berkeley: University of California Press.

Feyerabend, Paul. (1988). *Against method: Outline of an anarchistic theory of knowledge* (rev. ed.). London: Verso.

Fine, Michelle. (1992). Passions, politics, and power: Feminist research possibilities. In Michelle Fine (Ed.), *Disruptive voices: The possibilities of feminist research* (pp. 205–231). Ann Arbor: University of Michigan Press.

Floreak, Michael J. (1989). Designing for the real world: Using research to turn a "target audience" into real people. *Technical Communication, 36*, 373–381.

Fonow, Mary Margaret, & Cook, Judith A. (Eds.). (1991). *Beyond methodology: Feminist scholarship as lived research*. Bloomington: Indiana University Press.

Foucault, Michel. (1983). The subject and power. In Hubert L. Dreyfus & Paul Rabinow, *Michel Foucault: Beyond structuralism and hermeneutics* (2nd ed., pp. 208–226). Chicago: University of Chicago Press.

Foucault, Michel. (1984a). Space, knowledge, and power. In Paul Rabinow (Ed.), *The Foucault reader* (pp. 239–256). New York: Pantheon.

Foucault, Michel. (1984b). What is an author? In Paul Rabinow (Ed.), *The Foucault reader* (pp. 101–120). New York: Pantheon.

Foucault, Michel. (1986). Of other spaces. *Diacritics, 16* (Spring), 22–27.

Foucault, Michel. (1987). The ethic of care for the self as a practice of freedom. In James Bernauer & David Rasmussen (Eds.), *The final Foucault* (J. D. Gauthier, S. J., Trans.) (pp. 1–20). Cambridge, MA: MIT Press.

Freire, Paulo. (1993). *Pedagogy of the oppressed* (rev. ed.) (Myra Bergman Ramos, Trans.). New York: Continuum.

Garver, Eugene. (1987). *Machiavelli and the history of prudence*. Madison: University of Wisconsin Press.

Geertz, Clifford. (1983). *Local knowledge: Further essays in interpretive anthropology*. New York: Basic Books.

Gere, Anne Ruggles (Ed.). (1993). *Into the field: Sites of composition studies*. New York: Modern Language Association of America.

Geuss, Raymond. (1981). *The idea of a critical theory: Habermas and the Frankfurt school*. Cambridge: Cambridge University Press.

Gilligan, Carol. (1982). *In a different voice: Psychological theory and women's development*. Cambridge, MA: Harvard University Press.

Gore, Jennifer. (1992). What we can do for you! What *can* "we" do for "you"?: Struggling over empowerment in critical and feminist pedagogy. In Carmen Luke & Jennifer Gore (Eds.), *Feminisms and critical pedagogy* (pp. 54–73). New York: Routledge.

Grabill, Jeff. (1997). *Rhetoric, community literacy, and professional communication*. Unpublished doctoral dissertation. Purdue University, West Lafayette, IN.

Gray, Matthew. (1995, July). Report on growth of the web. http://www.netgen.com/info/growth.html.

Greenbaum, Joan, & Kyng, Morten (Eds.). (1991). *Design at work: Cooperative design of computer systems*. Hillsdale, NJ: Erlbaum.

Gross, Alan G. (1994). Review: Theory, method, practice. *College English, 56*, 828–840.

Gruber, Sibylle. (1995). Re: Ways we contribute: Students, instructors, and pedagogies in the computer-mediated writing classroom. *Computers and Composition, 12*, 61–78.

Gutièrrez, Gustavo. (1973). *A theology of liberation*. Maryknoll, NY: Orbis.

Habermas, Jürgen. (1990). *Moral consciousness and communicative action* (Christian Lenhardt & Shierry Weber Nicholsen, Trans.). Cambridge, MA: MIT Press.

Halio, Marcia Peoples. (1990a, January). Student writing: Can the machine maim the message? *Academic Computing, 4*, 16–19, 45, 52–53.

Halio, Marcia Peoples. (1990b). Maiming re-viewed. *Computers and Composition, 7*(3), 103–107.

Halpern, Jeanne W. (1988). Getting in deep: Using qualitative research in business and technical communication. *Journal of Business and Technical Communication, 2*, 22–43.

Hammersley, Martyn. (1992). *What's wrong with ethnography? Methodological explorations*. London: Routledge.

Handa, Carolyn (Ed.). (1990). *Computers and community: Teaching composition in the twenty-first century*. Portsmouth, NH: Boynton/Cook.

Harding, Sandra. (1986). *The science question in feminism*. Ithaca, NY: Cornell University Press.

Harding, Sandra. (1987a). Introduction: Is there a feminist method? In Sandra Harding (Ed.), *Feminism and methodology: Social science issues* (pp. 1–14). Bloomington: Indiana University Press.

Harding, Sandra (Ed.). (1987b). *Feminism and methodology: Social science issues.* Bloomington: Indiana University Press.

Harkin, Patricia. (1991). The postdisciplinary politics of lore. In Patricia Harkin & John Schilb (Eds.), *Contending with words: Composition and rhetoric in a post-modern age* (pp. 124–138). New York: Modern Language Association of America.

Harkin, Patricia, & Schilb, John. (1991). *Contending with words: Composition and rhetoric in a postmodern age.* New York: Modern Language Association of America.

Hartman, Karen, et al. (1991). Patterns of social interaction and learning to write: Some effects of network technologies. *Written Communication, 8,* 79–113.

Hassan, Ihab. (1993). Toward a concept of postmodernism. In Joseph Natoli & Linda Hutcheon (Eds.), *A postmodern reader* (pp. 273–286). Albany, NY: SUNY at Albany Press.

Hawisher, Gail E. (1989). Research and recommendations for computers and composition. In Gail E. Hawisher & Cynthia L. Selfe (Eds.), *Critical perspectives on computers and composition instruction* (pp. 44–69). New York: Teachers College Press.

Hawisher, Gail E. (1992a). Electronic meetings of the minds: Research, electronic conferences, and composition studies. In Gail E. Hawisher & Paul LeBlanc (Eds.), *Re-imagining computers and composition: Teaching and research in the virtual age* (pp. 81–101). Portsmouth, NH: Boynton/Cook.

Hawisher, Gail E. (1992b, Spring). Cross-disciplinary perspectives: Computer-mediated communication (CMC), electronic writing classes, and research. *SIGCUE Outlook, 21,* 45–52.

Hawisher, Gail E., & LeBlanc, Paul (Eds.). (1992). *Re-imagining computers and composition: Teaching and research in the virtual age.* Portsmouth, NH: Boynton/Cook.

Hawisher, Gail E., & Selfe, Cynthia L. (Eds.). (1989). *Critical perspectives on computers and composition instruction.* New York: Teachers College Press.

Hawisher, Gail E., & Selfe, Cynthia L. (Eds.). (1991). *Evolving perspectives on computers and composition studies: Questions for the 1990s.* Urbana, IL: NCTE.

Hawisher, Gail E., & Sullivan, Patricia. (in press). Women on the networks: Searching for an e-space of their own. In Susan Jarratt & Lynn Worsham (Eds.), *Feminism and composition.* New York: Modern Language Association of America.

Heidegger, Martin. (1977). The question concerning technology. *The question concerning technology and other essays* (pp. 3–35). New York: Garland.

Heim, Michael. (1987). *Electric language: A philosophical study of word processing.* New Haven, CT: Yale University Press.

Herndl, Carl G. (1993). Teaching discourse and reproducing culture: A critique of research and pedagogy in professional and non-academic writing. *College Composition and Communication, 44,* 349–363.

Herring, Susan C. (1993). Gender and democracy in computer-mediated communication. *EJC/REC 3* (2).

Holdstein, Deborah H. (1989). Training college teachers for computers and writing. In Gail E. Hawisher & Cynthia L. Selfe (Eds.), *Critical perspectives on computers and composition instruction.* (pp. 126–139). New York: Teachers College Press.

Hollingsworth, Sandra. (1994). Feminist pedagogy in the research class: An example of teacher research. *Educational Action Research, 2,* 49–70.

Holtzblatt, Karen, & Jones, Sandra. (1993). Contextual inquiry: A participatory design technique for system design. In D. Schuler & A. Namioka (Eds.), *Participatory design: Principles and practice.* Englewood Cliffs, NJ: Prentice Hall.

hooks, bell. (1981). *Ain't I a woman: Black women and feminism.* Boston: South End Press.

hooks, bell. (1989). *Talking back: Thinking feminist, thinking black.* Boston: South End Press.

Horkheimer, Max. (1972). *Critical theory: Selected essays* (Matthew J. O'Connell et al., Trans.). New York: Herder and Herder.

Howard, Tharon Wayne. (1992). *The rhetoric of electronic communities.* Unpublished doctoral dissertation, Purdue University, West Lafayette, IN.

Huckin, Thomas. (1987, March). *Surprise value in scientific discourse.* Paper presented at the Conference on College Composition and Communication, Atlanta.

Irigaray, Luce. (1993). *An ethics of sexual difference* (Carolyn Burke & Gillian C. Gill, Trans.). Ithaca, NY: Cornell University Press.

Jaggar, Alison M. (1992). Feminist ethics. In Lawrence C. Becker & Charlotte B. Becker (Eds.), *Encyclopedia of ethics,* Vol. 1 (pp. 361–370). New York: Garland.

Janangelo, Joseph. (1991). Technopower and technoppression: Some abuses of power and control in computer-assisted writing environments. *Computers and Composition, 9,* 47–64.

Johnson, Robert. (1991). *Rhetoric and use: Toward a theory of user-centered computer documentation.* Unpublished doctoral dissertation, Purdue University, West Lafayette, IN.

Johnson-Eilola, Johndan. (1995, March). *Little machines: Rearticulating hypertext users.* Paper presented at Conference on College Composition and Communication, Washington, DC.

Johnson-Eilola, Johndan. (1996, March). *Out of bounds: The politics of technology.* Paper presented at Conference on College Composition and Communication, Milwaukee, WI.

Jonsen, Albert R., & Toulmin, Stephen. (1988). *The abuse of casuistry: A history of moral reasoning.* Berkeley: University of California Press.

Kaplan, Nancy. (1991). Ideology, technology, and the future of writing instruction. In Gail E. Hawisher & Cynthia L. Selfe (Eds.), *Evolving perspectives on computers and composition studies: Questions for the 1990s.* (pp. 11–42). Urbana, IL: NCTE & Computers and Composition.

Kaplan, Nancy, & Moulthrop, Stuart. (1990). Other ways of seeing. *Computers and Composition, 7*(3), 89–102.

Keen, Peter G. W. (1987). Telecommunications and organizational choice. *Communication Research, 14,* 588–606.

Keller, Evelyn Fox. (1985). *Reflections on gender and science.* New Haven, CT: Yale University Press.

Keller, Evelyn Fox. (1992). *Secrets of life, secrets of death: Essays on language, gender, and science.* New York: Routledge.

Kerlinger, Fred N. (1973). *Foundations of behavioral research* (2nd ed.). New York: Holt, Rinehart, & Winston.

Kiefer, Kathleen. (1991). Computers and teacher education in the 1990s and beyond. In Gail E. Hawisher & Cynthia L. Selfe (Eds.), *Evolving perspectives on computers and composition studies: Questions for the 1990s.* (pp. 117–131). Urbana, IL: NCTE & Computers and Composition.

Kinneavy, James L. (1971). *A theory of discourse: The aims of discourse.* New York: Norton.

Kinneavy, James L. (1986). *Kairos*: A neglected concept in classical rhetoric. In Jean Dietz Moss (Ed.), *Rhetoric and praxis: The contribution of classical rhetoric to practical reasoning* (pp. 79–105). Washington, DC: Catholic University Press.

Kirsch, Gesa E. (1993). *Women writing the academy: Audience, authority, and transformation.* Carbondale: Southern Illinois University Press.

Kirsch, Gesa E., & Ritchie, Joy S. (1995). Beyond the personal: Theorizing a politics of location in composition research. *College Composition and Communication, 46,* 7–29.

Kleiber, N., & Light, L. (1978). *Caring for ourselves.* Vancouver, BC: University of British Columbia Press.

Klem, Elizabeth, & Moran, Charles. (1992). Teachers in a strange LANd: Learning to teach in a networked writing classroom. *Computers and Composition, 9*(3), 5–22.

Klem, Elizabeth, & Moran, Charles. (1995). "Whose machines are these?" Politics, power, and the new technology. In Patricia A. Sullivan & Donna J. Qualley (Eds.) *Pedagogy in the age of politics: Writing and reading (in) the academy* (pp. 73–87). Urbana, IL: NCTE.

Kling, Rob. (1980). Social analyses of computing: Theoretical perspectives in recent empirical research. *Computing Surveys, 12,* 61–110.

Kogen, Myra (Ed.). (1989). *Writing in the business professions.* Urbana, IL: NCTE and ABC.

Komsky, Susan H. (1991). A profile of users of electronic mail in a university: Frequent versus occasional users. *Management Communication Quarterly, 4,* 310–340.

Kothenbeutel, Karen Lee. (1988). Planning and conducting research. In Patty G. Campbell, Thomas Housel, & Kitty O. Locker (Eds.), *Conducting research in business communication* (pp. 1–15). Urbana, IL: Association for Business Communication.

Kuhn, Thomas S. (1970). *The structure of scientific revolutions* (2nd ed.). Chicago: University of Chicago Press.

Landauer, Thomas K. (1995). *The trouble with computers: Usefulness, usability, and productivity.* Cambridge, MA: MIT Press.

Landow, George P. (1992). *Hypertext: The convergence of contemporary critical theory and technology.* Baltimore, MD: Johns Hopkins University Press.

Lather, Patti. (1986). Research as praxis. *Harvard Educational Review, 56,* 257–277.

Lather, Patti. (1991). *Getting smart: Feminist research and pedagogy with/in the postmodern.* London: Routledge.

Lather, Patti. (1992). Post-critical pedgogies: A feminist reading. In Carmen Luke & Jennifer Gore (Eds.), *Feminisms and critical pedagogy* (pp. 120–137). New York: Routledge.

Latour, Bruno. (1987). *Science in action: How to follow scientists and engineers through society.* Cambridge, MA: Harvard University Press.

Lauer, Janice M. (1984). Composition studies: A dappled discipline. *Rhetoric Review, 3,* 20–29.

Lauer, Janice M., & Asher, J. William. (1988). *Composition research: Empirical ,*
New York: Oxford University Press.

Lauer, Janice M., & Sullivan, Patricia. (1993). Validity and reliability as social constructions. In Nancy Roundy Blyler & Charlotte Thralls (Eds.), *Professional communication: The social perspective* (pp. 163–176). Newbury Park, CA: Sage.

Laurel, Brenda. (1991). *Computers as theatre.* Reading, MA: Addison-Wesley.

Lave, Jean, & Wenger, Etienne. (1991). *Situated learning: Legitimate peripheral participation.* Cambridge: Cambridge University Press.

LeBlanc, Paul. (1990). Competing ideologies in software design for computer-aided composition. *Computers and Composition, 7*(2), 7–19.

LeBlanc, Paul J. (1993). *Writing teachers writing software: Creating our place in the electronic age.* Urbana, IL: NCTE & Computers and Composition.

Lincoln, Yvonna S., & Guba, Egon G. (1985). *Naturalistic inquiry.* Beverly Hills, CA:
Sage.

Lobkowicz, Nicholas. (1967). *Theory and practice: History of a concept from Aristotle to
Marx.* Notre Dame, IN: University of Notre Dame Press.

Lopez, Elizabeth Sanders. (1995). *The geography of computer writing spaces: A critical
postmodern analysis.* Unpublished doctoral dissertation, Purdue University, West
Lafayette, IN.

Lorde, Audre. (1984). *Sister outsider: Essays and speeches.* New York: Crossing Press.

Luke, Carmen, & Gore, Jennifer (Eds.). (1992). *Feminisms and critical pedagogy.* New
York: Routledge.

Lunsford, Andrea A., & Ede, Lisa. (1990). *Singular texts/plural authors: Perspectives on
collaborative writing.* Carbondale: Southern Illinois University Press.

Lyon, Arabella. (1992). Interdisciplinarity: Giving up territory. *College English, 54,* 681–
693.

Lyotard, Jean-François. (1984). *The postmodern condition: A report on knowledge* (Geoff
Bennington & Brian Massumi, Trans.). Minneapolis: University of Minnesota
Press.

Lyotard, Jean-François, & Thébaud, Jean-Loup. (1985). *Just gaming* (Wlad Godzich,
Trans.). Minneapolis: University of Minnesota Press.

MacIntyre, Alasdair. (1984). *After virtue: A study in moral theory* (2nd ed.). Notre Dame,
IN: University of Notre Dame Press.

Mackay, Wendy E. (1988). Diversity in the use of electronic mail: A preliminary inquiry.
ACM Transactions on Office Information Systems, 6, 380–397.

Maher, Frances A., & Tetreault, Mary Kay Thompson. (1994). *The feminist classroom.*
New York: Basic Books.

Malone, Thomas W. (1983). How do people organize their desks? Implications for the
design of office information systems. *ACM Transactions on Office Information Systems, 1,* 99–112.

Meeker, Mary, & DePuy, Chris. (1996). *The Internet report.* New York: Harper Business.

Miles, Matthew B., & Huberman, A. Michael. (1994). *Qualitative data analysis: A source-
book of new methods* (2nd ed.). Newbury Park, CA: Sage.

Miller, Carolyn R. (1989). What's practical about technical writing? In Bertie E. Fearing &
W. Keats Sparrow (Eds.), *Technical writing: Theory and practice* (pp. 14–24). New
York: Modern Language Association of America.

Miller, Leslie. (1995, August 28). For online users, connection is empowerment. *USA Today*, 10A.

Mirel, Barbara. (1996a, March). *Writing for problem-solving aspects of computer literacy: Theories to guide practice.* Paper presented at Conference on College Composition and Communication, Milwaukee, WI.

Mirel, Barbara. (1996b). Writing and database technology: Extending the definition of writing in the workplace. In Patricia Sullivan & Jennie Dautermann (Eds.), *Electronic literacies in the workplace: Technologies of writing* (pp. 91–114). Urbana, IL: NCTE and Computers and Composition.

Moran, Charles. (1992). Computers and the writing classroom: A look to the future. In Gail E. Hawisher & Paul LeBlanc (Eds.), *Re-imagining computers and composition: Teaching and research in the virtual age* (pp. 7–23). Portsmouth, NH: Boynton/ Cook.

Moulthrop, Stuart. (1991). The politics of hypertext. In Gail E. Hawisher & Cynthia L. Selfe (Eds.), *Evolving perspectives on computers and composition studies: Questions for the 1990s* (pp. 253-271). Urbana, IL: NCTE & Computers and Composition.

Muller, Michael J, & Kuhn, Sarah (guest Eds.). (1993, June). Special issue: Participatory design. *Communications of the ACM, 36*(4), 24–103.

Neubarth, Michael. (1995, April). Web fever: Catch it! The fourth media. *Internet World, 6*, 4.

Newkirk, Thomas. (1996). Seduction and betrayal in qualitative research. In Peter Mortensen & Gesa E. Kirsch (Eds.), *Ethics and representation in qualitative studies of literacy* (pp. 3–6). Urband, IL: NCTE.

Nicholson, Linda J. (Ed.). (1990). *Feminism/postmodernism.* London: Routledge.

Nielsen, Jakob. (1990). *Hypertext & hypermedia.* Boston: Academic Press.

Nielsen, Jakob. (1993). *Usability engineering.* Boston: Academic Press.

Noddings, Nel. (1984). *Caring: A feminine approach to ethics and moral education.* Berkeley: University of California Press.

Nord, Walter J., & Jermier, John M. (1992). Critical social science for managers? Promising and perverse possibilities. In Mats Alvesson & Hugh Willmott (Eds.), *Critical management studies* (pp. 202–222). London: Sage.

Norman, Donald A. (1988). *The psychology of everyday things.* New York: Basic Books.

North, Stephen M. (1987). *The making of knowledge in composition: Portrait of an emerging field.* Upper Montclair, NJ: Boynton Cook.

Nydahl, Joel. (1991). Ambiguity and confusion in word-processing research. *Computers and Composition, 8*(3), 21–37.

Oakley, Ann. (1974). *The sociology of housework.* London: Martin Robertson.

Odell, Lee, & Goswami, Dixie (Eds.). (1985). *Writing in nonacademic settings.* New York: Guilford Press.

Ohmann, Richard. (1985). Literacy, technology, and monopoly capital. *College English, 47*, 675–689.

Olsen, Leslie A. (1989). Computer-based writing and communication: Some implications for technical communication activities. *Proceedings of the International Technical Communication Conference, 36*, RT115–RT121.

Ong, Walter J., S.J. (1977). *Interfaces of the word: Studies in the evolution of consciousness and culture.* Ithaca, NY: Cornell University Press.

Ong, Walter J., [J.] (1982). *Orality and literacy: The technologizing of the word*. London: Methuen.

Papa, Michael J. (1990). Communication network patterns and employee performance with new technology. *Communication Research, 17*, 344–368.

Phelps, Louise Wetherbee. (1988). *Composition as a human science: Contributions to the self-understanding of a discipline*. New York: Oxford University Press.

Phelps, Louise Wetherbee. (1991). Practical wisdom and the geography of knowledge in composition. *College English, 53*, 863–885.

Phelps, Louise Wetherbee. (1992, Winter). A constrained vision of the writing classroom. *ADE Bulletin, 103*, 13–20.

Piller, Charles. (1992, September). Separate realities: The creation of the technological underclass in America's public schools. *Macworld*, 218–231.

Porter, James E. (1989). Assessing readers' use of computer documentation: A pilot study. *Technical Communication, 36*, 422–423.

Porter, James E. (1990). *Divisio* as em-/de-powering topic: A basis for argument in rhetoric and composition. *Rhetoric Review, 8*, 191–205.

Porter, James E. (1992a). *Audience and rhetoric: An archaeological composition of the discourse community*. Englewood Cliffs, NJ: Prentice Hall.

Porter, James E. (1992b, May). *Network communities and the development of the electronic writer*. Paper presented at the Conference on Computers and Writing, Indianapolis, IN.

Porter, James E. (1993). *Rhetorics of electronic writing*. Paper presented at the Conference on Computers and Writing, Ann Arbor, MI.

Porter, James E. (1995, March). *Ethical literacy*. Paper presented at Conference on College Composition and Communication, Washington, DC.

Porter, James E. (in press). *Rhetorical ethics and internetworked writing*. Greenwich, CT: Ablex.

Porter, James E., & Sullivan, Patricia A. (1994). Repetition and the rhetoric of visual design. In Barbara Johnstone (Ed.), *Repetition in discourse: Interdisciplinary perspectives (Vol. 1)*, (pp. 114–129). Norwood, NJ: Ablex.

Porter, James E., & Sullivan, Patricia. (1996). Working across methodological interfaces: The study of computers and writing in the workplace. In Patricia Sullivan & Jennie Dautermann (Eds.), *Electronic literacies in the workplace: Technologies of writing* (pp. 294–322). Urbana, IL: NCTE and Computers and Composition.

Poster, Mark. (1989). *Critical theory and poststructuralism: In search of a context*. Ithaca, NY: Cornell University Press.

Poster, Mark. (1990). *The mode of information: Poststructuralism and social context*. Chicago: University of Chicago Press.

Poster, Mark. (1995). *The second media age*. Cambridge, MA: Polity Press.

Provenzo, Eugene F., Jr. (1992). The electronic panopticon: Censorship, control, and indoctrination in a post-typographic culture. In Myron C. Tuman (Ed.), *Literacy online: The promise (and peril) of reading and writing with computers* (pp. 167–188). Pittsburgh: University of Pittsburgh Press.

Rawls, John. (1971). *A theory of justice*. Cambridge, MA: Belknap Press.

Reinharz, Shulamit. (1992a). *Feminist methods in social research*. New York: Oxford University Press.

Reinharz, Shulamit. (1992b). The principles of feminist research: A matter of debate. In Cheris Kramerae & Dale Spender (Eds.), *The knowledge explosion: Generations of feminist scholarship* (pp. 423–437). New York: Teachers College Press.

Rice, Ronald E. (1982). Communication networking in computer-conferencing systems: A longitudinal study of group roles and system structure. In Michael Burgoon (Ed.), *Communication Yearbook, 6*, 925–944.

Rice, Ronald E., & Shook, Douglas E. (1988). Access to, usage of, and outcomes from an electronic messaging system. *ACM Transactions on Office Information Systems, 6*, 255–276.

Roman, Leslie G. (1992). The political significance of other ways of narrating ethnography: A feminist materialist approach. In Margaret D. LeCompte, Wendy L. Millroy, & Judith Preissle (Eds.), *The handbook of qualitative research in education* (pp. 555–594). San Diego: Academic Press.

Roman, Leslie G., & Apple, Michael W. (1990). Is naturalism a move away from positivism? Materialist and feminist approaches to subjectivity in ethnographic research. In Eliot W. Eisner & Alan Peshkin (Eds.), *Qualitative inquiry in education: The continuing debate* (pp. 38–73). New York: Teachers College Press.

Romano, Susan. (1993). The egalitarianism narrative: Whose story? Which yardstick? *Computers and Composition, 10*, 5–28.

Rorty, Richard. (1991). Feminism and pragmatism. *Michigan Quarterly Review, 30*, 231–258.

Rose, Gillian. (1993). *Feminism and geography: The limits of geographic knowledge.* Minneapolis: University of Minnesota Press.

Sampson, Geoffrey. (1985). *Writing systems.* Stanford, CA: Stanford University Press.

Schmitz, Joseph, & Fulk, Janet. (1991). Organizational colleagues, media richness, and electronic mail: A test of the social influence model of technology use. *Communication Research, 18*, 487–523.

Schön, Donald A. (1983). *The reflective practitioner: How professionals think in action.* New York: Basic Books.

Scott, Charles E. (1990). *The question of ethics: Nietzsche, Foucault, Heidegger.* Bloomington: Indiana University Press.

Selfe, Cynthia L. (1992). Preparing English teachers for the virtual age: The case for technology critics. In Gail E. Hawisher & Paul LeBlanc (Eds.), *Re-imagining computers and composition: Teaching and research in the virtual age* (pp. 24–42). Portsmouth, NH: Boynton/Cook.

Selfe, Cynthia L. (1996, March). *The gendering of technology: Images of women, men, and technology.* Paper presented at Conference on College Composition and Communication, Milwaukee, WI.

Selfe, Cynthia L., & Hilligoss, Susan (Eds.). (1994). *Literacy and computers: The complications of teaching and learning with technology.* New York: Modern Language Association of America.

Selfe, Cynthia L., & Meyer, Paul R. (1991).Testing claims for on-line conferences. *Written Communication, 8*(2), 163–192.

Selfe, Cynthia L., & Selfe, Richard J., Jr. (1994). The politics of the interface: Power and its exercise in electronic contact zones. *College Composition and Communication, 45*, 480–504.

Sibley, David. (1995). *Geographies of exclusion: Society and difference in the west*. London: Routledge.

Simon, Herbert A. (1969). *The sciences of the artificial*. Cambridge, MA: MIT Press.

Simpson, Mark. (1989). *Shaping computer documentation for multiple audiences: An ethnographic study*. Unpublished doctoral dissertation, Purdue University, West Lafayette, IN.

Slatin, John, et al. (1990). Computer teachers respond to Halio. *Computers and Composition, 7*(3), 73-79.

Smith, Christian. (1991). *The emergence of liberation theology: Radical religion and social movement theory*. Chicago: University of Chicago Press.

Smith, Dorothy E. (1987). *The everyday world as problematic: A feminist sociology*. Boston: Northeastern University Press.

Smith, Dorothy E. (1990). *The conceptual practices of power: A feminist sociology of knowledge*. Boston, MA: Northeastern University Press.

Smith, Paul. (1988). *Discerning the subject*. Minneapolis: University of Minnesota Press.

Soja, Edward W. (1989). *Postmodern geographies: The reassertion of space in critical social theory*. London: Verso.

Sosnoski, James J. (1991). Postmodern teachers in their postmodern classrooms: Socrates begone! In Patricia Harkin & John Schilb (Eds.), *Contending with words: Composition and rhetoric in a postmodern age* (pp. 198–219). New York: Modern Language Association of America.

Spender, Dale. (1995). *Nattering on the net: Women, power and cyberspace*. Melbourne, AU: Spinifex.

Spilka, Rachel (Ed.). (1993). *Writing in the workplace: New research perspectives*. Carbondale: Southern Illinois University Press.

Sproull, Lee, & Kiesler, Sara. (1991a). *Connections: New ways of working in the networked organization*. Cambridge, MA: MIT Press.

Sproull, Lee, & Kiesler, Sara. (1991b, September). Computers, networks, and work. *Scientific American, 265*, 116–123.

Stanley, Liz (Ed.). (1990a). *Feminist praxis: Research, theory, and epistemology in feminist sociology*. London: Routledge.

Stanley, Liz. (1990b). Feminist praxis and the academic mode of production: An editorial introduction. In Liz Stanley (Ed.), *Feminist praxis: Research, theory, and epistemology in feminist sociology* (pp. 3–19). London: Routledge.

Stanley, Liz, & Wise, Sue. (1990). Method, methodology and epistemology in feminist research processes. In Liz Stanley (Ed.), *Feminist praxis: Research, theory and epistemology in feminist sociology* (pp. 20–60). London: Routledge.

Stanley, Liz, & Wise, Sue. (1993). *Breaking out again: Feminist ontology and epistemology* (new ed.). London: Routledge.

Steinfield, Charles W. (1985). Computer-mediated communication in an organizational setting: Explaining task-related and socioemotional uses. In Margaret L. McLaughlin (Ed.), *Communication Yearbook, 9*, 777–804.

Steinfield, Charles W. (1992). Computer-mediated communications in organizational settings: Emerging conceptual frameworks and directions for research. *Management Communication Quarterly, 5*, 348–365.

Strauss, Anselm L. (1987). *Qualitative analysis for social scientists*. Cambridge: Cambridge University Press.

Suchman, Lucy A. (1987). *Plans and situated actions: The problem of human-machine communication*. Cambridge: Cambridge University Press.

Sullivan, Patricia A. (1992). Feminism and methodology in composition. In Patricia A. Sullivan & Gesa Kirsch (Eds.), *Methods and methodology in composition research* (pp. 37–61). Carbondale: Southern Illinois University Press.

Sullivan, Patricia A. (1989a). Beyond a narrow conception of usability. *IEEE Transactions on Professional Communication, 32*, 256–264.

Sullivan, Patricia. (1989b). Human-computer interaction perspectives on word processing issues. *Computers and Composition, 6*(3), 11–33.

Sullivan, Patricia. (1991). Taking control of the page: Electronic writing and word publishing. In Gail E. Hawisher & Cynthia L. Selfe (Eds.), *Evolving perspectives on computers and composition studies: Questions for the 1990s* (pp. 43–64). Urbana, IL: NCTE & Computers and Composition.

Sullivan, Patricia. (1993a, May). *Uses of method in computers and composition studies*. Paper presented at the Conference on Computers and Writing, Ann Arbor, MI.

Sullivan, Patricia A. (1993b, June). Studying electronic communities. *The Bulletin of the Association for Business Communication, 56*(2), 41–42.

Sullivan, Patricia. (1995, March). *Methodology and situated practice in computers and writing: Studying teachers in networked classes*. Paper presented at Conference on College Composition and Communication, Washington, DC.

Sullivan, Patricia & Dautermann, Jennie (Eds.). (1996). *Electronic literacies in the workplace: Technologies of writing*. Urbana, IL: NCTE and Computers and Composition.

Sullivan, Patricia, & Porter, James E. (1990a). How do writers view usability information? A case study of a developing documentation writer. *SIGDOC '90 Conference Proceedings, 14*, 29–35.

Sullivan, Patricia, & Porter, James E. (1990b). User testing: The heuristic advantages at the draft stage. *Technical Communication, 37*, 78–80.

Sullivan, Patricia A., & Porter, James E. (1993a). On theory, practice, and method: Toward a heuristic research methodology for professional writing. In Rachel Spilka (Ed.), *Writing in the workplace: New research perspectives* (pp. 220–237). Carbondale: Southern Illinois University Press.

Sullivan, Patricia A., & Porter, James E. (1993b). Remapping curricular geography: Professional writing in/and English. *Journal of Business and Technical Communication, 7*, 389–422.

Swales, John, & Najjar, Hazem. (1987). The writing of research article introductions. *Written Communication, 9*, 175–191.

Takayoshi, Pamela. (1994a). Building new networks from the old: Women's experiences with electronic communications. *Computers and Composition, 11*, 21–35.

Takayoshi, Pamela Denise. (1994b). *Theorizing technocentricism in computers and composition: Conflicting values, competing visions, and pedagogical interventions*. Unpublished doctoral dissertation, Purdue University, West Lafayette, IN.

Taylor, H. Jeanie, Kramarae, Cheris, & Ebben, Maureen (Eds.). (1993). *Women, information technology, and scholarship*. Urbana, IL: Center for Advanced Studies.

Tuman, Myron C. (1992). *Word perfect: Literacy in the computer age*. Pittsburgh: University of Pittsburgh Press.

Turner, Stephen. (1994). *The social theory of practices: Tradition, tacit knowledge, and presuppositions*. Chicago: University of Chicago Press.

Van Maanen, John. (1988). *Tales of the field: On writing ethnography*. Chicago: University of Chicago Press.

Vatz, Richard E. (1973). The myth of the rhetorical situation. *Philosophy and Rhetoric, 6*, 154–161.

Vitanza, Victor J. (1991). "Some more" notes, toward a "third" sophistic. *Argumentation, 5*, 117–139.

Vitanza, Victor J. (1994). Concerning a postclassical *ethos* as para/rhetorical ethics, the "selphs," and the excluded third. In James S. Baumlin & Tita French Baumlin (Eds.), *Ethos: New essays in rhetorical and critical theory* (pp. 380–431). Dallas: Southern Methodist University Press.

Walzer, Arthur E., & Gross, Alan. (1994). Positivists, postmodernists, Aristotelians, and the Challenger disaster. *College English, 56*, 420–433.

Warry, Wayne. (1992). The eleventh thesis: Applied anthropology as praxis. *Human Organization, 51*, 155–163.

Webb, Eugene T., Campbell, Donald T., Schwartz, Richard D., Sechrest, Lee, & Grove, Janet Belew. (1981). *Nonreactive measures in the social sciences* (2nd ed.). Boston: Houghton Mifflin.

Werlen, Benno. (1993). *Society, action, and space: An alternative human geography* (Gayna Walls, Trans.). London: Routledge.

Westkott, Marcia. (1977). Feminist criticism of the social sciences. *Harvard Educational Review, 49*, 422–430.

Whiteside, John, Bennett, J., & Holtzblatt, Karen. (1988). Usability engineering: Our experience and evolution. In Mark Helander (Ed.), *Handbook of human computer interaction*. New York: North-Holland.

Winner, Langdon. (1991, Winter). Artifact/ideas and political culture. *Whole Earth Review, 73*, 18–24.

Winograd, Terry. (1995). Heidegger and the design of computer systems. In Andrew Feenberg & Alastair Hannay (Eds.), *Technology and the politics of knowledge* (pp. 108–127). Bloomington: Indiana University Press.

Winograd, Terry, & Flores, C. Fernando. (1986). *Understanding computers and cognition: A new foundation for design*. Norwood, NJ: Ablex.

Yahoo. (1995, August). Yahoo's list of web page design and layout resources. http://www.yahoo.com/Computers_and_Internet/Internet/World_Wide_Web/Page_Design_and_Layout/.

Yates, Joanne. (1989). *Control through communication: The rise of system in American management*. Baltimore, MD: Johns Hopkins University Press.

Yin, Robert K. (1994). *Case study research: Design and methods* (rev. ed.). Thousand Oaks, CA: Sage.

Young, Iris Marion. (1990). *Justice and the politics of difference*. Princeton, NJ: Princeton University Press.

Youra, Steven. (1990). Computers and student writing: Maiming the Macintosh (a response). *Computers and Composition, 7*(3), 81–88.

Zuboff, Shoshana. (1988). *In the age of the smart machine: The future of work and power*. New York: Basic Books.

Author Index

Subject Index

About the Authors

Patricia Sullivan teaches graduate rhetoric courses at Purdue University, where she directed the technical writing program for twelve years. Her co-edited book with Jennie Dautermann, *Electronic Literacies in the Workplace: Technologies of Writing* (NCTE and Computers and Composition, 1996), examines how technology affects writing practices in workplace contexts. With Gail Hawisher, she is working on a book exploring women's lives on electronic networks.

James Porter, who has been at Purdue University since 1988, teaches in the Purdue rhetoric Ph.D. program and directs the business writing program. His book *Rhetorical Ethics and Internetworked Writing* (Ablex, in press) develops rhetoric theory as a heuristic for addressing ethical and legal problems writers face in cyberspace.

Collaborating since 1989, Sullivan and Porter have co-authored numerous articles and chapters on methodology, computers and writing, and professional writing. In 1994, their article "On Theory, Practice, and Method" won the NCTE award for Best Article in Philosophy/Theory of Technical and Scientific Communication.